The Feminist Critique of Language

The Feminist Critique of Language

A reader

Edited by Deborah Cameron

Routledge

London and New York

First published 1990
by Routledge
11 New Fetter Lane, London EC4P 4EE

Simultaneously published in the USA and Canada
by Routledge
a division of Routledge, Chapman and Hall, Inc.
29 West 35th Street, New York, NY 10001

The collection as a whole © 1990 Routledge

Typeset by LaserScript Limited, Mitcham, Surrey.
Printed in Great Britain by Biddles Ltd, Guildford and Kings Lynn.

British Library Cataloguing in Publication Data

The feminist critique of language: a reader. (World and word series)
1. English language, Grammar: Gender
I. Cameron, Deborah II. Series 428.2

Library of Congress Cataloging in Publication Data

The Feminist critique of language
Bibliography: p.
Includes index.
1. Language and languages–Sex differences. 2. Women–Language. I.
Cameron, Deborah
P120.S48F46   1990   408.2   89-6306

ISBN 0-415-04259-3
ISBN 0-415-04260-7 (pbk.)

General editor's preface

The *World and Word* series, as its title implies, is based on the assumption that literary texts cannot be studied in isolation. The series presents to students, mainly of English literature, documents and materials which will enable them to have first-hand experience of some of the writing which forms the context of the literature they read. The aim is to put students in possession of material to which they cannot normally gain access so that they may arrive at an independent understanding of the interrelationships of literary texts with other writing.

There are to be twelve volumes, covering topics from the Middle Ages to the twentieth century. Each volume concentrates on a specific area of thought in a particular period, selecting from religious, philosophical, or scientific works, literary theory or political or social material, according to its chosen topic. The extracts included are substantial in order to enable students themselves to arrive at an understanding of the significance of the material they read and to make responsible historical connections with some precision and independence. The task of compilation itself, of course, predetermines to a great extent the kind of connections and relationships which can be made in a particular period. We all bring our own categories to the work of interpretation. However, each compiler makes clear the grounds on which the choice of material is made, and thus the series encourages the valuable understanding that there can be no single, authoritative account of the relationships between world and word.

Each volume is annotated and indexed and includes a short bibliography and suggestions for further reading. The *World and Word* series can be used in different teaching contexts, in the students' independent work, in seminar discussion, and on lecture courses.

Isobel Armstrong
University of Southampton

Contents

Contents

Prefatory note

'The feminist critique of language' is a convenient label for what has become a vast body of literature; selecting a limited number of excerpts has not been easy, and there are bound to be inclusions which some readers will find eccentric, as well as omissions they will find unaccountable. Obviously I must take responsibility for the choices I have made; but it may be helpful to know what practical and pedagogic criteria I have used.

Briefly, then, I have prioritized papers which are either not readily available at all, or else are unlikely to be available to literature students in the normal course of events (for instance because they are buried in social science texts), or which are available only without much-needed annotation. Conversely, I have sometimes refrained from reprinting papers which are available in a recent, annotated edition. For example, I have not included anything by Julia Kristeva because students will undoubtedly have access to Toril Moi's useful *Kristeva Reader* (1986). Where I have reprinted more familiar material, it is either because existing editions do not treat it from the point of view of the feminist critique of language, or because there is some special virtue in juxtaposing it with other pieces to form a microcosm of important debates.

These considerations apart, I have tried in my selection to represent the most significant trends in the feminist critique of the last fifteen years, covering all the topics I think will prove to be of lasting importance. I have tried to arrange and introduce them in such a way that the book as a whole gives a coherent overview.

If I have succeeded in any of these aims it is partly thanks to the help and support of a number of colleagues. I am indebted in particular to

Isobel Armstrong, who suggested the project and supported it through thick and thin; to Sarah Turvey who made useful comments on the introduction and whose perspective as a literature teacher has been invaluable; and to all those people who by sharing their views on language and gender have helped me both to clarify my thoughts and find the best ways of expressing them.

Acknowledgements

The editor and publishers would like to thank the following copyright holders for permission to reprint material:

The Estate of Virginia Woolf and The Hogarth Press for 'Women and fiction' and 'Dorothy Richardson and the woman's sentence' by Virginia Woolf; Praeger Publishers for 'The silence is broken' by Josephine Donovan; Verso for 'Language and gender' by Cora Kaplan; Century Hutchinson Ltd for 'Woman's word' by Annie Leclerc; The editorial collective of *Ideology and Consciousness* for 'Women's exile': an interview with Luce Irigaray; SEFT (Society for Education in Film and Television) Ltd for 'Linguistic, social, and sexual relations: a review of Dale Spender's *Man Made Language*' by Maria Black and Rosalind Coward; Daw Books Ltd for extract from *Native Tongue* by Suzette Haden Elgin; Virago Press for extract from *Silences* by Tillie Olsen; Cambridge University Press for 'Androcentrism in prescriptive grammar' by Ann Bodine; Penguin Books Ltd and Basic Books Inc., Publishers for 'A person paper on purity in language' by Douglas R. Hofstadter; Harper & Row Publishers, Inc. for extract from *Language and Woman's Place* by Robin Lakoff; Pergamon Press for 'Gossip: notes on women's oral culture' by Deborah Jones.

Every effort has been made to obtain permission to reproduce copyright material. If any proper acknowledgement has not been made, or permission not received, we would invite copyright holder to inform us of the oversight.

Introduction: why is language a feminist issue?

Why is language a feminist issue? To readers well-versed in modern literary and social theory, the question may seem naive, the answer obvious; others may find the whole issue obscure, or consider it a distraction from 'serious' politics. Yet what cannot be disputed is that contemporary feminisms (and I use the plural advisedly here) have indeed placed language on the political agenda. A 'feminist critique of language' now exists; its influence on public, and especially academic discourse has grown to the point where people with an interest in literary or social theory cannot just dismiss it, but must try to grasp its meaning and assess its implications.

One serious obstacle to intelligent understanding is that feminist views on language are very diverse, reflecting not only political differences within feminism itself but also the great proliferation of 'discourses'– traditions, theoretical frameworks, academic disciplines – in which language is discussed in the modern age. Although I have spoken of 'the' feminist critique of language, this is really a kind of shorthand, since the critique is fragmented: its strands are not unified, nothing is settled. And this recognition that the ground is still shifting beneath our feet has certain implications for anyone who sets out to edit a collection like this one. I cannot assume the conventional authority of someone 'summing up' from a safe historical distance. Nor can I pretend to a disinterested stance in a debate which is so very much alive and ongoing. I have therefore conceived my task in a rather different way, and set out, precisely, to document diversity. In my selection (and it is a selection, with all the non-neutrality the word implies) I have tried to show how varied and complex are feminist views on language. Yet I have also accepted a certain responsibility to guide the reader through

1

this diversity. The purpose of this introductory piece is to suggest some frameworks, historical and theoretical, in which we can order and make sense of different views.

Critique

We may begin the process of 'making sense' with some discussion of the title I have given this volume. What is a 'feminist critique of language'? What, indeed, is a 'critique' of anything? For many readers, the word *critique* will carry off-putting overtones of trendy left-wing jargon. I have deliberately chosen to use it, however, because it has two meanings and both of them are relevant.

The first meaning of *critique* is the more familiar: nowadays the term is very often synonymous with the related word *criticism* as most of us use it, in the sense of 'negative assessment or evaluation'. This is apposite, for many feminists are indeed highly critical of language as we know it. Language for women is 'not good enough', and one constant theme of the feminist critique is the need to change words and make them fitter for our use. Readers will doubtless be acquainted with some of the ways in which feminist activists have challenged, and to some extent altered, conventional usage: the rejection of generic *he* and *man*, for example, or of titles which indicate women's marital status. They may also have encountered in literary discourse the idea of women's dissatisfaction with the language of literature; their quest for new metaphors and ways of writing which reflect female lives and bodies as conventional language cannot. All this implies a negative assessment of existing linguistic practice, a critical approach to the way language has been used.

But *critique* also has a more specialized meaning, apart from this project of complaint and reform. In philosophy, to undertake a critique of something is to examine the conditions on which it exists, calling into question the assumptions it is based on. Some strands of feminism can fairly be said to have produced a critique of language in this second sense as well. They have come up with novel theories and perspectives on language as a social and cultural institution, questioning, for instance, our common-sense assumption that the sexes share 'a common language'. It is feminism, moreover, which has given new urgency to the old debate on 'linguistic determinism' – the question of how far linguistic structures underpin, as opposed to just reflecting, our perceptions of the world.

2

In putting together this collection of writings I have tried to do justice to both kinds of feminist critique. I have included both theoretical writings and more practical or polemical linguistic manifestos; I have also put in some reflections by women writers on their own linguistic practice and how they feel about it.

But simply listing these different kinds of writing does not unravel the fiendish complexities of the debate which together they represent. Within the categories of 'theory' or 'polemic' (and the boundaries between them are in any case blurred) there are many differing approaches and concerns, which need to be distinguished and placed in context. It would have been possible to organize this book around the identification of 'currents' and an anatomy of their differences. In the end, though, I decided against such a procedure: the result, apart from being tedious and dry, would have been to obscure what the currents have in common. And despite my awareness of disagreement and fragmentation, I would want to insist that there is much common ground. From interestingly different preconceptions and perspectives, feminist writers on the subject of language return to the same major themes and concerns.

I have structured this volume around three themes in particular: the theme of silence and exclusion from language, which also raises the question of finding an authentic female voice; the theme of 'naming' or representation, in which the meaning of gender is constructed and contested; and the theme of behavioural differences in language, their relation to male dominance and female culture. Each of these topics occupies a part of the book, and the excerpts I have chosen to exemplify each one show how one basic theme supports many variations. At some points, the extracts themselves can be read as a debate between differing positions. In order to make possible a broadly informed reading of each section as a whole, I want now to introduce the three themes in turn, drawing attention to the problems and debates they imply.

Speech and silence: the quest for a female voice in culture

As I have observed elsewhere the idea of 'silence' recurs in women's writing.[1] But what do we mean when we refer to women's 'silence'? It cannot be that women are always and everywhere silent, nor (obviously) that they lack the ability to use language. Language is in one sense the inalienable birthright of every human being, regardless of gender; some forms of linguistic activity, moreover, are popularly associated with women as much as or possibly even more than with men (for example 'gossip', storytelling, private letters, and diaries).[2] But this list of 'female' genres gives a valuable clue to the constitution of 'women's silence'. For none of these genres are especially prestigious, and some, like gossip, are actually disparaged. They are *private* forms of language, confined to the space of the home or village community; in the public domain, and especially the domain of culture (by which I mean a society's representation of itself in rituals, institutions, codified knowledge, and creative art), these genres have no currency, let alone value.

The silence of women is above all an absence of female voices and concerns from high culture. If we look at a society's most prestigious linguistic registers – religious ceremonial, political rhetoric, legal discourse, science, poetry – we find women's voices for the most part silent – or rather, *silenced*, for it is not just that women do not speak: often they are explicitly *prevented* from speaking, either by social taboos and restrictions or by the more genteel tyrannies of custom and practice. Even where it seems that women could speak if they chose, the conditions imposed on their lives by society may make this a difficult or dangerous choice. Silence can also mean censoring yourself for fear of being ridiculed, attacked, or ignored.

Let us look, briefly, at some examples of silencing and how it is done. In the field of public speaking and rhetoric, it is taboo and custom we are dealing with above all. In traditional societies, restrictions may be formulated as rules with serious penalties attached to violation: anthropologists have reported societies, for instance, where women are forbidden to speak outside the private house, or in the presence of male relatives and superordinates, or where they must avoid certain words and expressions.[3] It has often been pointed out, and in my view quite correctly, that these clear-cut restrictions have their analogues in modern western cultures. Consider, for instance, the fact that swearing and other taboo ('obscene' or 'explicit') language is still thought more inappropriate for women (and in their presence) than for men; or the unease and hostility that still exists towards women stand-up comics and political orators. (Anyone who doubts this last point should reflect on the negative feelings so often expressed about the verbal style of Margaret Thatcher, which far exceed in their vehemence our assessment of any male speaker. Indeed, some of the peculiarities of the Thatcher style have evidently been evolved as strategies for coping with prejudice against female speakers – for example, the self-conscious lowering of the voice pitch.)

4

Another good example is the current debate over whether women should be ordained as priests. Opposition to sex-equality in this sphere manifests an irrational dread of women taking over priestly and ritual functions, including the linguistic ones of public prayer, preaching, and saying the liturgy. Readers will recall the strict prohibitions on women's speech recorded in the scriptures, and Dr Johnson's remark about the unnaturalness of women preaching (like a dog walking on its hind legs). Is it too strong to see this not merely as 'tradition' but as taboo? Even secular social rituals – wedding receptions for example – allot the role of speaker specifically to men, and for women to challenge this (for a bride to speak at her own reception, say) is still a daring move.

Writing, and particularly the production of literature, is subject to a different set of exclusions. Perhaps the most sweeping of these is the exclusion of women from the knowledge and skills needed to write at all. Writing is not an organic growth out of general linguistic capabilities, but a technology; like most technologies it has been monopolized by the powerful. Women are not the only social group to be affected disproportionately by illiteracy. But gender differences in literacy rates are striking enough to call for comment, and the pattern whereby women are less literate than men applies across the social and geographic spectrum. The greatest sufferers in this as in other things are poor Black women: as Alice Walker asks,

> What did it mean for a black woman to be an artist in our grand-mothers' time? In our great-grandmothers' day? It is a question with an answer cruel enough to stop the blood....How was the creativity of the black woman kept alive, year after year and century after century, when for most of the years black people have been in America, it was a punishable crime for a black person to read and write?[4]

In the case of Black women and men under slavery, literacy was not merely unavailable to them but actually forbidden on pain of punishment. This is a very significant fact which throws light on the continuing illiteracy of women: for although high rates of female illiteracy may be partly explained by economic factors (where education is a scarce resource it is thought more worthwhile to educate boys), there are political factors involved in it too. Powerful groups have quite specific fears that the ability to read and write, should it spread among the powerless, will facilitate opposition and eventually mass revolt. We see this not only in the practice of American slave-owners but also, for example, among the English bourgeoisie of the nineteenth century.

Although industrialization required certain levels of literacy among workers, the ruling class attempted to restrict this to a minimum, fearing that any more would give access to subversive ideas. Some women's literacy projects have reported similar fears expressed by the men of the community.

I have dwelt on this issue of illiteracy because in global and historical terms, it has been crucial in silencing women and denying them opportunities for creative expression (although Alice Walker makes it clear that Black women's creativity *was* kept alive, clearly the artistic impulse could not be channelled into the production of literature till literacy was permitted). In modern societies, the language of permanence and authority is always written language: if women are illiterate, or less at home with writing, they will not be able to share fully in the culture and, specifically, they will not play a full part in shaping it.

But though literacy is an obvious prerequisite for women's writing, illiteracy is not the only obstacle to it. As Virginia Woolf pointed out in *A Room of One's Own*, most women, even those of the privileged classes, lack the economic independence and leisure time which are needed for sustained literary effort.[5] Other women, like the writer and critic Tillie Olsen, have alluded to the practical and psychological difficulties of writing while caring for young children.[6] There is a general assumption that women's time and energy are endlessly available for ministering to the needs of others, and women themselves feel this constraint on their endeavours. The wifely, daughterly, or sisterly devotion which sustained a writer like William Wordsworth contrasts sharply with the trials of a Jane Austen or Elizabeth Gaskell, snatching time to think and write from the duties of a household. And let us not forget women such as Alice Walker's grandmother, for whom *any* time of leisure was stolen from a life of unending drudgery.

Even those women who have had the time and means to write have faced other barriers and 'incitements to silence'. If women's utterance is not forbidden, it is often ignored; and if not ignored, then received with howls of execration. It is the fear of censure which leads to self-censorship, a phenomenon amply attested in the history of women's writing.

It is well-known, for example, that many women writers in the nineteenth century adopted male pen-names, both to ensure that their work would receive serious critical attention untainted by stereotypes of women's inferior skill, and also to escape the charge of 'coarseness' or indecency which fell on women dealing with the literary themes of sexuality and passion. Certain forms or genres were thought unseemly and inappropriate for women writers. Cora Kaplan, introducing Elizabeth Barrett Browning's epic *Aurora Leigh*, observes that despite the great achievement of this poem, critical opinion has preferred to represent its author as a lyric poet, remembering her particularly for her love poems to Robert Browning – lyrics and love poetry are more suitably 'feminine'. (Ironically, *Aurora Leigh* discusses this very issue.) Kaplan also quotes a number of contemporary reviews which complain of the unfemininity of Barrett Browning's heroine, and of coarseness in her language.[7]

Yet if women writers must take pains to avoid being unfeminine, they must also avoid being too explicitly, uncomfortably feminine: many women have felt constrained to keep silent about specifically female experience and concerns, since these have been defined as outside the 'human values' literature deals with.

The pressure to avoid discussing female experience is not confined to the literary domain. It is felt throughout public discourse and to some extent in private discourse too. In the early years of the modern Women's Liberation Movement women organized consciousness raising (CR) groups and 'speakouts' where the aim was to discuss and bear witness to experiences unspoken or unmentionable previously – experiences like incest and backstreet abortion, as well as less obviously taboo subjects from our lives. This was perceived as a political act of breaking silence, painful but liberating. It challenged prevailing views of the world, and lessened the isolation of individual women.

Exactly the same political responsibility for breaking silence faces the feminist producer of literary discourse, but to do so is, if anything, even more difficult for her. Both the traditional themes of the literary work and the traditional language in which it is couched seem not to have been made for the expression of our concerns. This, combined with the self-censorship many women have felt obliged to practise, raises an issue which has become central in feminist analyses of women's silence: the quest for an authentic 'women's language' or 'feminine writing'. Feminists in some traditions have posed the question whether it is enough for women to speak and write as men do: for if we are 'allowed in' to literature and culture only on condition that we accept conventional (i.e., masculine) ways of expressing ourselves, we are simply exchanging one silence for another, albeit manifested in a more subtle form. That is what the French writer Hélène Cixous means when she speaks of some women 'doing men's writing for them'.[8]

7

A number of women, particularly but not exclusively in France, have advocated that we find ways of writing which acknowledge and attempt to embody women's *difference*. Annie Leclerc (see below, pp. 74–9) calls for a literature of what has remained unwritten: the reality and the pleasures of the female body. The male literary establishment does not want women to discuss these things openly; but Annie Leclerc robustly maintains that

> it's too bad for him, but I must talk about the pleasures of my body, no, not those of my soul, my virtue or my feminine sensitivity, but the pleasures of my woman's belly, my woman's vagina, my woman's breasts, luxuriant pleasures that you can't even imagine.

In stressing the need to speak of the body and not those vaguely spiritual qualities ('soul', 'sensitivity') beneath which women's sexuality is often concealed, Leclerc does of course echo other woman writers, notably Virginia Woolf in her essay 'Professions for women'.[9]

'Difference' in women's writing does not only refer to what is written about, but also to the language in which it is written. For many women, the kind of writing that addresses female sexuality and experience requires a new form of language, a radical remaking of literary style in the image of woman rather than man. Again, the inadequacy of 'male' language is not a new preoccupation for women writers, though their views on what would constitute a female alternative have varied at different historical periods. In her interesting essay (see below, pp. 41–56), Josephine Donovan quotes writers of the Renaissance in England like 'Jane Anger', Margaret Cavendish, and Dorothy Osborne, who criticized the flowery 'euphuistic' and 'Ciceronian' style favoured by many men of the early modern period. Donovan suggests that women's preference for the 'plain style' was related to their lack of any training in classical languages and the rhetorical tradition of the ancients. Female education was vernacular education, and the literary genres which came to be associated with women (the novel in particular) were those which grew out of private vernacular writing (letters/diaries) and drew little or nothing from classical models. Early women writers like Cavendish and Osborne forged a style which was artless and informal where men's seemed pedantic and strained.

Virginia Woolf, writing early this century, expresses views on male style which are strikingly similar to her foresisters' criticisms of their male contemporaries. Both Woolf and her fellow modernist Dorothy

Richardson deliberately tried in their fiction to get away from male subject-matter and what they regarded as male sentence structure – 'too loose, too heavy, too pompous for a woman's use'. (It should be pointed out, though, that despite the similarity of their criticisms of male style, Woolf and Richardson's 'female sentence' was quite different from the 'plain style' of Cavendish and Osborne.)

The conviction that existing style and even grammar are male in form persists to the present day. It is trenchantly expressed by Luce Irigaray, for instance, in her assertion that 'all western discourse presents a certain isomorphism with the masculine sex' (see below pp. 80–96). She adds that women's language, when we unearth it from its present repressed position, will be unlike the 'subject, predicate' or 'subject, verb, object' of grammatical tradition. This very radical vision of feminine language is shared by many in France. Writing about developments there in the 1970s, Shoshana Felman sums up their preoccupations:

> The challenge facing the woman today is nothing less than to reinvent language... to speak not only against but outside the structure... to establish a discourse the status of which would no longer be defined by the phallacy of male meaning.[10]

This current in the feminist critique of language is based on accepting a theory about language to be found in the writings of psychoanalysts who follow the late Jacques Lacan. Without going too deeply into this theory now (it is outlined in the paper by Cora Kaplan, below pp. 57–69, and readers may also refer to a number of other sources)[11] language for the Lacanian constitutes a 'symbolic order' which is the foundation of culture, and it is as s/he acquires language that the child becomes a cultural being. But language acquisition is affected by gender. Because in a patriarchal culture the most privileged symbol or *signifier* is the phallus, the order of language is a masculine order dominated by the phallus; hence those who do not possess the phallus – women – remain marginal to language, *in* the culture (since women are compelled to learn to speak) but not entirely *of* it. It is from these ideas that Felman's phrase 'the phallacy of male meaning' or Irigaray's 'isomorphism with the masculine sex' gain their significance.

Feminine writing, then, is *outside the structure*: but to different degrees, depending on which theorist you read. Irigaray speaks of a language in which the masculine structure has entirely broken down; another writer in the psychoanalytic tradition, Julia Kristeva, talks about pre-symbolic features 'disrupting' discourse, producing the oddness and fragmentation typical of modernist and symbolist poetry.[12] Some women, including Richardson and Woolf, are particularly concerned with expressing in their language a less linear conception of time and space. In the writing of many women influenced by these ideas, there is a challenge to the notion of 'rational discourse', an interest in playing with the forms of language so that its less rational aspects, like puns and parapraxes, are foregrounded. There are also moves towards breaking down the conventions of what you can talk about in literature, and how. (It should also be noted that this 'feminine' sort of writing need not be confined to *women* writers, and that those women who advocate it often hold up men as models of what they are trying to achieve: Julia Kristeva discusses Mallarmé and Lautréamont, while Dorothy Richardson admired Proust and Joyce. What most feminists of this type would insist on, however, is that 'feminine' writing done by either sex is progressive because it challenges certain myths (rationality, unity) that are essentially patriarchal.)

The ideas I have been discussing here are not without their critics. Many feminists of a more sociological turn of mind would probably agree with the American critic Elaine Showalter that

> The appropriate task for feminist criticism is to concentrate on women's access to language...on the ideological and cultural determinants of expression [i.e., the social rather than the psychic]. The problem is not that language is insufficient to express women's consciousness but that women have been denied the full resources of language and have been forced into silence, euphemism and circumlocution.[13]

It is worth looking at some objections along these lines, since this is one way of demonstrating the diversity of the feminist critique of language and the variety of approaches to a problem – that of silence and exclusion – which all feminists readily acknowledge and discuss.

The first objection is encapsulated in the question, should feminists in fact be looking for an authentic women's language or writing? The current in feminism which advocates this is one which, heavily reliant on Freudian categories, places emphasis on differences between the two genders (not, it should be said, crude biological differences but differences constructed in psychic development and family relations). But many feminisms, while obviously concerned with 'difference' in the sense of inequality, would prefer to stress the underlying similarity of men and women. Dividing the world into masculine and feminine spheres, and justifying this on the grounds of (natural) sex difference is an ancient strategy of the male oppressor; it is the business of feminism to call it into question, but notions of women's or feminine language just aid and abet anti-feminist thinking.

Then there are the themes of 'feminine writing' – the body, sexuality, irrationality. As a number of critics have pointed out, this too is quite close to traditional anti–feminism, in which women are identified with sex, body, passion while men are identified with reason and the mind.

The question of irrationality is especially vexing. It is possible – some would say, crucial – to assert that women have the right to participate in rational discourse, and that in doing so they in no way abdicate their femininity. Simone de Beauvoir, for instance, explicitly rejected the idea that rationality and everything else our culture values were inherently masculine: she said they were human, universal, but dishonestly claimed by the patriarchs for themselves. Although many feminists would emphasize the sexism of our values and of what counts as true knowledge, great art, etc., they would probably agree with de Beauvoir's contention that things like 'rationality' should not be gendered, and the same would apply to 'female' qualities like emotion. The whole spectrum of human possibilities should rather be opened up to the whole of humanity.

A second objection to 'feminine writing', which occurs with some force to a linguist, if not to a literary critic, is that much of the feminist project of Irigaray *et al.* is completely utopian: it stirs the imagination but has little concrete pay off, because it tends to misconceive the nature of language. Of course conventions of usage and style change: the modernism of Richardson, Woolf, and Joyce serves as an illustration. And it is obviously possible, not to mention desirable, to bring new topics and viewpoints into the literary domain. But the potential for 'reinventing language' in the literal sense some writers seem to intend this is negligible. On one hand, the form of natural languages is given (it appears) by human mental capacities. So Irigaray's vision of a totally different language, outside the grammatical structures we know, cannot be a description of an actual possibility. On the other hand – and this is an even more important point – language is irreducibly a social practice, grounded in history. Mere individual acts of will do not change it, nor can it be 'reinvented' from scratch. Whatever changes in perception and expression we manage collectively to bring about, we will always carry with us the baggage of history in the domain of language as everywhere else. We must be aware of this point in our struggles, or we will end up like feminist Humpty Dumpties: 'when I use a word it means what I choose it to mean, neither more nor less'.[14] In the second part of this introduction and of the book, we will be concerned with a feminist historical understanding of language, and with the possibilities for intervention in linguistic practice.

'Naming' and representation: the struggle for meaning

We have been looking at women's aspirations to be speakers and writers in all domains of culture. Now we must consider a slightly different issue: not women speaking but women spoken about. Language, as we have observed, is a major component in any human culture. It encodes the culture's values and preoccupations, and transmits these, furthermore, to each new generation. It is thus of the utmost importance for feminists to examine how issues of gender are represented in languages. Like other representations (for example, those of the visual arts), linguistic representations both give a clue to the place of women in the culture and constitute one means whereby we are kept in our place.

Many strands in the feminist critique of language have specifically concerned themselves with representation. They have concluded, on the whole, that our languages are sexist: that is, they represent or 'name' the world from a masculine viewpoint and in accordance with stereotyped beliefs about the sexes. Mary Daly points out that in the cherished mythology of the Judeo-Christian world it is 'man' in the person of Adam who gives names to God's creation.[15] And this male monopoly of naming has serious consequences.

Many feminists have made the claim that the names we give our world are not mere reflections of reality, nor arbitrary labels with no relation to it. Rather, names are a culture's way of fixing what will actually count as reality in a universe of overwhelming, chaotic sensations, all pregnant with a multitude of possible meanings.

In fact this is far from being a novel idea. Whether linguistic categories define, as opposed to reflecting perception is a question that recurs in western discourse on language. In modern linguistics the fullest and most influential statement of a 'determinist' position comes from the anthropological linguists Sapir and Whorf, who wrote in the early twentieth century in America.[16] They suggested that the extreme divergence anthropologists found between the perceptions of Europeans

12

and native Americans might be related to differences in the structure of Amerindian and 'standard average European' languages. Members of different cultures and speech communities may have wildly differing notions of such apparent human fundamentals as the nature of time and space, the composition of the colour spectrum, the division between animate and inanimate, and so on. For a Whorfian one powerful explanation of this would lie in the underlying grammatical and semantic categories provided by different languages – categories according to which we cannot help organizing our experience.

Although most present-day linguists reject, or at the very least are sceptical about strong determinist theses, a number of strands in the feminist critique of language have adopted Whorfian views enthusiastically. (See, for instance, the extracts from Dale Spender, below pp. 102–10, who is probably their most thorough-going feminist exponent.) The distinctive contribution made by these feminists is to assert first, that many languages have an underlying semantic or grammatical rule whereby male is positive and female negative, so that the tenets of male chauvinism are encoded into language; and second, that the reason why languages are structured in this sexist way is that their rules and meanings have been literally 'man made': women have been excluded from naming and definition.

If one consequence of this exclusion is the sexism of our existing expressions (a topic to which we shall shortly return), another, according to several writers, is an *absence* of words for certain feelings and ideas, those the male language-makers have chosen not to 'name' because they do not fit in with the official male worldview. Since feelings and ideas without words to express them may remain fleeting, inchoate, and unrecognized by the culture at large, our languages are less than perfect vehicles for expressing women's most pressing concerns (a link appears here with the debate on silence and authenticity). It is interesting to note that in feminist utopias – imaginary ideal worlds like those of Charlotte Perkins Gilman's *Herland*, Marge Piercy's *Woman on the Edge of Time*, and Monique Wittig's *Les Guerrillères* – there is often some attempt at a modified language. A female utopia could not be content with what we have now. One recent science-fiction novel specifically deals with the theme of women inventing a new language in order to change the (oppressive) world they live in. A sample of this imaginary language (Láadan) from Suzette Haden Elgin's *Native Tongue* is reprinted in this book (see below, pp. 160–3).

The feminist critique of language is not, of course, united on the question of whether language does create reality. Feminist versions of Whorfian determinism beg a number of questions, and these are debated. Powerful arguments exist against determinism *per se*: the fact that we can learn new languages, add new concepts to language, translate fairly successfully from one language to another, and so on. Moreover, there is surely something very bizarre about Spender's vision of men, or an elite of them, getting round a table to decide on the rules of language. I will come back to this point later on in the discussion, and suggest a way in which the idea of men controlling meaning and usage might be made more precise and more in line with what we know about the world.

However, it is very important to note that one does not have to be in the least determinist to accept that language is in many ways sexist. Language could be seen as a *reflection* of sexist culture; or (in my view a more satisfactory position) it could be seen as a carrier of ideas and assumptions which become, through their constant re-enactment in discourse, so familiar and conventional we miss their significance. Potentially, the ideas embedded in our usage could be challenged; actually, it is rare for this to happen. Thus sexism is not merely reflected but acted out and thus reinforced in a thousand banal encounters.

Before returning to this abstract issue it is worth looking more closely at *what* assumptions are being reinforced in the language as it stands. There is a slippery heterogeneity about so-called 'sexist language': it is not just a case of certain words being offensive, but of sexism entering into many levels of language from morphology (for example, word endings) which is usually seen as part of a language's core, through to stylistic conventions in specific 'fields' of discourse, which are much less general, more conscious, and more context-bound. We must be careful to consider different fields of discourse in different terms, since traditions of sexism in discussions of poetry are not the same as those in, for instance, rape reporting. The underlying assumptions are different, too: they may even be at odds with each other (as in the stereotype of woman as silent, which contrasts with the stereotype of woman as inveterate talker). The point I am trying to make here is really that 'sexist language' cannot be regarded as simply the 'naming' of the world from one, masculist perspective; it is better conceptualized as a multifaceted phenomenon occurring in a number of quite complex systems of representation, all with their places in historical traditions.

Some examples may illustrate what I mean by 'multifaceted' and reveal the importance of specific histories. One of the most familiar instances of sexism in English is the way that *man*, pronominalized as *he*, has been represented as synonymous with humanity. Thus there is an English grammatical rule that all generic or indefinite referents are of the masculine gender; the (generic) child of the psychology textbook and the writer or artist of literary criticism are conventionally male – the norm, with women as exceptions.

That this does have real effects is pointed out by Tillie Olsen (see below, pp. 164–5). Olsen observes that the constant reiteration of *he* in relation to writers makes it doubly hard for women to conceive of themselves as 'real' writers who are not at the same time freaks. She cites a poem by a woman, Denise Levertov, where the poet is personified as a man, and suggests that this constitutes a painful alienation of the woman artist, and yet another source therefore of female literary silence. Olsen also shows how the notion of the artist as male is paralleled by an idea of his raw material, his inspiration, and so on as female (another version of the classic 'man = active, woman = passive' opposition). She quotes a particularly offensive conceit of the poet Auden, in which he compares the poet to a husband impregnating his wife, language:

> The poet is the father who begets the poem which the language bears. At first sight this would seem to give the poet too little to do and the language too much, till one remembers that, as the husband, it is he, not the language, who is responsible for the success of their marriage....

In a single analogy, Auden manages to wipe out women's creativity and reduce them to passive objects in relation not just to art but also sex and reproduction! Furthermore, while the analogy would not be meaningful without certain pre-existing conventions of the culture, Auden here is doing his bit to make sure these sexist assumptions are perpetuated and recirculated in discourse. His language both reflects and reinforces sexist definitions of gender.

The idea of women as passive sexual objects is to be found expressed linguistically in various ways. One of the most obvious places where it is pervasive is the lexicon (vocabulary). Feminists have systematically researched the history and current prevalence of sexist terminology in the field of human sexuality. They have shown how the language used to describe sexual intercourse, whether clinical or colloquial, incorporates a view of activity as male ('penetration' rather than 'enclosure'; men 'screwing' where women 'get laid'). They have also pointed out that women are linguistically identified with the sexual: as Muriel Schulz (see below, pp. 134–47) points out, words originally neutral in both meaning and sex reference take on sexual connotations when they 'specialize' to refer to women (illustrative examples include *professional* and *tramp*, which have a specifically female meaning of 'prostitute or loose woman' in addition to their more general, ungendered senses). Words like this also take on negative connotations, since the sexual woman is synonymous with the whore. The existence of a rich vocabulary denoting women as whores, discussed from a historical viewpoint by Schulz, has tangible consequences for women now, since words like *slag* with no masculine equivalent are routinely used to harass women and to police the boundaries of acceptable female sexual behaviour.[17]

Linguistic conventions mark women not just as sex objects but as male property. This fact has been manifested in different conventions at different periods: for example, eighteenth-century slang referred to female genitals as 'the commodity', a mode of speech which no longer exists (though compare a phrase like 'I *had* her' meaning 'we had intercourse').[18] In our own time, a clear example of women being represented as male property appears in our naming conventions. Women traditionally take their surname from the man to whom they belong: the changing name at marriage is symbolic of the passage from father's property to husband's. The titles Miss and Mrs further indicate whether a woman is still on the market or not. It is significant that these conventions persist – albeit not totally unchallenged – after the legal status of women as men's chattels has been abolished and supposedly forgotten.

In fact, our linguistic habits often reflect and perpetuate ideas about things which are no longer embodied in law, but which continue to have covert significance in the culture. This is one reason why feminists have often paid detailed attention to language and discourse: our ways of talking about things reveal attitudes and assumptions we might well consciously disown, thus testifying to the deep-rootedness of sexism. An example may make this point less obscure. Consider the following two reports of an incident involving a married couple whose house was broken into. The first is taken from a so-called 'quality' newspaper, the *Daily Telegraph;* the second is from a 'popular' tabloid, the *Sun.* I reproduce them both to show that we are dealing not with the idiosyncrasy of some individual journalist, but with a convention of this genre, or what some theorists would call a 'discursive practice'.

> A man who suffered head injuries when attacked by two men who broke into his home in Beckenham, Kent, early yesterday, was pinned down on the bed by intruders who took it in turns to rape his wife.
>
> *(Daily Telegraph)*

> A terrified 19-stone husband was forced to lie next to his wife as two men raped her yesterday.
>
> *(Sun)*

What is happening in these reports? My interpretation would be that the act of rape is being represented as a crime against a man rather than a woman. It is relevant to recall that *rape* was originally synonymous with *theft*; in our culture once, and in some cultures still, to rape a woman was to rob her father or husband of her value by rendering her unchaste (hence the common practice of forcing the rapist of a virgin to marry his victim: after all, no one else would want 'damaged goods'). This perception of rape is supposed to have been supplanted by a view of it as an assault on a woman's bodily integrity; yet these reports suggest things are more complex than that.

There are a number of linguistic features which license my interpretation that the reports are making rape into a crime against a man. For example, the experience of the man in this incident is foregrounded in both reports. He is the first person to be mentioned, and the grammatical subject of the main clause. Significantly, too, he is the subject of the verbs *suffered* and *was forced*. A feminist would want to ask *who* is forced and who suffers in a rape: the *Sun* and the *Daily Telegraph* convey that it is the man. The woman – in each case referred to as 'his wife' – is tucked away at the end of a long complex sentence. Her rape is mentioned in a dependent clause, rather than in the main thread of the sentence. In the *Daily Telegraph* it is third in order of importance, behind the man's head injuries and the violation of 'his home' (note: not hers). In the *Sun* a similar ordering of events gives the impression that the rape itself was less appalling than the fact that the husband was forced to witness it.

This kind of analysis shows the limitations of considering sexism in representation exclusively in terms of specific single words or expressions. Apart from the lack of symmetry between *man* and *wife* in the

Daily Telegraph report, there is nothing here for a conventional feminist critique to get hold of: no generic masculines, no overtly derogatory descriptions ('blonde' or 'sexy' for example), just a series of syntactic and textual choices that add up to a sexist and androcentric worldview. Examples like these have led some feminists, including myself, to question the centrality of 'naming' in our critique of language, and to call for a rather broader focus on practices of *representation*. A theory which reduces words to 'names' will not help us come to grips with what is offensive about rape reporting or Auden's discussion of poetry: as Black and Coward have strongly argued in response to Dale Spender (see below, pp. 111–33), it is much more theoretically and practically satisfactory to challenge particular 'discursive practices' in which sexist assumptions are embodied by linguistic choices, than to keep on asserting that 'language' is globally and generally sexist in itself.

This brings us back to the work of Dale Spender and her notion of male-controlled or 'man-made' language. I have already said that the picture Spender's work sometimes conjures up of men deciding what words mean while women cook their dinner is bizarre; it is reminiscent of Humpty Dumpty in its lack of attention to the complex history of languages. But I think there is a way to make the picture more realistic (and to be fair to Spender, this is sometimes implicit in her own remarks: I am making her something of a 'fall-gal' here for the purpose of setting out my argument more clearly).

One way in which Spender's idea of 'man-made language' *is* realistic is in recognizing the importance of human agency in constructing and changing linguistic practice. Some ways of talking about language portray it as a sort of triffid: an organic growth that develops a life and will of its own. This might be a useful image for discussing certain linguistic processes (for example, some aspects of sound change), but it is hardly applicable to the linguistic representation of gender. Here, we need to look at languages as cultural edifices whose norms are laid down in things like dictionaries, grammars, stylebooks, and glossaries – all of which have historically been compiled by men, and conservative men at that. The areas covered by rules and conventions of this type may not exhaust the whole of usage, but they do regulate both what we might call 'official' language and what people think is 'correct' or 'good style'. In order for your discourse to be appropriate and authoritative, especially if you happen to be a professional user of language (teacher, bureaucrat, journalist, etc.), you must obey the rules of the codified tradition. Nor does this apply only in technologically advanced societies which support great literary and other traditions. The proverbs, stories, and conventional similes in which unlettered peoples express their cultural wisdom are equally codified and binding on speakers.

Yet why insist on this point with such force? The reason is that to detach language from its historical, cultural, and social roots, to think of it as outside individual and societal control, is a certain route to political quietism – a sense that nothing can really be changed. In certain strands of opposition to the feminist critique of language we find exactly this sort of retreat from political action. We are assured that, yes, the language is sexist and this is a very regrettable thing: but sexist conventions 'crept into' the language and have been entrenched there since time immemorial. To get rid of them is not possible; we will just have to wait until under the impact of social change they creep out again of their own accord. (To which one might reply by asking what on earth *is* this utterly abstract social change that does not involve people deliberately changing things, including conventions of linguistic usage?) If, on the other hand, we acknowledge that the conventions of representation have been historically constructed, it is evident that they can also be de- and reconstructed. It is evident, moreover, that the current feminist critique has made a certain amount of progress in this de- and reconstruction.

A pertinent instance here is the representation of male-as-norm in the use of generic *he* and *man*. Tillie Olsen refers to this as one of the 'entrenched, centuries-old oppressive power realities, early on incorporated into language' (see below, p. 164). But Ann Bodine (see below, pp. 166–86) has undertaken an historical investigation which shows that the generic masculine was only fully established as a norm of correctness fairly late in the history of English by concerted activity on the part of conservative prescriptive grammarians. It should also be noted that the generic masculine is currently in the process of having its status as a mark of correctness undermined by concerted activity on the part of *feminists*, who have battled for the right to use *she* or *they*, and even to make these the norm for all writers.[19] Authoritative grammars of English compiled by linguists are having to recognize this change of direction.[20] And while feminists would doubtless have pressed on with it regardless, it is worth pointing out that work like Bodine's gives us a valuable weapon in the struggle against sexism. Whenever we are told that generic *he* is an inalienable part of the structure of our language, we can reply that on the contrary it is a man-made convention, and a relatively recent one at that.

Prescriptive grammar is not the only male-controlled metalinguistic practice to feel the feminist squeeze. Recognizing the power of such practices to regulate, if not language then the codified norms of 'The Language', feminists are hitting back with their own critical rewritings of things like the dictionary. In the introduction to *A Feminist Dictionary* (see below, pp. 148–59), Cheris Kramarae and Paula Treichler draw attention to the authoritarian and sexist nature of mainstream lexicography; in the body of the dictionary they demonstrate their own anti-sexist and pluralist alternatives.

Feminist activity has, at the very least, sensitized speakers and writers to the non-neutral nature of representation. What was previously unnoticed and unquestioned in our usage is now the site of a struggle for meaning, in which our notions of the natural, the masculine and feminine, the elegant and the offensive, can be challenged and eventually changed. Real debate is going on in the discourses of religion, law, and science as well as in traditional literary domains. Feminist meanings may not be dominant in culture – it is hard to make a meaning stick against the social grain – but they do call into question the absolute authority of those meanings which have been taken for granted. The screams of protest issuing from traditionalists, to the effect that language change is ugly, trivial, and socially divisive make it clear that our meanings *are* impinging on the culture to a point where our critique can no longer be passed over in silence.

Dominance and difference: power and culture in women's linguistic behaviour

The third set of debates I want to look at in this volume concern the differing styles of language – particularly speech – used by women and men. These debates, while sometimes referred to in passing by writers about literature, are carried on mostly by social scientists and can be inaccessible to people outside. Nevertheless, they are both interesting in themselves and relevant to a broad understanding of the feminist critique of language. They also provide yet another perspective on women's exclusion from some areas of language, and on cultural representations of the feminine.

It is important to be aware that discussion of differences in the linguistic behaviour of the sexes has a lengthy history. Contemporary debates both draw on and react against a rich and complex heritage of 'folklinguistic' speculation (folklinguistics is, as the term suggests, people's unscientific, common-sense knowledge about language). This heritage can be unearthed by studying a large body of comment on the English language going back as far as the fourteenth century. Historians of English use this tradition as a source of evidence on the status of the vernacular, the extent of regional variation, and the degree of anxiety about linguistic matters at different periods. But it also contains many interesting remarks about gender differences and women's language. From these it appears it has long been received wisdom that women and men differ greatly in their usage.

Jonathan Swift, for example, in his letter to the Earl of Oxford of 1712, *A Proposal for Correcting, Improving and Ascertaining the English Tongue*, includes a long digression on an experiment he claims to have conducted, asking women and men to write down the first letters that came into their heads: he reports that

> upon reading this Gibberish we have found that which the Men had writ, by the frequent encountering of rough consonants to sound like High Dutch, and the other by the Women, like Italian, abounding in vowels and liquids.[21]

Swift's conclusion is that since the sexes are phonologically complementary – 'women do naturally discard the consonants, as we do the vowels' – it is desirable for both sexes to participate in polite conversation in order to keep the language balanced. (Incidentally, Swift's association of men with consonants and Germanic languages where vowels and Romance languages connoted femininity was a recurring theme in discussions of language right up to the present century.)

Swift's *Proposal* is rather unusual in that it does not simply deplore the malign influence of women on language. Most commentators of his and other times do sternly deplore it; but the relation of their criticisms to linguistic reality may be judged from the fact that as views on language alter, so do the sins of which women stand accused.

For instance, eighteenth-century texts are preoccupied above all with 'ascertaining' the language – that is, fixing it so that like Greek and Latin, the dead classical tongues, it would be the same for all time. The idea that, in Pope's phrase, 'such as Chaucer is shall Dryden be' (i.e., incomprehensible to succeeding ages) struck terror in the hearts of the era's prescriptivists. They were therefore highly critical of those who introduced ephemeral words, creating an English in a state of constant flux. Needless to say, these wanton innovators were popularly supposed to be female rather than male. 'That we are indebted to the ladies for most of these ornaments to our language', wrote Richard Cambridge with heavy irony, 'I readily acknowledge'.[22]

But concepts of what should be valued in a language altered as time went on. In the age of Darwin, languages came to be regarded as natural organisms which evolved and adapted. Innovation, instead of threatening a language, became the mark of its success in adapting to new conditions. And at this point, women mysteriously lost their ascribed incorrigible tendency to innovate. By 1922 we find the linguist Otto Jespersen castigating women for their lack of innovation, calling their language 'languid and insipid' and referring to men as 'the chief renovators of language' (see below, p. 212).

Jespersen's notorious chapter 'The Woman' in his *Language: Its Nature, Development and Origin* encapsulates, albeit with a scholarly gloss, the received wisdom amassed over more than a century. Its main motifs will be depressingly familiar: women speakers and writers are, it appears, conservative, timorous, overly polite and delicate, trivial in their subject matter, and given to simple, repetitive or incomplete/illogical sentence structures ('like a set of pearls joined together on a string of *ands*'), softly spoken, and soft in the head. Jespersen here recycles mere popular prejudice – he makes no attempt to produce evidence for his claims except, interestingly, from the speech of characters in literature written by men – and for this he has been censured and ridiculed by feminists. Yet every discourse incorporates elements of what it opposes and aims to replace. The feminist critique of language is no exception, and the stereotypes ingrained in the linguistic tradition return to haunt us in various guises.

Thus the attentive reader may already have noticed that Jespersen's catalogue in many of its details is not unlike some *feminist* conceptions of women's language. The 'set of pearls' may well recall Virginia Woolf's quest for a less heavy and pompous sentence, like the 'elastic', 'enveloping' structure for which she praises Dorothy Richardson's writing. The irrationality of women's discourse, to which Jespersen calls attention, has its feminist admirers, as we have already observed; and it is particularly telling that Jespersen should oppose the 'grammatical' organization of male language to the 'emotional' organization of women's through the use of stress and pitch variation, since this same distinction is made by Julia Kristeva to mark the break between the 'masculine' symbolic and the 'feminine' semiotic. Nor do these echoes occur only in one type of highly literary feminist analysis.

In her pioneering study of the early 1970s, *Language and Woman's Place* (see below, pp. 221–33), the linguist Robin Lakoff also echoes Jespersen in her claim that certain features are typical of women's speech: overpoliteness, heavily qualified statements, 'empty' vocabulary, and trivial subject matter. Like Jespersen, Lakoff relied on her own intuitions and casual observation. But unlike Jespersen, Lakoff wrote from a feminist perspective – as did Kristeva and Virginia Woolf. Perhaps when we imagine a feminine language, we are more influenced than we realize by a tradition of comment on sex differences which we did not create and which is blatantly antifeminist.

Faced with this centuries-old tradition of comment, a feminist critique could do several things. One option, for instance, would be to challenge the stereotypes: to say, 'nonsense, of course women don't talk like that'. Certain stereotypes are indeed no longer current: Swift's claim about women's affinity for vowels seems merely silly now to even the most diehard chauvinist, while Jespersen's remarks about women's lesser brain-power leave contemporary readers embarrassed or incredulous. Yet on the whole, the feminist critique has accepted that stereotypes may contain a measure of truth. It has opted therefore for a different strategy: reinterpretation of what stereotype behaviours mean. This reinterpretation has, however, taken two distinct forms.

The first retains a traditional, negative evaluation of women's language. Lakoff, for instance, acknowledges female linguistic inadequacies as pointed out by people like Jespersen; but she carefully explains these inadequacies in political and cultural terms, rather than seeing them as natural sex differences. Lakoff maintains that women are forced to learn a weak, trivial, and deferential style as part of their socialization, which is essentially a training in how to be subordinate. In other words, she regards women's style as a reflex of their powerlessness and men's power over them. I shall refer to this as the 'dominance approach'; and while Lakoff's version of it is not the only one, or indeed the most popular one among feminists today, it is still an important way of understanding sex differences in verbal style.

An alternative approach is again to acknowledge that women use language in a different way from men, and perhaps in the very way the stereotypes suggest, but to reinterpret this in a more positive light, as an authentic manifestation of a female culture. There are clearly elements of this 'difference approach' in the work of Luce Irigaray or Annie Leclerc, and it is strongly argued from a different viewpoint by Deborah Jones in her article 'Gossip: notes on women's oral culture' (see below pp. 242–50). The 'difference approach' says that if we can stop assessing things by sexist male standards, the features now labelled 'trivial' and 'deferential' will appear as 'women-centred' and 'supportive'.

Which of these approaches should be preferred by feminists? In my view, a meaningful and effective feminist critique will incorporate elements of both, as well as maintaining a certain scepticism about the actual facts concerning male and female use of language. To discover which stereotypes are baseless and which have some truth in them is an essential precondition for further discussion: there is little point in revaluing a speech style that has never existed outside the antifeminist imagination (though of course false stereotypes are interesting as clues to our *ideology* of femininity and sex difference). Investigation of actual behaviour is also necessary in so far as it confirms that 'women' and 'men' are not homogeneous groups: class, ethnic, and cultural divisions are important too, and the speech of middle-class western Europeans cannot simply be generalized to all groups of women. It is an empirical question of some significance whether stylistic features exist which are cross-cultural markers of femininity. At present, too little research has been done for any firm conclusion to be drawn on that point.

Nevertheless, we know enough about some speech communities for questions of explanation and interpretation to arise. Having rejected some stereotypes as baseless, what of the differences that do exist between male and female verbal styles?

Let me stress first of all that the differences are quantitative not absolute. There is little warrant for notions of a separate women's language, or even what used to be called a 'genderlect' (i.e., a distinctive dialect used by one gender). Linguists have not found, for example, that men never use hedges like *sort of, y' know, well;* rather, they have found in a number of communities that women tend to use more of them than men. It should also be noted that these results are statistical averages for groups: there will be some individual women who use fewer hedges than some men. What we are dealing with is not an iron law of behaviour but in technical language, a 'sex-preferential tendency'.

But these quantitative findings are not the result of random chance. They need to be explained and placed in social context. Here the 'dominance' and 'difference' approaches come into play. Does the fact that women use hedges more than men reflect the verbal inadequacy attendant on their socially subordinate position? Or is it a manifestation of female values evolved outside mainstream culture, more supportive and less self-aggrandizing than the unqualified statements valued in male discourse?

Both approaches have been used by researchers. Early feminist work done at the same time as Lakoff's, or in its wake, tended to focus on the effects of male dominance on interaction between women and men. One typical, and notorious, finding of this era was Zimmerman and West's results for interruptions in conversation.[23] They found that, overwhelmingly, men interrupted women; that this related to social dominance and not some invariable masculine style was suggested by the very low incidence of interruption in all-male conversations.

This sort of research, while it explained its findings in terms of sexual inequalities, nevertheless diverged from Lakoff's idea of a weak and deferential women's style which girls learnt as part of their early socialization. The work of Pamela Fishman (see below, pp. 234–41) represents a more sophisticated version of the 'dominance approach' in which women's style is seen as the outcome of power struggles and negotiations which are played out under the surface of conversation. Rather than belonging inalienably to the woman, 'female' stylistic features belong to the context in which she is trying to interact with a male superordinate. Thus women ask more questions than men (Fishman's major finding, often replicated since), not because insecurity is part of our psychology and therefore of our speech style (as Lakoff had suggested), but because men in a dominant position often refuse to take responsibility for the smooth conduct of interpersonal relations (what Fishman calls doing the 'interactional shitwork'). Asking them a question is thus an effective strategy for forcing them to acknowledge and contribute to the talk. It can be argued that features like question-asking are not deferential at all; on the contrary, they provide a means for the socially powerless to assert some kind of control over particular conversations.

Recently, however, there has been something of a return to the idea of a female style learnt in childhood. This time it comes from proponents of the 'difference approach'. Feminist researchers have suggested that women do organize their talk differently from men – they are more co-operative and less hierarchical, more supportive of their interlocutors and less concerned with competing for the floor. The evidence for this claim comes from studies of all-female groups (for example, 'rap' and CR groups – unfortunately parallel studies of all-male groups are rare).

But why should women in these groups have a different and more co-operative style of talk than men? According to some recent commentators, because the sexes form separate subcultures with separate norms.[24] This is crucially the case in childhood: girls play with other girls, boys with other boys. Girls' and boys' peer groups are organized differently, and this is reflected in their patterns of speech. For most of the cultures sociolinguistics has studied, mainly in western Europe and North America but including various class and ethnic groups, boys form large, hierarchically organized gangs whereas girls have looser groupings based on pairs or small clusters of 'best friends'. Among boys, therefore, there is competition for powerful positions in the hierarchy, and this encourages assertive talk, putting people down, giving orders, and so on. Among girls, there is more mutual support and less need for individual self-assertion. Girls' speech is marked by intimacy and self-disclosure, and by great concern for others. These early patterns persist into adulthood, and this explains not only certain actual differences, but the different expectations the sexes have of talk.

Both the 'dominance' and the 'difference' perspectives are valuable in two ways. At a theoretical level, they allow us to perceive women as complex social beings who are more than just victims of our conditioning, or of men. Women's speech appears as a way of negotiating powerlessness, or indeed as a positive identification with alternative values. At a political level, each approach underpins important demands. One strategy feminists have used is to develop more assertive styles, the better to prevent ourselves being constantly interrupted and ignored in verbal encounters. This is certainly necessary and effective. But we have also been critical of the notion that confrontational, unsupportive styles of discourse are always appropriate. These styles are often used in public arenas, even 'progressive' ones like trades unions and left-wing groups. Not only do they disadvantage women, who are more likely than men to find them alien and intimidating, they are also destructive of group solidarity and democratic spirit, and thus hinder the achievement of collective goals. Here, as elsewhere in feminist politics, two differing approaches go hand in hand: we can work towards appropriating men's prerogatives at the same time as we insist that the rules of the entire game should be changed.

* * *

The debate on women's language and language about women – what it is, what it should be, what it could be – still has a long way to go. As I suggested at the start of this essay, it is a live issue rather than a dead controversy. But although it may be too soon to assess the full effects of the feminist critique on our everyday speech and our literary production, it is certainly not too soon to perceive that there have been changes. However different things may look in a few years, however inadequate this volume may come to seem as a guide, the debate will continue to be grounded in its own history, and therefore to proceed broadly along the lines I have tried to draw here.

Of course there will continue to be differences of emphasis within the critique, and real theoretical and political disagreements, just as there are now. One of my own cherished hopes for the future, however, is that differing currents will come to be more familiar with each other's preoccupations, political aims, and theoretical assumptions. At present, there is too little cross-fertilization: sociolinguists are rarely well-versed in feminist criticism or psychoanalysis, while students of literature do not read sociolinguistics or anthropology. An important part of the intellectual context for the feminist critique – the history of linguistic thought in the west – continues to be obscure for most linguists and most critics.

I believe that we must make the effort to broaden our horizons; not only to acknowledge diversity in principle, but to come to terms with a wider range of writings in practice. In compiling this volume I have tried to take a small step in the right direction by bringing together different approaches, concerns, and academic disciplines, encompassing both the literary and the social scientific. I hope that readers will find they are excited by the scope and the vitality of the feminist critique of language.

Notes

1 Deborah Cameron, *Feminism and Linguistic Theory* (London: Macmillan, 1985), p. 5.

2 The meaning of diaries for women is discussed by Rebecca Hiscock, 'Listening to her self', in Graham McGregor and R. S. White (eds), *The Art of Listening* (London: Croom Helm, 1986).

3 Some examples are given by Jespersen (this volume, pp. 201–20); more up-to-date discussion can be found in Ann Bodine, 'Sex differentiation in language', in B. Thorne and N. Henley (eds), *Language and Sex: Difference and Dominance* (Rowley, Mass.: Newbury House, 1975).

4 Alice Walker, *In Search of our Mother's Gardens* (London: Women's Press, 1984), pp. 233–4.

5 Virginia Woolf, *A Room of One's Own and Three Guineas* (London: Hogarth Press, 1984).

6 Tillie Olsen, *Silences* (London: Virago Press, 1980).

7 Elizabeth Barrett Browning, *Aurora Leigh and Other Poems*, introduced by Cora Kaplan (London: Women's Press, 1978).

8 Hélène Cixous, 'The laugh of the medusa', in Elaine Marks and Isabelle de Courtivron (eds), *New French Feminisms* (London: Harvester Press, 1981).

9 Virginia Woolf, 'Professions for women', *Collected Essays*, vol. II (London: Hogarth Press, 1966).

10 Shoshana Felman, 'Women and madness', *Diacritics* 5, (1975).

11 See Cameron, *Feminism and Linguistic Theory*, ch. 7; or for a detailed exposition, Rosalind Coward and John Ellis, *Language and Materialism* (London: Routledge & Kegan Paul, 1977).

12 See Toril Moi (ed.), *The Kristeva Reader* (Oxford: Basil Blackwell, 1986), and also Moi's *Sexual/Textual Politics* (London: Methuen, 1985), for illuminating comments on the work of Kristeva.

13 Elaine Showalter, 'Feminist criticism in the wilderness', *Critical Inquiry* 8 no. 2 (1981), p. 193.

14 Lewis Carroll, *Through the Looking Glass* (London: Dent, 1976).

15 Mary Daly, *Beyond God the Father* (London: Women's Press, 1986).

16 See Benjamin Lee Whorf, *Language, Thought and Reality*, ed. J. Carroll (Cambridge, Mass: MIT Press, 1976).

17 This is cogently discussed by the sociologist Sue Lees in *Losing Out* (London: Hutchinson, 1986).

18 The meaning of eighteenth-century sexual slang is touched on by Anna Clark, *Women's Silence, Men's Violence* (London: Pandora, 1987).

19 See, for instance, the practical handbook by Casey Miller and Kate Swift, *A Handbook of Nonsexist Writing* (London: Women's Press, 1980).

20 For example, R. Quirk *et al*, *A Comprehensive Grammar of the English Language* (London: Longman, 1986).

21 Jonathan Swift, *A Proposal for Correcting, Improving and Ascertaining the English Tongue*, in *Prose works of Jonathan Swift* vol. IV, ed. H. Davis (Oxford: Basil Blackwell, 1957), p. 13.

22 From Susie Tucker, *English Examined: Two Centuries of Comment on the Mother Tongue* (Cambridge: Cambridge University Press, 1961) p. 93.

23 Don Zimmerman and Candace West, 'Sex roles, interruptions and silences in conversation', in Barrie Thorne and Nancy Henley (eds), *Language and Sex: Difference and Dominance* (Rowley, Mass.: Newbury House, 1975), pp. 105–29.

24 Two papers which have been very influential in arguing this case are Marjorie Goodwin, 'Directive response sequences in girls' and boys' task activities', in S. McConnell-Ginet *et al.* (eds), *Women and Language in Literature and Society* (New York: Praeger, 1980), pp. 157–73; and Daniel Maltz and Ruth Borker, 'A cultural approach to male/female misunderstanding', in John Gumperz (ed.), *Language and Social Identity* (Cambridge: Cambridge University Press, 1982), pp. 195–216.

Part One

SPEECH AND SILENCE

Introduction

The first three papers reprinted here deal with the nature of, and reasons for women's 'silence' – their virtual absence from literary domains before the seventeenth century and their apparent preference thereafter for particular genres and styles (especially for novels rather than essays or poetry).

Virginia Woolf, writing in 1929, stresses the material and social constraints on women up until her own time: the lack of education, the domestic responsibilities, the sanctions attendant on 'unwomanly' aspirations, and the restricted experiences available for women artists to draw on. Josephine Donovan takes a similarly sociological point of view, but focuses in more detail on women's participation in private writing (for example, letters, diaries, autobiography) and their lack of access to the classical models which dictated both the subject-matter and the style of more public literature. She argues that when classical authority declined in the intellectual shifts of a post-Cartesian era, women were well placed to produce new forms of writing, specifically the novel.

Cora Kaplan, in contrast, while acknowledging the historical and material factors just mentioned, attempts a psychoanalytically informed account of women's silence. She claims that as the most concentrated and prestigious form of symbolic language, poetry is forbidden to women on a deeper level than mere 'lack of access', and that individual women must internalize the prohibition on poetic utterance. Hence the ambivalent or defiant feelings expressed so often by early women poets. Whereas Woolf hints that women writers of this century have partly resolved their troubled relationship to language and literature, and looks forward to a full resolution in the future, Kaplan sees this troubled relationship as integral to patriarchal cultures, reproduced with each generation in the formation of our psychic identities. Thus language remains '[women's] as a consequence of being human, and at the same time not theirs as a consequence of being female'.

In the next three pieces we turn to the question of what feminine language is, or could be if it were not silenced and repressed. We begin once again with Virginia Woolf and her discussion of the style of Dorothy Richardson, the so-called 'women's sentence'. These short extracts remind us of the strong connection that still exists between notions of feminine style and the modernist dislike of realist modes. To 'be rid of realism' is equated with the disruption or subversion of patriarchy with its myth of the rational, unitary human subject.[1] (This equation may appear problematic, even ironic, in view of Josephine Donovan's contention that the realist narrative historically represented a favouring of women's writing habits.)

The other two authors in this section write in the French tradition, though from differing perspectives. Annie Leclerc in *Parole de Femme* claims the right to talk about the female body openly and explicitly. The interview with Luce Irigaray is a less polemical piece; it is not the most recent expression of Irigaray's complex views on feminine language and its repression, but it is an outstandingly clear exposition. In it all the themes of the section come together: the question of 'difference', the psychic versus social repression of woman's language, the relation of language to the body, and so on. 'Women's exile' is her cultural Otherness, a condition of being shut out from the endless conversation of men which defines what is beautiful, important, and true. The feminists writing here have advocated that women challenge the male monopoly of discourse, but they ask us to be sure to speak with our own authentic voices.

Note

1 This case is vigorously argued in Toril Moi, *Sexual/Textual Politics* (London: Methuen, 1985).

1

Women and fiction

Virginia Woolf

The Forum, *March 1929, reprinted in V. Woolf,* Collected Essays, *vol. II (London: Hogarth Press 1966).*

The title of this article can be read in two ways; it may allude to women and the fiction that they write, or to women and the fiction that is written about them. The ambiguity is intentional, for in dealing with women as writers, as much elasticity as possible is desirable; it is necessary to leave oneself room to deal with other things besides their work, so much has that work been influenced by conditions that have nothing whatever to do with art.

The most superficial enquiry into women's writing instantly raises a host of questions. Why, we ask at once, was there no continuous writing done by women before the eighteenth century? Why did they then write almost as habitually as men, and in the course of that writing produce, one after another, some of the classics of English fiction? And why did their art then, and why to some extent does their art still, take the form of fiction?

A little thought will show us that we are asking questions to which we shall get, as answer, only further fiction. The answer lies at present locked in old diaries, stuffed away in old drawers, half obliterated in the memories of the aged. It is to be found in the lives of the obscure – in those almost unlit corridors of history where the figures of generations of women are so dimly, so fitfully perceived. For very little is known about women. The history of England is the history of the male line, not of the female. Of our fathers we know always some fact, some distinction. They were soldiers or they were sailors; they filled that office or they made that law. But of our mothers, our grandmothers, our great-grandmothers, what remains? Nothing but a tradition. One was beautiful; one was red-haired; one was kissed by a Queen. We know nothing of them except their names and the dates of their marriages and the number of children they bore.

Thus, if we wish to know why at any particular time women did this or that, why they wrote nothing, why on the other hand they wrote masterpieces, it is extremely difficult to tell. Anyone who should seek among those old papers, who should turn history wrong side out and so construct a faithful picture of the daily life of the ordinary woman in Shakespeare's time, in Milton's time, in Johnson's time, would not only write a book of astonishing interest, but would furnish the critic with a weapon which he now lacks. The extraordinary woman depends on the ordinary woman. It is only when we know what were the conditions of the average woman's life – the number of her children, whether she had money of her own, if she had a room to herself, whether she had help in bringing up her family, if she had servants, whether part of the housework was her task – it is only when we can measure the way of life and the experience of life made possible to the ordinary woman that we can account for the success or failure of the extraordinary woman as a writer.

Strange spaces of silence seem to separate one period of activity from another. There was Sappho and a little group of women all writing poetry on a Greek island 600 years before the birth of Christ. They fall silent. Then about the year 1000 we find a certain court lady, the Lady Murasaki, writing a very long and beautiful novel in Japan. But in England in the sixteenth century, when the dramatists and poets were most active, the women were dumb. Elizabethan literature is exclusively masculine. Then, at the end of the eighteenth century and in the beginning of the nineteenth, we find women again writing – this time in England – with extraordinary frequency and success.

Law and custom were of course largely responsible for these strange intermissions of silence and speech. When a woman was liable, as she was in the fifteenth century, to be beaten and flung about the room if she did not marry the man of her parents' choice, the spiritual atmosphere was not favourable to the production of works of art. When she was married without her own consent to a man who thereupon became her lord and master, 'so far at least as law and custom could make him', as she was in the time of the Stuarts, it is likely she had little time for writing, and less encouragement. The immense effect of environment and suggestion upon the mind, we in our psychoanalytical age are beginning to realize. Again, with memoirs and letters to help us, we are beginning to understand how abnormal is the effort needed to produce a work of art, and what shelter and what support the mind of the artist requires. Of those facts the lives and letters of men like Keats and Carlyle and Flaubert assure us.

Thus it is clear that the extraordinary outburst of fiction in the beginning of the nineteenth century in England was heralded by innumerable slight changes in law and customs and manners. And women of the nineteenth century had some leisure; they had some education. It was no longer the exception for women of the middle and upper classes to choose their own husbands. And it is significant that of the four great women novelists – Jane Austen, Emily Brontë, Charlotte Brontë, and George Eliot – not one had a child, and two were unmarried.

Yet, though it is clear that the ban upon writing had been removed, there was still, it would seem, considerable pressure upon women to write novels. No four women can have been more unlike in genius and character than these four. Jane Austen can have had nothing in common with George Eliot; George Eliot was the direct opposite of Emily Brontë. Yet all were trained for the same profession; all, when they wrote, wrote novels.

Fiction was, as fiction still is, the easiest thing for a woman to write. Nor is it difficult to find the reason. A novel is the least concentrated form of art. A novel can be taken up or put down more easily than a play or a poem. George Eliot left her work to nurse her father. Charlotte Brontë put down her pen to pick the eyes out of the potatoes. And living as she did in the common sitting-room, surrounded by people, a woman was trained to use her mind in observation and upon the analysis of character. She was trained to be a novelist and not to be a poet.

Even in the nineteenth century, a woman lived almost solely in her home and her emotions. And those nineteenth-century novels, remarkable as they were, were profoundly influenced by the fact that the women who wrote them were excluded by their sex from certain kinds of experience. That experience has a great influence upon fiction is indisputable. The best part of Conrad's novels, for instance, would be destroyed if it had been impossible for him to be a sailor. Take away all that Tolstoy knew of war as a soldier, of life and society as a rich young man whose education admitted him to all sorts of experience, and *War and Peace* would be incredibly impoverished.

Yet *Pride and Prejudice, Wuthering Heights, Villette*, and *Middlemarch* were written by women from whom was forcibly withheld all experience save that which could be met with in a middle-class drawing-room. No first-hand experience of war, or seafaring, or politics, or business was possible for them. Even their emotional life was strictly regulated by law and custom. When George Eliot ventured to live with Mr Lewes without being his wife, public opinion was scandalized. Under its pressure she withdrew into a suburban seclusion which, inevitably, had the worst possible effects upon her work. She wrote that unless people asked of their own accord to come and see her, she never invited them. At the same time, on the other side of Europe, Tolstoy was living a free life as a soldier, with men and women of all classes, for which nobody censured him and from which his novels drew much of their astonishing breadth and vigour.

But the novels of women were not affected only by the necessarily narrow range of the writer's experience. They showed, at least in the nineteenth century, another characteristic which may be traced to the writer's sex. In *Middlemarch* and in *Jane Eyre* we are conscious not merely of the writer's character, as we are conscious of the character of Charles Dickens, but we are conscious of a woman's presence – of someone resenting the treatment of her sex and pleading for its rights. This brings into women's writing an element which is entirely absent from a man's, unless, indeed, he happens to be a working man, a negro, or one who for some other reason is conscious of disability. It introduces a distortion and is frequently the cause of weakness. The desire to plead some personal cause or to make a character the mouthpiece of some personal discontent or grievance always has a distressing effect, as if the spot at which the reader's attention is directed were suddenly twofold instead of single.

The genius of Jane Austen and Emily Brontë is never more convincing than in their power to ignore such claims and solicitations and to hold on their way unperturbed by scorn or censure. But it needed a very serene or a very powerful mind to resist the temptation to anger. The ridicule, the censure, the assurance of inferiority in one form or another which were lavished upon women who practised an art, provoked such reactions naturally enough. One sees the effect in Charlotte Brontë's indignation, in George Eliot's resignation. Again and again one finds it in the work of the lesser women writers – in their choice of a subject, in their unnatural self-assertiveness, in their unnatural docility. Moreover, insincerity leaks in almost unconsciously. They adopt a view in deference to authority. The vision becomes too masculine or it becomes too feminine; it loses its perfect integrity and, with that, its most essential quality as a work of art.

The great change that has crept into women's writing is, it would seem, a change of attitude. The woman writer is no longer bitter. She is no longer angry. She is no longer pleading and protesting as she writes. We are approaching, if we have not yet reached, the time when her writing will have little or no foreign influence to disturb it. She will be able to concentrate upon her vision without distraction from outside. The aloofness that was once within the reach of genius and originality is only now coming within the reach of ordinary women. Therefore the average novel by a woman is far more genuine and far more interesting today than it was a hundred or even fifty years ago.

But it is still true that before a woman can write exactly as she wishes to write, she has many difficulties to face. To begin with, there is the technical difficulty – so simple, apparently; in reality, so baffling – that the very form of the sentence does not fit her. It is a sentence made by men; it is too loose, too heavy, too pompous for a woman's use. Yet in a novel, which covers so wide a stretch of ground, an ordinary and usual type of sentence has to be found to carry the reader on easily and naturally from one end of the book to the other. And this a woman must make for herself, altering and adapting the current sentence until she writes one that takes the natural shape of her thought without crushing or distorting it.

But that, after all, is only a means to an end, and the end is still to be reached only when a woman has the courage to surmount opposition and the determination to be true to herself. For a novel, after all, is a statement about a thousand different objects – human, natural, divine; it is an attempt to relate them to each other. In every novel of merit these different elements are held in place by the force of the writer's vision. But they have another order also, which is the order imposed upon them by convention. And as men are the arbiters of that convention, as they have established an order of values in life, so too, since fiction is largely based on life, these values prevail there also to a very great extent.

It is probable, however, that both in life and in art the values of a woman are not the values of a man. Thus, when a woman comes to write a novel, she will find that she is perpetually wishing to alter the established values – to make serious what appears insignificant to a man, and trivial what is to him important. And for that, of course, she will be criticized; for the critic of the opposite sex will be genuinely puzzled and surprised by an attempt to alter the current scale of values, and will see in it not merely a difference of view, but a view that is weak, or trivial, or sentimental, because it differs from his own.

37

But here, too, women are coming to be more independent of opinion. They are beginning to respect their own sense of values. And for this reason the subject-matter of their novels begins to show certain changes. They are less interested, it would seem, in themselves; on the other hand, they are more interested in other women. In the early nineteenth century, women's novels were largely autobiographical. One of the motives that led them to write was the desire to expose their own suffering, to plead their own cause. Now that this desire is no longer so urgent, women are beginning to explore their own sex, to write of women as women have never been written of before; for of course, until very lately, women in literature were the creation of men.

Here again there are difficulties to overcome, for, if one may generalize, not only do women submit less readily to observation than men, but their lives are far less tested and examined by the ordinary processes of life. Often nothing tangible remains of a woman's day. The food that has been cooked is eaten; the children that have been nursed have gone out into the world. Where does the accent fall? What is the salient point for the novelist to seize upon? It is difficult to say. Her life has an anonymous character which is baffling and puzzling in the extreme. For the first time, this dark country is beginning to be explored in fiction; and at the same moment a woman has also to record the changes in women's minds and habits which the opening of the professions has introduced. She has to observe how their lives are ceasing to run underground; she has to discover what new colours and shadows are showing in them now that they are exposed to the outer world.

If, then, one should try to sum up the character of women's fiction at the present moment, one would say that it is courageous; it is sincere; it keeps closely to what women feel. It is not bitter. It does not insist upon its femininity. But at the same time, a woman's book is not written as a man would write it. These qualities are much commoner than they were, and they give even to second- and third-rate work the value of truth and the interest of sincerity.

But in addition to these good qualities, there are two that call for a word more of discussion. The change which has turned the English woman from a nondescript influence, fluctuating and vague, to a voter, a wage-earner, a responsible citizen, has given her both in her life and in her art a turn towards the impersonal. Her relations now are not only emotional; they are intellectual, they are political. The old system which condemned her to squint askance at things through the eyes or through the interests of husband or brother, has given place to the direct and practical interests of one who must act for herself, and not merely influence the acts of others. Hence her attention is being directed away from the personal centre which engaged it exclusively in the past to the impersonal, and her novels naturally become more critical of society, and less analytical of individual lives.

We may expect that the office of gadfly to the state, which has been so far a male prerogative, will now be discharged by women also. Their novels will deal with social evils and remedies. Their men and women will not be observed wholly in relation to each other emotionally, but as they cohere and clash in groups and classes and races. That is one change of some importance. But there is another more interesting to those who prefer the butterfly to the gadfly – that is to say, the artist to the reformer. The greater impersonality of women's lives will encourage the poetic spirit, and it is in poetry that women's fiction is still weakest. It will lead them to be less absorbed in facts and no longer content to record with astonishing acuteness the minute details which fall under their own observation. They will look beyond the personal and political relationships to the wider questions which the poet tries to solve – of our destiny and the meaning of life.

The basis of the poetic attitude is of course largely founded upon material things. It depends upon leisure, and a little money, and the chance which money and leisure give to observe impersonally and dispassionately. With money and leisure at their service, women will naturally occupy themselves more than has hitherto been possible with the craft of letters. They will make a fuller and a more subtle use of the instrument of writing. Their technique will become bolder and richer.

In the past, the virtue of women's writing often lay in its divine spontaneity, like that of the blackbird's song or the thrush's. It was untaught; it was from the heart. But it was also, and much more often, chattering and garrulous – mere talk spilt over paper and left to dry in pools and blots. In future, granted time, and books, and a little space in the house for herself, literature will become for women, as for men, an art to be studied. Women's gift will be trained and strengthened. The novel will cease to be the dumping-ground for the personal emotions. It will become, more than at present, a work of art like any other, and its resources and its limitations will be explored.

From this it is a short step to the practice of the sophisticated arts, hitherto so little practised by women – to the writing of essays and criticism, of history and biography. And that, too, if we are considering the novel, will be of advantage; for besides improving the quality of the novel itself, it will draw off the aliens who have been attracted to fiction by its accessibility while their hearts lay elsewhere. Thus will the novel be rid of those excrescences of history and fact which, in our time, have made it so shapeless.

So, if we may prophesy, women in time to come will write fewer novels, but better novels; and not novels only, but poetry and criticism and history. But in this, to be sure, one is looking ahead to that golden, that perhaps fabulous, age when women will have what has so long been denied them – leisure, and money, and a room to themselves.

2

The silence is broken

Josephine Donovan

Reprinted from S. McConnell-Ginet, R. Borker, and N. Furman (eds), Women and Language in Literature and Society *(New York: Praeger 1980).*

Had she been born in 1827, Dorothy Osborne would have written novels; had she been born in 1527, she would never have written at all. But she was born in 1627, and at that date though writing books was ridiculous for a woman there was nothing unseemingly in writing a letter. And so by degrees the silence is broken ...

(Virginia Woolf)[1]

Had Shakespeare had a sister of equal genius, she would not have written masterpieces. In all likelihood, as Virginia Woolf pointed out in *A Room of One's Own*, she would never have written a line. Yet roughly two centuries later women were creating masterworks of prose fiction. Indeed, women so dominated the early history of the novel that it was thought to be a 'female thing'.[2] My interest here is to examine some of the possible explanations for women's rapid move from relative literary obscurity into the limelight of literary production, an abrupt shift accomplished in a few hundred years. *Central question*

Let us begin with Shakespeare's hypothetical sister: we know that she would have been denied access to training in the Latin rhetorical tradition, which at this time was a *sine qua non* for the construction of critically acceptable *oeuvres*. However 'small' Shakespeare's Latin is claimed to be, and however 'lesse' his Greek, he nevertheless was thoroughly initiated into that tradition. T. W. Baldwin has exhaustively demonstrated the extent of Shakespeare's classical education by examining the grammar school curriculum to which young males of the period were exposed.[3] While there is no record of which school Shakespeare attended, or if he attended any school, there is overwhelming evidence of such training in the plays themselves. Shakespeare was, in short, exposed to the Latin rhetorical patterns of *classical education for ♂ — denied to ♀*

such authors as Cato, Terence, Ovid, Virgil, Horace and Seneca, as well as to the classic ancient authorities on rhetoric such as the author of the *Ad Herennium*, Cicero, and Quintilian. With a few minor exceptions most of the major English writers up to the eighteenth century (that is, up to Defoe and Richardson) received a similar training. Shakespeare's sister, however, would have been denied access to this tradition for girls were not permitted into the Latin schools.

Walter J. Ong characterized the Latin schooling system, as it developed through the Middle Ages, as a male initiation rite. In an article entitled 'Latin language study as a Renaissance puberty rite', Ong notes how from roughly 500 to 700 AD Latin no longer functioned as a vernacular spoken language. Instead a split occurred between spoken Latin, which eventually developed into the modern romance languages, and written Latin, or what Ong calls Learned Latin.

Ong

> Learned Latin, which moved only in artificially controlled channels *through the male world of the schools*, was no longer anyone's mother tongue, in a quite literal sense. Although from the sixth or eighth century to the nineteenth Latin was spoken by millions of persons, *it was never used by mothers cooing to their children*.[4]

Latin had become a male, public language, which existed only within the academic institutions. Women could only learn vernaculars and for centuries were denied access to the world of formal, public communication (including literature). As Ong notes, until the nineteenth century learning Latin meant entrance into the male educated elite. Latin had become a *'sex-linked language, a kind of badge of masculine identity'*.[5]

> Under these circumstances learning Latin took on the characteristics of a puberty rite, a *rite de passage* or initiation rite: it involved isolation from the family, *the achievement of identity in a totally male group* (the school), the learning of a body of relatively abstract tribal lore inaccessible to those outside the group.... The Latin world was a man's world.[6]

Intellectual education for women was scanty at best until the nineteenth century. Eileen Power notes that while there may have been some attendance by girls at elementary schools up through the fifteenth century, this practice, especially in England, was not widespread. Nor was the curriculum extensive.[7] While women of the middle class were often literate in the vernacular, it is only among the aristocracy or indeed in courtly circles that an occasional women received a formal, classical education.

It is true, however, that treatises favouring the education of women began appearing with some regularity from the early Renaissance on. Christine de Pisan (1364–1430), for example, issued her treatise on the education of women in the early fifteenth century. Renaissance humanists such as More, Erasmus, and Vives also favoured education for women, but none of them really conceived of female education as being truly equal to the male. For, as Diane Valeri Bayne points out, while they

> take exception to the contemporary beliefs by asserting women's capability for learning, [they] were traditional in judging the domestic role as the only one which women, educated or not, were suited to play. Thus, the curriculum suggested by Vives for girls is considerably less than that recommended for boys.[8]

In her *Doctrine for the Lady of the Renaissance* Ruth Kelso also emphasizes that the education for women – even of the leisured class – was primarily designed to make them entertaining wives and good mothers.[9]

Nevertheless, education of women of the courtly class at least became an ideal in the Renaissance. And in rare cases where women were highly educated they did in fact produce works of literature which were considered critically acceptable. One good example is Louise Labé (1526?–66), a poet of the 'School of Lyons', whose father decided to educate her 'à la mode italienne', which meant a regimen almost equal to male education, including training in Latin and Greek.[10] Her sonnet sequence, still considered a significant classic of French literature, was modelled upon Petrarch's but is rhetorically considerably less artificial than his, with fewer elaborate conceits and with a more direct, fresh, and therefore seemingly more authentic description of experience.[11]

In England the situation was similar to that on the continent. As Myra Reynolds notes, 'Learning was a kind of high-class individual accomplishment purely for home consumption. . . . [It] belonged only to the daughters of the nobility or of the very rich. Even within these bounds it was sporadic.'[12] *education only for the rich*

The importance of training in Latin rhetoric eventually diminished as a result of philosophical shifts that occurred in the sixteenth and seventeenth centuries. The gradual and highly complex transition from the classical–medieval worldview to the modern involved among other things an increasing de-emphasis upon 'looking to the ancients' for models in form and style. At the same time there developed an increasing focus upon the self and the powers of the individual imagination as the source of aesthetic truth.

The novel could only emerge after this philosophical groundwork had been laid. Only in a post-Cartesian world would a form like the novel have legitimacy. This is because the novel asserts the value of the experience of one individual. The experiential details of everyday life have become legitimate sources of verification (as opposed to citations gleaned from Latin *auctores*).

Pointing to Descartes's determination 'to accept nothing on trust', Ian Watt notes in his study of the novel that the *Discourse on Method* (1637) paved the way for 'the modern assumption whereby the pursuit of truth is conceived of as a wholly individual matter, *logically independent of the tradition of past thought*'.[13]

> The novel is the form of literature which most fully reflects this individualistic and innovating reorientation. Previous literary forms had reflected the general tendency of their cultures to make conformity to traditional practice the major test of truth: . . . the merits of the author's treatment were judged largely according to a view of literary decorum derived from the accepted models in the genre. This literary traditionalism was first and most fully challenged by the novel, whose primary criterion was truth to individual experience. . . .[14]

The epistemological shift towards empirical observation and induction that occurred in the seventeenth century thus provided a philosophical justification for the new genre.

From the beginning there had been an association of women with the sentimental novel, both as readers and as writers. As Michael Danahy suggests, this association relied upon stereotypes of what is the feminine.[15] In France, it stemmed from the assumption that women are authorities on love, an emotion that played a central role in the French novelistic tradition.[16] In England too vast numbers of sentimental novels were written and read by women, especially in the eighteenth century.[17]

Mrs Eliza Haywood, one of the most popular of these sentimental novelists of the early eighteenth century, explained why as a writer she was drawn to the new form:

But as I am a Woman, and consequently depriv'd of those Advantages of Education which the other Sex enjoy, I cannot . . . imagine it in my Power to soar to any Subject higher than that which Nature is not negligent to teach us.

Love is a topick which I believe few are ignorant of; there requires no aids of Learning. . . .[18]   *Need no formal education to write about love*

Haywood's statement suggests that it was a lack of education rather than any particular affinity with sentiment that led women to dwell upon feeling in their fiction.

But there is another reason why women writers should have gravitated to the novel. It was a new form, not known in antiquity. Therefore, there were really no classical models nor critical rules that one would have to know in order to practise its writing. As early as 1594 Torquato Tasso remarked how women favoured new forms (in this case, the heroic romance) and defended them against the classicists.[19]

To be sure there were attempts to appropriate classical models for the novel. Dr Johnson called it a 'comedy of romance', thus returning to an Aristotelian genre, the comedy. Henry Fielding called the novel 'a comic epic in prose', thus returning to another Aristotelian genre, the epic. But these attempts were strained, and ultimately unsuccessful. Critical judgements on the novel could not be rooted in ancient authority.

The novel broke with classical doctrine in another important way. It violated the concept of the separation of styles. For, according to classical rhetorical doctrine the domestic world was not considered appropriate matter for serious or 'high' literary attention. Comedy was the form appropriate for the everyday 'bourgeois' world (women's world) and the style appropriate for comedy was the low style.

The novel, therefore, according to classical doctrine, could not be considered an important, 'high' work of literature, because it dealt with common, everyday matters and in the 'plain style'. The persistence of this prejudice against the novel may be seen in an observation made by LeSage in 1715 regarding the literary taste of his epoch with its marked preference for classical genres.

At that time they read almost nothing but serious pieces. Comedies were scorned. They thought the best comedy or the brightest, most ingenious novel a feeble production unworthy of praise. Whereas the slightest serious work – an ode, an eclogue, a sonnet – was considered the highest effort of the human spirit.[20]

elite men stayed away from the novel

Ironically, this attitude kept male writers of the educated elite from appropriating the novel as 'theirs'. This meant that even though critically disparaged, it was nevertheless a genre which women and other cultural outsiders (less well-educated men) were free to use.

The freedom which the novelist enjoyed meant that s/he could borrow or invent techniques taken from everyday life (which was of course the primary source for the subject-matter of the novel, as well). A good example of an important novelistic technique which did not have a classical antecedent is the epistolary convention. As Mme de Staël remarked: 'the ancients would never have thought of giving their fiction such a form [because it] always presupposes more sentiment than action'.[21] *epistolary technique*

This technique developed in part from what had become a popular feminine pastime in the late seventeenth century, 'amateur' letter-writing.[22] While the familiar letter was a classical genre, the prototype of which was Cicero's *Epistulae ad Familiares* (still a model for schoolboys in the seventeenth century), the form had been considerably bowdlerized by a series of letter-writing manuals written in the 1600s. These provided correspondents with models of letters and style to be used in stock situations.[23] Because of these models it was no longer necessary to receive formal rhetorical training in order to write acceptable, if informal, prose.

Samuel Richardson, one of the earliest English novelists, had in fact been commissioned by two booksellers to compose a letter-writing manual. This apparently gave him the idea of using the epistolary convention in *Pamela* (1740). He eventually published the manual as *Letters Written To and For Particular Friends* in 1741. Richardson himself was not formally educated. Ellen Moers suggests that it was probably his own status as a cultural outsider that led him to identify with women as a class.[24] This status might also explain his willingness to use a non-traditional style and genre. For, as Watt points out, the use of the letter-writing style permitted Richardson to 'break with the traditional decorums of prose',[25] a move which may have been a conscious and deliberate one on Richardson's part.

There is at least a strong suggestion in *Clarissa* that he regarded his own literary style as infinitely superior to those of the classically educated. . . . Anna Howe [a character in *Clarissa*] tells us that '*mere* scholars' too often 'spangle over their productions with *metaphors*; they rumble into *bombast*: the *sublime* with them, lying in *words* and not in sentiment'; while others 'sinking into the classical pits, there poke and scramble about never seeking to show genius of their own.'[26]

Pamela itself became a model for the 'familiar' style – a mode emulated by Fanny Burney, the first important female novelist in England, in her first novel, *Evelina* (1778). Burney has Evelina's mentor enjoin her against writing letters which are 'correct, nicely grammatical, and run in smooth periods'. Rather he urges her to 'dash away, whatever comes uppermost'.[27] Jane Austen also used the epistolary convention in *Eleanor and Marianne*, a precursor of her first published novel, *Sense and Sensibility*.

Many of the English women prose writers of the seventeenth century are known for their correspondence. The first English woman whose letters were preserved and eventually published was Lady Brilliana Harley (1600–43). Other notable female letter-writers of the period include: Margaret Lucas Cavendish, the Duchess of Newcastle (1624–74), Katherine Fowler Philips, (1631–64), Dorothy Osborne (Temple) (1627–95), Aphra Behn (1640–89) (known primarily for her plays and novels), and somewhat later, Lady Mary Wortley Montagu (1689–1762). Of these only Cavendish's works were substantially published in her lifetime.[28] Most of the others were not published until the nineteenth century.

The unseemliness of a woman daring to publish in the seventeenth century is signalled to us in the dismay expressed by Katherine Philips when an unauthorized edition of her poems was published in 1664:

> To me . . . who never writ any line in my life with any intention to have it printed. . . . This is a most cruel accident, and hath made so proportionate an impression upon me, that really it hath cost me a sharp fit of sickness since I heard it.[29]

The Duchess of Newcastle, however, was considerably less coy on the subject of publication than the others. 'All I desire', she is said to have remarked, 'is fame.'[30] This is undoubtedly one of the reasons she was dubbed 'Mad Madge' by her contemporaries.

The other major secular prose writing done by English women in the seventeenth century was the autobiography or memoir. Here again we see a transitional genre, one that is fundamentally private or family-oriented, but which provides an experience in writing that is not far removed from the experience of writing a novel. The earliest novels, those of Defoe, for example, follow an essentially autobiographical pattern: '[Defoe's] total subordination of the plot to the pattern of the autobiographical memoir is as defiant an assertion of the primacy of individual experience in the novel as Descartes' *cogito ergo sum* was in philosophy.'[31]

The earliest extant autobiography in English was written by a woman, Margery Kempe (*c.* 1373). Since she was illiterate, this work was dictated. Women writers of the seventeenth century who produced memoirs and autobiographies include: Alice Thornton (1627–1707), the Duchess of Newcastle, Mary Boyle, Countess of Warwick (1624–78), Lucy Apsley, Mrs Hutchinson (1620–?), Ann Harrison, Lady Fanshawe (1625–80), Martha, Lady Giffard (1639–1722), and Mary De la Riviere Manley (1663–1724).

Women had in letter-writing, and the autobiography or memoir, genres which were not subject to critical censure, because they were not published. The emergence of the novel, in part from these semi-private genres, gave women a non-traditional form with which to work and relieved them of the fear of not living up to classical doctrine. By the mid-eighteenth century even critics were no longer judging according to classical rules. As Fielding remarked, critics were permitted to practise 'without knowing one word of the ancient laws'.[32]

The demise of classical authority was encouraged by the gradual replacement of literary patrons by capitalist booksellers as the primary source of remuneration for writers. Booksellers who themselves had little or no classical training and who were interested primarily in marketing to a large audience were not concerned about classical doctrine. They were in fact quite willing to pander to a reading public that was by the turn of the seventeenth century predominantly female. The market was such that a periodical completely devoted to women's interests appeared in 1692, the *Ladies Mercury*. Booksellers also quickly discerned the 'profitable connection between women and sentimental epistolary fiction',[33] the other genre dominated by women writers in the eighteenth century.

The breakdown of classical control over literature and the emergence of a non-traditional genre like the novel were therefore developments favourable to an out-group like women. No longer could educational conditions force them to automatic literary exile, for they, as well as any male, had access to the experiential details of daily life and therefore access to resources of legitimate literary expression.

48

Women were in fact in an ideal situation – the centre of the family – to observe the everyday details of domestic life which became prime matter for the English 'indoor' novel. And, since by the end of the century it was no longer expected that this 'matter' be conveyed through a Ciceronian medium, through the 'grand style', women could write in a vernacular close to the style in which they spoke without fear of critical chastisement. *change in style*

There is considerable debate as to the exact reasons for the transition to the 'plain style', and indeed as to when it occurred. The authority on the subject, Morris Croll, viewed the change as a 'battle' that occurred during the late sixteenth and seventeenth centuries out of which the 'plain style' emerged 'triumphant'. On one side of the battle lines were the traditionalists who favoured a Ciceronian, or 'grand', or 'Asiatic' style.[34] John Lily's *Euphues* and Sidney's *Arcadia* exemplify this style. On the other side were the anti-Ciceronians, Montaigne, Bacon, who adopted a more conversational, less artificial form of rhetoric. Croll thus dated the emergence of the new 'modern' style at 1600.

Croll's views have been disputed by R. F. Jones who maintained that the term 'anti-Ciceronian' is a misnomer, as it implies a reversion to the anti-Ciceronian authors of antiquity, namely Seneca and Tacitus, as models; instead, he asserted, the proponents of the plain style were in fact primarily under the influence of the new scientific epistemology, the Baconian 'new philosophy', and were not looking to the ancients for models.[35] Jones dated the triumph of the new style at around 1660.

From our perspective the Jones date seems the more credible. For it is only around the time of the Restoration that women writers (specifically Margaret Cavendish and Dorothy Osborne) began to write in a consciously plain style. Margaret Cavendish's biographer notes a stylistic transition in her works from the fancifully original style of her early work to the 'flatter, cautious . . . ordinary'[36] prose of her later writing (late 1660s to early 1670s).

While her style had never been Latinate and her preference had always been for 'the natural and most usual way of speaking',[37] she was nevertheless directly affected by the growing predisposition among scientific writers towards a simple style. Thomas Sprat had articulated this tendency in 1667 when he called for the use of a plain simple prose in scientific treatises in his *History of the Royal Society*.

One feature of the new style was the 'loose period'. It stands opposed to the Ciceronian rounded period, which implied a closed, 'circular', or syllogistic logic, congenial to a worldview which rested upon a closed

(margin annotation: closed v. open period)

system of verities, and therefore upon a closed circle of initiates or cultural insiders. This was the design of all ancient and medieval societies, which were rigidly class structured and which rested upon an educated elite of males. The 'loose period', on the other hand, attempted

> to express . . . the order in which an idea presents itself when it is first experienced. It begins, therefore, without premeditation, stating its idea in the first form that occurs; the second member is determined by the situation in which the mind finds itself after the first has been spoken; and so on throughout the period. Each member being an emergency of the situation.[38]

Such a stylistic method implies an inductive, empiric logic, appropriate to seventeenth-century European society, which had shifted towards the experientially verifiable and away from received premises as the source of truth. It also implies a spontaneous, unpractised quality, which when valued, obviates the necessity for formal rhetorical training. Again, women as cultural outsiders stood to benefit from this kind of stylistic shift. For in the epistolary style, as in the loose period, 'everything was subordinated to the aim of expressing the ideas passing in the mind at the moment of writing'.[39] That the 'dashaway' epistolary style with its 'breathless, disorganized "artless" informality'[40] became identified as a female style is not surprising.

Margaret Cavendish, interestingly enough, anticipated the rationale for the 'artless' style nearly a century before it found expression in Richardson's novels. A collection of her poems published in 1653 included this critical prescription:

> Give me the style that Nature frames, not art,
> For art doth seem to take the pedant's part;
> And what seems noble, which is easy, free,
> Not to be bound with o'er-nice pedantry.[41]

(margin annotation: women's use of plain style ~ lack of education)

While it would not be wholly accurate to assume a continuing tradition among women writers of a less artificial rhetoric than male writers, there are nevertheless several critical statements made by women writers over the centuries which suggest at least a preference for the *genus humile*. This preference may well have been the result of women's historical lack of access to formal training in rhetoric.[42]

We find, for example, that a woman named 'Jane Anger' (presumably a pseudonym) wrote a feminist critique of John Lily in 1589.[43] In this tract Anger gave strong criticism of the artificial,

50

Euphuistic style of her opponent's work, asserting that it was characteristically male.

> The desire that every man has to show his true vein in writing is unspeakable, and their minds are so carried away with the manner, as no care at all is had of the matter. They run so into rhetoric as often times they overrun the bounds of their own wits and go they know not whither.[44]

Less than a century later Dorothy Osborne (Temple) also urged the adoption of the plain style, and disdained artificial circumlocution. Significantly, her comments came in defence of letter-writing, a predominantly feminine genre which provided women with a useful apprenticeship in 'amateur' writing before it was acceptable for them to be professional writers.

> All letters, methinks, should be free and easy as one's discourse; not studied like an oration, nor made up of hard words like a charm. 'Tis an admirable thing to see how some people will labour to find out terms that may obscure a plain sense, like a gentleman I knew, who would never say 'the weather grew cold', but that 'winter begins to salute us.' I have no patience for such coxcombs, and cannot blame an old uncle of mine that threw the standish at his man's head because he writ a letter for him where instead of saying . . . 'that he would have writ himself, but that he had gout in his hand' he said 'that the gout would not permit him to put pen to paper'. . . .[45]

At about the same time the Duchess of Newcastle attempted to deflect critical censure of her style in her Preface to the *Sociable Letters* (published in 1664). She attributes her lapses to a lack of education, but asserts that the style or 'wordative part' is not important; what matters is the content. *content over style*

> They may say some Words are not Exactly Placed, which I confess to be very likely, and not only in that, but in all the rest of my Works there may be such Errors, for I was not Bred in an University, or a Free-School, to learn the Art of Words; neither do I take it for a Disparagement of my Works, to have the Forms, Terms, Words, Numbers, or Rhymes found fault with . . . for I leave the Formal, or Wordative part to Fools, and the Material or Sensitive part to Wise men.[46]

clever double bind

A century later we find Mary Wollstonecraft in her introduction to *A Vindication of the Rights of Women* (1792) consciously rejecting Ciceronian rhetoric, opting again for the plain style which she feels is appropriate to a work which urges that women be seen as rational agents rather than foppish supernumeraries.

> I shall disdain to cull my phrases or polish my style. I aim at being useful, and sincerity will render me unaffected; for wishing rather to persuade by the force of my argument than dazzle by the elegance of my language, I shall not waste my time in rounding periods, or in fabricating the turgid bombast of artificial feelings. . . I shall try to avoid . . . flowery diction. . . .[47]

A number of very specific historical developments explain why women were unable to compete in the construction of literary masterworks until the nineteenth century. Shakespeare's sister would have been denied access to Latin rhetorical training and hence to the symbolic tools with which to create public art. Only when the Latin influence had weakened, when serious prose was being written in the vernaculars, in a non-traditional form, and only after the rhetoric of the home and of the forum had once again merged could women hope to have equal access to the means of literary creation.

Since women had been excluded from the educated elites until this time and since their premises had never been included in the closed circle of knowledge that dominated western culture for centuries, it is not surprising that few women produced cultural works. However, once epistemological assumptions had shifted so as to allow a literary legitimacy to non-traditional modes, and new conceptions of reality, women were in a position to put forth their own works of literature.

In the mid-seventeenth century women writers like Dorothy Osborne and Margaret Cavendish are at a kind of intermediate stage. They are writing in semi-private genres, but they *are* writing – in the vernacular and for the most part in the plain style which is beginning to 'triumph' – perhaps indeed because of them. From 1660 to 1800 women wrote more than one-third of the published works of prose fiction in English.[48] By the end of the eighteenth century women novelists predominated; they were writing 'the better novels' of the time.[49]

From the first English women who began to appropriate the means of literary production for themselves, Osborne and Cavendish, to Jane Austen stretches a little more than a century. Three to four generations of women writers learning to master the trade passed between. But without their practice, without their having taken advantage of women's newly achieved access to the materials of the trade, we might never have had a Jane Austen, a Charlotte Brontë, a George Eliot, or indeed, a Virginia Woolf.

Notes

1 Virginia Woolf, 'Dorothy Osborne's *Letters*', *Collected Essays* (London: Chatto & Windus, 1967), vol. 3 p. 60.

2 To borrow from Michael Danahy's recent article on the subject, 'Le roman est-il chose femelle?' *Poetique* 25 (1976), pp. 85–106.

3 T. W. Baldwin, *William Shakespere's Small Latine & Lesse Greeke* (Urbana: University of Illinois, 1944). See especially vol. 1. chs 22–30; vol. 2 chs 31–50.

4 Walter J. Ong, S. J., *The Presence of the Word* (New Haven: Yale University Press, 1967), pp. 250–1 (my emphasis). I would like to acknowledge Barbara Nauer who suggested this and other readings to me and who encouraged me to write an earlier version of this article.

5 ibid., p. 250 (my emphasis).

6 ibid., p. 251 (my emphasis).

7 Eileen Power, *Medieval Women* (Cambridge: Cambridge University Press, 1975), p. 84.

8 Diane Valeri Bayne, 'Richard Hyrde and the More Circle', *Moreana* 12 no. 45 (February 1975), p. 13.

9 Ruth Kelso, *Doctrine for the Lady of the Renaissance* (Urbana: University of Illinois Press, 1956). See especially ch. 4, 'Studies'.

10 Dorothy O'Connor, *Louise Labé, sa vie et son oeuvre* (Paris: Les presses françaises, 1926), p. 54.

11 I have detailed the evidence for this assertion in 'The love sonnets of Louise Labé', unpub. article. See below for further discussion of women's inclination toward a less artificial rhetoric.

12 Myra Reynolds, *The Learned Lady in England 1650–1760* (Boston: Houghton Mifflin, 1920), p. 427. Indeed, those rare pieces of secular literature created by women before the late seventeenth century were written by women of the upper or courtly class, as, for example, in England, Lady Elizabeth Tanfield Carey (1585–1639) or Lady Mary Sidney Wroth, the Countess of Montgomery (fl. 1621). For other examples, see Mary R. Mahl and Helene Koon (eds) *The Female Spectator, English Women Writers before 1800* (Old Westbury: The Feminist Press, 1977).

One study shows that even in the nineteenth century only 20 per cent of women writers had any sort of formal schooling. See Elaine Showalter, *A Literature of Their Own* (Princeton: Princeton University Press, 1977), pp. 40–1.

13 Ian Watt, *The Rise of the Novel, Studies in Defoe, Richardson and Fielding* (Berkeley: University of California Press, 1957), p. 13 (my emphasis).

14 ibid., p. 13.

15 Michael Danahy 'Le roman est-il chose femelle?', p. 91. Danahy also suggests, however, that the novel was more accessible to women than other forms of literature such as drama where 'social and moral prohibitions' tended to exclude them, or even poetry, rooted as it was in oral and religious traditions which were pre-eminently male (p. 93).

16 See Georges May, *Le Dilemme du roman au XVIIIe siècle* (New Haven: Yale University Press, 1963), especially ch. 8, 'Féminisme et roman', for a discussion of the French connection between women and the novel.

17 See Harrison Steeves, *Before Jane Austen, The Shaping of the English Novel in the Eighteenth Century* (New York: Holt, Rinehart & Winston, 1965), pp. 161–2.

18 Dedication to *The Fatal Secret* (1724), as cited in Robert Adams Day, *Told in Letters, Epistolary Fiction Before Richardson* (Ann Arbor: University of Michigan 1966), p. 81.

19 Torquato Tasso, 'Discourses on the heroic poem', *Literary Criticism from Plato to Dryden*, ed. Allan H. Gilbert (Detroit: Wayne University Press, 1962), p.465.

20 As cited in Georges May, *Le Dilemme du roman au XVIIIe siècle*, p. 6 (my translation). The sonnet is not, of course, a classical genre, but it was nevertheless by this time considered 'high' literature.

21 As cited in Watt, *The Rise of the Novel*, p. 176.

22 ibid., p. 193.

23 Nathalie Wurzbach (ed.), *The Novel in Letters* (London: Routledge & Kegan Paul 1969), pp. xiii–xiv. See also Day, ch. 4.

24 Ellen Moers, *Literary Women* (Garden City: Doubleday 1977), p. 175. Frederick R. Karl, *The Adversary Literature: The English Novel in the Eighteenth Century, A Study in Genre* (New York: Farrar, Straus & Giroux 1974) also notes this identification, p. 130 n. 1.

25 Watt, *The Rise of the Novel*, p. 194.

26 ibid., p. 194.

27 Moers, *Literary Women*, p. 97.

28 Cavendish's letters were probably written for publication; indeed, they were probably fictitious, as Delores Palomo demonstrated in her paper, 'Margaret Cavendish and the letter essay', presented at the Modern Language Association convention, 1977. Cavendish did not, however, follow the Ciceronian epistolary form but rather pioneered the informal epistolary essay.

29 As cited in Reynolds, *The Learned Lady in England*, p. 58.

30 As cited in Woolf 'The Duchess of Newcastle', *Collected Essays*, vol. 3, p. 51.

31 Watt, *The Rise of the Novel*, p. 15.

32 ibid., p. 58.

33 Day, *Told in Letters*, p. 76.

34 Morris Croll, *Style, Rhetoric and Rhythm, Essays*, ed. J. Max Patrick, Robert O. Evans, John M. Wallace, and R. J. Schoek (Princeton: Princeton University Press 1966), p. 68.

35 Jones's views are summarized in Robert Adolph, *The Rise of Modern Prose Style* (Cambridge, Mass.: MIT Press 1968), pp. 4–5, 19–20.

36 Douglas Grant, *Margaret the First* (Toronto: University of Toronto Press 1957), p. 211.

37 *Natural Pictures*, p. c5^v, as cited in Grant, p. 210.

38 Croll, *Style, Rhetoric and Rhythm*, p. 224.

39 Watt, *The Rise of the Novel*, p. 194.

40 Moers, *Literary Women*, p. 97.

41 As cited in Grant, *Margaret the First*, p. 127.

42 Indeed, it has been suggested that the entire tradition of English prose was initiated by two women (Margery Kempe and Julian of Norwich) because they were not comfortable with Latin composition. See Robert Karl Stone, 'Middle English prose style: Margery Kempe and Julian of Norwich' (Ph.D. dissertation, University of Illinois 1962), pp. 2–3.

43 Helen Andrews Kahin suggests that the work in question is Lily's *Euphues his Censure to Philautus*, which includes much misogynist material. See her 'Jane Anger and John Lily', *Modern Language Quarterly* 8 (March 1947), pp. 31–5.

44 Jane Anger 'Protection for Women', *by a Woman writt*, ed. Joan Goulianos (Indianapolis: Bobbs-Merrill 1973), p. 24.

45 *The Love Letters of Dorothy Osborne to Sir William Temple*, ed. Israel Hollancz (London: De La More Press 1903), p. 146.

46 Margaret Cavendish, 'The Preface', *CCXI Sociable Letters* (London: William Wilson 1664; reprint ed. Menston: The Scolar Press, 1969). Significantly, the duchess also rejects the heroic or gallant epistolary style, which had become somewhat faddish, especially in France.

> These Letters are an Intimation of a Personal Visitation and Conversation, which I think is Better (I am sure more profitable) than those Conversations that are an Imitation of Romancial Letters, which are but Empty Words, and Vain Compliments.

(See also Letters XXI, LXXXI.)
See Wurzbach (ed.) *The Novel in Letters* for a selection of romantic epistles of the period. The prototype of this genre was the *Lettres portugaises* (1669), allegedly written by a nun to her lover. The romanesque mode seems to have been established in France (with La Calprenède's and Mlle. de Scudery's mid-century novels setting the fashion). Before and during the Restoration the heroic romance crossed the channel; its influence can be seen in writers like Aphra Behn and Mary Manley.

47 Mary Wollstonecraft, *A Vindication of the Rights of Women* (Baltimore: Penguin 1975), p. 82.

48 George Watson (ed.), *The New Cambridge Bibliography of English Literature* vol. 2 (1660–1800) (Cambridge: Cambridge University Press 1971), col. 975–1014, lists approximately 760 entries of 'minor fiction'. Of these 265 works, or approximately 35 per cent of the total, were written by women. Many other authors are anonymous; these may well have been women. By the end of the eighteenth century at least half the entries are works by women. The total number of entries (760) represents a selection of roughly one-fifth the total published prose fiction of the period 1660–1800. A majority of the 760 entries in the *New Cambridge Bibliography* are sentimental novels in the epistolary mode.

49 Harrison Steeves, *Before Jane Austen*, pp. 330, 362. Of the standard histories of the early novel only Steeves gives serious attention to the emergence of the female novelists. Other works consulted and not mentioned elsewhere include Arnold Kettle, *An Introduction to the English Novel*, vol. 1 (2nd edn) (London: Hutchinson 1967); Walter Allen, *The English Novel, A Short Critical History* (New York: Dutton 1955); and Edward Wagenknecht, *Cavalcade of the Novel* (New York: Holt, Rinehart & Winston, 1954).

3

Language and gender

Cora Kaplan

This essay was written for a conference on patriarchy held in London in the spring of 1976. It represents my first enthusiastic attempts to use psychoanalytic theory in cultural criticism. The theoretical sections of the essay are, not surprisingly, fairly rough, a congested paraphrase of my sources. But the application of the theory, which has been better synthesized by others, seems to me still useful, especially since poetry is still a field much neglected by feminist critics. I have updated the theoretical references. Reprinted from Sea Changes (London: Verso 1986).

Poetry is a privileged metalanguage in western patriarchal culture. Although other written forms of high culture – theology, philosophy, political theory, drama, prose fiction – are also, in part, language about language, in poetry this introverted or doubled relation is thrust at us as the very reason-for-being of the genre. Perhaps because poetry seems, more than any other sort of imaginative writing, to imitate a closed linguistic system it is presented to us as invitingly accessible to our understanding once we have pushed past its formal difficulties. Oddly we still seem to expect poetry to produce universal meanings. The bourgeois novel is comfortably established as a genre produced by and about a particular class, but there is an uneasy feel about the bourgeois poem. Poetry is increasingly written by members of oppressed groups, but its popular appeal is so small in western society today that its shrinking audience may make its elitism or lack of it a non-issue. Its appeal may have diminished in relation to other literary forms but its status and function in high culture continues to be important. This paper examines women's poetry as part of an investigation of women's use of high language, that is, the language, public, political and literary, of patriarchal societies.

A study of women's writing will not get us any closer to an enclosed critical practice, a 'feminist literary criticism'. There can in one sense be no feminist literary criticism, for any new theoretical approach to literature that uses gender difference as an important category involves a profoundly altered view of the relation of both sexes to language, speech, writing and culture. For this reason I have called my paper 'Language and gender' rather than 'Women and poetry', although it grew out of work on a critical anthology of English and American women's poetry that I introduced and edited a few years ago.[1] Some of the problems raised there still seem central to me – the insertion of female-centred subject-matter into a male literary tradition, the attendant problems of expressing this matter in a formal symbolic language, the contradictions between the romantic notion of the poet as the transcendent speaker of a unified culture and the dependent and oppressed place of women within that culture. New problems have occurred to me as equally important. The difficulty women have in writing seems to me to be linked very closely to the rupture between childhood and adolescence, when, in western societies (and in other cultures as well) public speech is a male privilege and women's speech restricted by custom in mixed sex gatherings, or, if permitted, still characterized by its private nature, an extension of the trivial domestic discourse of women. For male speakers after puberty, the distinction between public and private speech is not made in nearly such a strong way, if at all. Obviously, in the twentieth century and earlier, such distinctions have been challenged and in some cases seem to be broken down, but the distinction is still made. The prejudice seems persistent and irrational unless we acknowledge that control of high language is a crucial part of the power of dominant groups, and understand that the refusal of access to public language is one of the major forms of the oppression of women within a social class as well as in trans-class situations.

A very high proportion of women's poems are about the right to speak and write. The desire to write imaginative poetry and prose was and is a demand for access to and parity within the law and myth-making groups in society. The decision to storm the walls and occupy the forbidden place is a recognition of the value and importance of high language, and often contradicts and undercuts a more radical critique in women's poetry of the values embedded in formal symbolic language itself. To be a woman and a poet presents many women poets with such a profound split between their social, sexual identity (their 'human' identity) and their artistic practice that the split becomes the insistent subject, sometimes overt, often hidden or displaced, of much women's poetry.

The first part of my paper will try out a theoretical account of the process by which women come to internalize the suppression and restriction of their speech. The second part* demonstrates how the struggle to overcome the taboo is presented as the hidden subject in poems that seem deliberately difficult and opaque.

* The second part of this essay has been omitted from this collection.

Do men and women in patriarchal societies have different relationships to the language they speak and write? Statements of such a difference, questions about its source, persistence and meaning run through
western writing since Greek times. Often buried in that larger subject,
the exploration and definition of gender difference in culture, it becomes
a distinct issue when women speak or write, and men protest, not only
or primarily at what they say, but at the act itself. Recently left feminists
have used work on ideology by the French political philosopher, Louis
Althusser, together with the psychoanalytic theories of Freud and his
modern French interpreter, Jacques Lacan, to clarify their understanding
of the construction of femininity.[2] Contemporary work on ideology in
France accepts Freud's theory of the unconscious and is concerned,
among other things, with the construction of the subject in culture.
Language is the most important of all the forms of human communication. Through the acquisition of language we become human and
social beings: the words we speak situate us in our gender and our class.
Through language we come to 'know' who we are. In elaborating and
extending Freud's work, Lacan emphasizes the crucial importance of
language as the signifying practice in and through which the subject is
made into a social being. Social entry into patriarchal culture is made in
language, through speech. Our individual speech does not, therefore,
free us in any simple way from the ideological constraints of our culture
since it is through the forms that articulate those constraints that we
speak in the first place.

The account that follows here is necessarily very schematized,
designed simply to show the crucial nexus between the acquisition of
subjectivity through language and the recognition of the social nature of
female identity.[3]

Every human child, according to Lacan, goes through an encounter
with his own image in the mirror, somewhere between 6 and 18 months,
which is particularly significant and a precondition of the acquisition of
subjectivity. For in that encounter the image is misrecognized as an ideal
whole – a counterpart, an Other, of the fragmented, feeling being.
During this period the child is angrily conscious of the capricious
comings and goings, which he is helpless to control, of persons on
whom he relies for physical care and emotional comfort. The perception
of the image in the mirror as both self and other, as the same and
different, the projection of an ideal form of the self through a spatial
relation acts as the basis for the acquisition of subjectivity, and is, as
well, the crude form, self and other for all intersubjective relations.

Although the child may learn words quite early, during the first year and a half of life, the mastery of language succeeds the mirror stage and is the true point at which subjectivity is attained. Nevertheless even the early use of very simple abstractions shows how the child gains some small form of control over the absence and presence of his caretaker. The classic example, taken from Freud, is the *fort/da* game, in which the child in the mother's absence, throws away an object 'fort' and retrieves it 'da' to symbolize and, in part, control, her absence and presence. As the child acquires more linguistic competence, for example the correct use of names and pronouns to differentiate self from others, he moves from the omnipotence implicit in the prelinguistic fantasy when he and the mirror image are one, to the necessary limitation of his own desires and powers when he acceded to language, to subjectivity and the world of social relations. In language the child acquires the necessary abstractions to situate himself in relation to others and to speak the particular meanings of his own experience in a public, socially understood discourse.[4]

For Lacan, language, adult or competent speech, is the Symbolic order. It embodies the abstracted relations of the laws of a particular culture. Language only exists through individual speech, so in each speech act the self and the culture speak simultaneously or, to put it another way, each time we speak we are also spoken: this formulation is abstract, but is not meant to be understood as a mechanical operation in which a ventriloquist culture moves our lips. Lacan uses and transforms the linguistic theories of Ferdinand de Saussure who makes the basic distinction between language and speech. Saussure also suggests that meanings, words, can only be understood as differences from other meanings. Meanings – signifiers – are part of chains – think of a sentence as a chain – and refer not to some fixed phenomenological object but to the meanings, either present or implied in the chain, which therefore make up the sense of the chain. To the extent that the words we choose have meanings other than the particular ones that an individual speech act intends, these absent but still invoked relations of meaning are responsible for a 'veering off of meaning' or 'the sliding of the signified under the signifier', of sense under meaning in any given signifying chain.[5] It will become clear quite soon how the distinction between language and speech, the definition of meanings as relations of difference and the crucial role of language in the development of the child's consciousness of self, relates to women's use of language.

Symbolic language, which includes everyday speech as well as written or imaginative forms, uses two basic tropes, metaphor and metonymy. These tropes 'present the most condensed expression of two basic modes of relation; the internal relation of similarity (and contrast) underlies the metaphor; the external relation of contiguity (and remoteness) determines the metonymy'.[6] While metaphor and metonymy are the stuff of poetry (Roman Jakobson, who I have quoted here, sees metaphor as the principal mode in romantic and symbolic poetry, and metonymy as the mode of the epic), these linguistic tropes are the modes through which we come to perceive all relations of difference, such as gender difference and the separation of the self from others. Lacan has identified these figures of speech with Freud's concept of the modes that occur in dreams. Metaphor equals condensation; metonymy equals displacement. Language like the unconscious resists interpretation even as, through dreams and in ordinary discourse it invites us to interpret it. We ought not to think of the use of metaphor and metonymy in imaginative genres as uniquely isolated or sophisticated. How men and women come to speak at all, how they see each other through speech, the social taboos on speech for children and women, all these relations bear upon the way in which individual poets are seen to 'create' new symbolic identifications and relations.

Having gone so deep into language we must now go back to the construction of the subject in culture, and pick up our child at what Freud and Lacan designate the Oedipal stage which is also the point at which the child's competence in speaking means that he has virtually entered the Symbolic order. Entry into the Symbolic order is necessary, says Lacan, for mental stability. If the subject cannot be located in linguistic abstraction, then in extreme cases, as observed in the broad disorder termed schizophrenia, words cannot be constructed in an individual discourse. The dislocated subject treats them as things, sounds, associations, and does not use them in a logical pattern to situate herself in her intersubjective (social) situation. The difference between male and female entry into the Symbolic has to do with the stage of development which overlaps the full acquisition of language, and through which the child accepts his or her gender identity – the Oedipal phase. In Lacan, the phallus (not to be confused with the actual penis) is the 'missing' signifier to which both sexes must reconcile their relationship. Full entry into the Symbolic does not depend on having or not having a penis, but on the symbolic interpretation a child places on its absence or presence in him/herself and in the two powerful figures of the mother and father. In order for women to identify finally with their mothers and take their place as female in culture they must accept the missing phallus as a permanent loss in themselves. According to Freud's account of the Oedipal resolution, the lack of a phallus in the mother is a nasty shock for both boys and girls. Boys repress their incestuous feelings for their mothers and their anger with their fathers as a result of the implied threat of castration – seen as already accomplished in the mother. At this point they accede to an identification with the father, which seals their gender identity and holds out the promise of a future alignment with authority, the Symbolic order, or law of the Father in place of the lost identification with the mother. Little girls, who must position themselves very differently in relation to the missing phallus, accept, sometimes reluctantly and with ongoing hostility, their likeness to the mother. The introduction of the father/phallus as the third term in the child's social world, breaks the early mother–child relationship for both sexes and brings on all the ensuing crises of identity through gender differentiation, so that all children lose the dyadic relation to the mother as they enter a wider society. Girls, as Freudian theory would have it, have a particular relation to loss or lack in that they must substitute for it, not the possession of the phallus but babies and/or an intersubjective relation with men (who are necessary for the production of babies).[7]

The phallus as a signifier has a central, crucial position in language, for if language embodies the patriarchal law of the culture, its basic meanings refer to the recurring process by which sexual difference and subjectivity are acquired. All human desire is, in Lacan's view, mediated through language, through the 'defiles of the signifier', and is expressed through the desire of the other – the projected ideal form of the imago (remember the model of the mirror phase) which becomes dispersed through our entry into the Symbolic in our real relation to others. Only if we accept the phallus as a privileged signification (a meaning which *does* relate to something outside itself) do we see that the little girl's access to the Symbolic, that is to language as the embodiment of cultural law, is always negative, or more neutrally, eccentric.

Even if we do accept the phallus as a privileged meaning, the concept of negative entry, as it has been posed so far seems at once too easy and too difficult to grasp. It is a convenient way of describing a phenomenon not yet fully understood or articulated in psychoanalytic theory. I would prefer, cautiously, to call the entry into the Symbolic 'different' rather than 'negative' for girls, since lack, in Lacanian theory, is as much an experience for men as for women. Also the production of subject as the place and origin of meanings (the entry into language) is necessary for both men and women. The formation of the unconscious in the first instance occurs when the child substitutes language for drives, demand for need, duplicating in the unconscious the prelinguistic arrangement of drives. A second stage of formation can be noted when abstractions, even those as simple but central as the fort/da game, allow the child to produce itself as the subject who controls absence. All of language can then be seen as an extended system of mastery over primary need which can never entirely succeed, since the repressed material 'escapes' through dreams, through slips of the tongue, and so on. Why should women whatever the relation of difference through which they enter the Symbolic be less adept at this system than men? Empirical studies that I have seen don't suggest that there is that much significant variation between male and female speech until puberty, if ever, although it is a subject only recently taken up in linguistics. I will return to this problem briefly in the next section, but I want to suggest tentatively here that it is at puberty, the second determining stage of gender identity in culture, that a distinction between male and female speakers is confirmed.

At puberty female social identity is sealed by the onset of menstruation and fertility, and here, in western culture, is where the bar against the public speech of females is made. Puberty and adolescence fulfil the promises of the Oedipal resolution. The male is gradually released from the restrictions of childhood, which include the restriction of his speech among adults. The girl's different relation to the phallus as signifier is made clear by a continued taboo against her speech among men. Male privilege and freedom can now be seen by the adult female to be allied with male use of public and symbolic language. In many cultures there is a strong taboo against women telling jokes. If we think of jokes as the derepressed symbolic discourse of common speech, we can see why jokes, particularly obscene ones, are rarely spoken from the perspective of femininity. Adult femininity thus requires (at least in western culture) an extension of the injunction: 'Children should be seen but not heard'. A sexual division of labour in the reproduction of ideology thus appears. Men reproduce it directly through the control of public speech, and women indirectly through the reproduction of children in the institution of the family. Since women have spoken and learned speech up to and through adolescence they continue to speak among themselves, and to their men in the domestic situation. It is a taboo which seems, in modern society, made to be broken by the demands of women themselves. When women are freed from constant reproduction, when they are educated equally with men in childhood, when they join the labour force at his side, when wealth gives them leisure, when they are necessary and instrumental in effecting profound social change through revolution – at these points women will protest and break down the taboo.

It should be clear to the reader that what I have produced so far is an account of a process by which women become segregated speakers, not an explanation of why this process should take place. Nor have I claimed for it a universal application, but limited myself to western societies. If we assume for the sake of the rest of my argument that the segregation of male and female speech, although apparent to little girls as they observe the social relations of adults and interact with them, is crucially and traumatically confirmed in adolescence, then we may say that the predominance of expressed male perspectives in common and high speech stems from the taboo after childhood. There are therefore two very important and distinct stages at which women's apparently weaker position in language is set. The first is at the Oedipal stage where the child, constructed as a speaking subject, must acknowledge social sex difference and align herself with women and restricted speech – a distinction blurred by the restrictions on children's speech. The second stage, puberty, further distinguishes girls from boys by the appearance of adult sex difference and access to public discourse for men.

This account makes some sense in psychic terms of the significant but statistically small presence of women as makers of high culture, of their anxiety about their precarious position, about their difficulties (which are often made into strengths) when using what is clearly in many ways a 'common' language. It is not an alternative to other sorts of social and political analysis of the oppression of women in patriarchal culture through more brutal means, and in other ideological forms.

The seventeenth century in England produced a number of important women poets whose first task seemed to be to challenge the bar against women as speakers and writers. Anne Bradstreet (1612–72) says

> I am obnoxious to each carping tongue
> Who sayes, my hand a needle better fits

and looks back towards a golden age when there was no bias

> But sure the antique Greeks were far more mild
> Else of our sex, why feigned they those nine
> And poesy made Calliope's own child;[8]

Anne Finch, Countess of Winchelsea (1661–1720) attacks with more vigour and subtlety symbolic associations as spoken from the masculine position. For example, a rose, a cupped flower has no gender in English but to male poets it often represents the female. Its metaphorical associations are with the female sexual organs, its metonymic associations are with muteness, frailty. In asserting her right to an original poetic gift Anne Finch rejects both the rose/woman image and woman's approved leisure occupation, embroidery.

> My hand delights to trace unusual things,
> And deviates from the known and common way;
> Nor will in fading silks compose
> Faintly the inimitable rose....[9]

The use of 'deviates' and 'inimitable' in this passage seems especially suggestive. She uses deviate when she might use wander or swerve or some softer verb. For women to write at all was to be deviant. The poet refuses to be positioned in mute nature. The rose is therefore 'inimitable'. 'Trace' and 'compose' are reversed and ironized; 'trace' used for creative writing and 'compose' for embroidery. It is a brave and largely successful attempt at challenging metaphor through the subtle inversion of a traditional poetic image, but it strikes me as damned hard work. And the sliding of meaning, the effect of metonymy, is obvious. In defying traditional male-centred associations she reminds us of them; they assert themselves as meanings in spite of her skill and care. The ghosts of the meanings she wishes to resist shadow her words.

There is a haunting painting by Odilon Redon of a woman's face in ivory cameo, further enclosed in a green oval mist. A wraithlike madonna, still, and at the same time full of intense activity, she holds two fingers to her lips, and, perhaps, a cupped paw to her ear. The picture is titled *Silence*. Enjoining silence, she is its material image. A speaking silence – image and injunction joined – she is herself spoken, twice spoken we might say – once by the artist who has located *his* silence in a female figure, and once again by the viewer who accepts as natural this abstract identification of woman = silence and the complementary imaging of women's speech as whispered, subvocal, the mere escape of trapped air ... shhhhhhhh.

More, her speech seems limited by some function in which she is wrapped as deeply as in the embryonic mist. Mother or nurse, the silence she enjoins and enacts is on behalf of some sleeping other. In enforcing our silence and her own she seems to protect someone else's speech. Her silence and muted speech, as I interpret it, is both chosen and imposed by her acceptance of her femininity. It has none of the illusory freedom of choice that we associate with a taciturn male. It is not the silence of chosen isolation either, for even in a painting significantly without other figures it is an inextricably social silence.

Redon's Madonna trails meanings behind it like the milky way. *Silence* makes a point central to my argument that it is perhaps difficult to make with any literary epigraph. Social silence as part of the constitution of female identity – i.e., subjectivity – is a crucial factor in her handling of written language. In an as yet almost unresearched area there is very little evidence to suggest that women's common, everyday speech is in any way less complex than men's, and some evidence to suggest that girls not only speak earlier than boys but develop linguistic complexity earlier too. It has been tentatively suggested that although girls are more 'verbal' (whatever that may mean) by the age of eleven or twelve, there is less meaning in their speech, though the phonemic complexity is greater. Robin Lakoff, in *Language and Woman's Place*,[10] does not adduce any particular evidence for her ideas or locate her women speakers in any class, race or locale, but suggests that women do speak a sort of second-class English which is more interrogatory, more full of 'empty' qualifiers ('lovely', 'kind of'), and, because vulgarity is censored, is super-genteel and grammatically more correct than men's speech. It is by no means clear that these observations would be true (if at all) of any group of women except perhaps upwardly mobile middle-class white American women, and if true of this group it seems much more likely to be related to a class plus gender instability than to be a particular quality of women's speech. In any case, recent debate over the language of class and of Black English has produced persuasive evidence that a restricted or alternative code does not necessarily produce restricted meanings. The variations that Lakoff lists as being special to women's speech seem very slight when compared to the variations of grammatical structure in Black English compared to standard English. Obviously the subject has barely been opened much less closed, but one might hazard that women speak the language of their class, caste, or race and that any common variants, which are in any case never fully observed, do not in themselves limit the meanings their speech can have. The sanction against female obscenity can have a particular application in the sanction against the telling of jokes and the use of wit by women, since dirty jokes are forms of common speech in which the repressed meanings of early sexual feelings are expressed in tight symbolic narratives.

It is the intra- and trans-class prejudice against women as speakers at all which seems most likely to erode women's use of 'high' language. This preference is connected with the patriarchal definition of ideal femininity. 'Silence gives the proper grace to women', Sophocles writes in *Ajax*. Its contradictions are expressed succinctly in the play, 'The Man who Married a Dumb Wife'. A famous physician is called in to cure the beautiful mute. He succeeds, she speaks, and immediately begins to prattle compulsively, until the husband bitterly regrets his humane gesture. His only wish is to have her dumb again so that he might love her as before. Women speak on sufferance in the patriarchal order. Yet although the culture may prefer them to be silent, they must have the faculty of speech in order that they may be recognized as human. One reading of the Dumb Wife, whose speech is her only flaw, is that the physician's alchemy was necessary to reassure the husband that he had married a human woman, although her unrestrained, trivial speech destroys his ability to see her as the ideal love object.

Elizabeth Barrett Browning comments bitterly on the prohibition against women as speakers of public language in her long feminist poem *Aurora Leigh*. Aurora, who defies society to become a major poet, recounts her education at the hands of her aunt who was a model of all that was 'womanly':

> I read a score of books on womanhood... – books that boldly
> > assert
> Their right of comprehending husband's talk
> When not too deep, and even of answering
> With pretty 'may it please you', or 'so it is', –
> Their rapid insight and fine aptitude,
> Particular worth and general missionariness,
> As long as they keep quiet by the fire
> And never say 'no' when the world says 'ay', ... their, in
> > brief,
> Potential faculty in everything
> Of abdicating power in it.

Aurora calls 'those years of education' a kind of water torture, 'flood succeeding flood/To drench the incapable throat ...'. The imposed silence is described as intersubjective, a silence whose effort is bent towards 'comprehending husband's talk'.[11] Women writers from the seventeenth century onwards (when women first entered the literary ranks in any numbers) comment in moods which range from abnegation to outright anger on the culture's prohibition against women's writing, often generalizing it to women's speech. They compare their situation to that of 'state prisoners, pen and ink denied' and their suppressed or faulty speech to the child's or the 'lisping boy's'. Emily Dickinson's 'They shut me up in Prose/As when a little Girl/They put me in the Closet – / Because they liked me "still" – '[12] condenses all these metaphors by connecting verbal imprisonment to the real restrictions of female childhood, and adds the point that the language most emphatically denied to women is the most concentrated form of symbolic language – poetry.

The consciousness of the taboo and its weight seemed to press heavily on the women who disobeyed it, and some form of apology, though tinged with irony, occurs in almost all of the women poets, as well as in many prose writers, whether avowed feminists or not, as an urgent perhaps propitiating preface to their speech. In the introduction to the anthology I ascribed this compulsion to an anticipatory response to male prejudice against women writers, and so it was. But it now seems to me that it goes much deeper, and is intimately connected as I have said with the way in which women become social beings in the first place, so that the very condition of their accession to their own subjectivity, to the consciousness of a self which is both personal and public is their unwitting acceptance of the law which limits their speech. This condition places them in a special relation to language which becomes theirs as a consequence of becoming human, and at the same time not theirs as a consequence of becoming female.

Notes

1 Cora Kaplan, *Salt and Bitter and Good: Three Centuries of English and American Women Poets*, (London and New York: Paddington Press, 1975).

2 Louis Althusser, 'Ideology and ideological state apparatus', and 'Freud and Lacan', in *Lenin and Philosophy and Other Essays*, (London: Verso, 1971); Jacques Lacan, *Ecrits: A Selection*, (London: Tavistock, 1977); Jacques Lacan, *The Four Fundamentals of Psycho-Analysis*, (Harmondsworth: Penguin 1977). See also Juliet Mitchell and Jacqueline Rose (eds), *Feminine Sexuality: Jacques Lacan and the école freudienne'*, (London: Macmillan, 1982).

3 Useful introductory syntheses of the Lacanian account of the construction of the subject in language are Chris Weedon, Andrew Tolson, and Frank Mort 'Theories of language and subjectivity', in Stuart Hall, Dorothy Hobson, Andrew Lowe and Paul Willis, (eds), *Culture, Media, Language*, (London:

Hutchinson, 1980); and Terry Eagleton, 'Psychoanalysis', *Literary Theory*, (London: Basil Blackwell, 1984). The substantial introductions by Juliet Mitchell and Jacqueline Rose to *Feminine Sexuality* situate the work of Freud and Lacan in relation to femininity.

4 Lacan, 'The mirror stage as formative of the function of the I', *Ecrits*, pp. 1–7.

5 Lacan, 'The agency of the letter in the unconscious or reason since Freud', *Ecrits*, pp. 146–78.

6 Roman Jakobson, *Studies in Child Language and Aphasia*, (The Hague: Mouton, 1971).

7 Lacan, 'The signification of the phallus', *Ecrits*, pp. 282–91.

8 Kaplan, *Salt and Bitter and Good*, p. 29.

9 ibid., p. 61.

10 Robin Lakoff, *Language and Woman's Place*, (New York: Harper & Row, 1975).

11 Elizabeth Barrett Browning, *Aurora Leigh and Other Poems*, ed. Cora Kaplan (London: Virago, 1978), first book, pp. 51–2.

12 Kaplan, *Salt and Bitter and Good*, p. 154.

4

Dorothy Richardson and the woman's sentence

Virginia Woolf

Reprinted from Contemporary Writers: Virginia Woolf *(London: Hogarth Press 1965).*

The Tunnel

Review of *The Tunnel* by Dorothy Richardson (*TLS*, 13 February 1919)

Although *The Tunnel* is the fourth book that Miss Richardson has written, she must still expect to find her reviewers paying a great deal of attention to her method. It is a method that demands attention, as a door whose handle we wrench ineffectively calls our attention to the fact that it is locked. There is no slipping smoothly down the accustomed channels; the first chapters provide an amusing spectacle of hasty critics seeking them in vain. If this were the result of perversity, we should think Miss Richardson more courageous than wise; but being, as we believe, not wilful but natural, it represents a genuine conviction of the discrepancy between what she has to say and the form provided by tradition for her to say it in. She is one of the rare novelists who believe that the novel is so much alive that it actually grows. As she makes her advanced critic, Mr Wilson, remark: 'There will be books with all that cut out – him and her – all that sort of thing. The book of the future will be clear of all that.' And Miriam Henderson herself reflects: 'but if books were written like that, sitting down and doing it cleverly and knowing just what you were doing and just how somebody else had done it, there was something wrong, some mannish cleverness that was only half right. To write books knowing all about style would be to become like a man'. So 'him and her' are cut out, and with them goes the old deliberate business: the chapters that lead up and the chapters that lead down; the characters who are always characteristic; the scenes that are passionate and the scenes that are humorous; the elaborate construction of reality; the conception that shapes and surrounds the whole. All these things are cast away, and there is left, denuded,

70

unsheltered, unbegun and unfinished, the consciousness of Miriam Henderson, the small sensitive lump of matter, half transparent and half opaque, which endlessly reflects and distorts the variegated procession, and is, we are bidden to believe, the source beneath the surface, the very oyster within the shell.

The critic is thus absolved from the necessity of picking out the themes of the story. The reader is not provided with a story; he is invited to embed himself in Miriam Henderson's consciousness, to register one after another, and one on top of another, words, cries, shouts, notes of a violin, fragments of lectures, to follow these impressions as they flicker through Miriam's mind, waking incongruously other thoughts, and plaiting incessantly the many-coloured and innumerable threads of life. But a quotation is better than description.

> She was surprised now at her familiarity with the details of the room ... that idea of visiting places in dreams. It was something more than that...all the real part of your life has a real dream in it; some of the real dream part of you coming true. You know in advance when you are really following your life. These things are familiar because reality is here. Coming events cast *light*. It is like dropping everything and walking backward to something you know is there. However far you go out you come back....I am back now where I was before I began trying to do things like other people. I left home to get here. None of those things can touch me here. They are mine.

Here we are thinking, word by word, as Miriam thinks. The method, if triumphant, should make us feel ourselves seated at the centre of another mind, and, according to the artistic gift of the writer, we should perceive in the helter-skelter of flying fragments some unity, significance, or design. That Miss Richardson gets so far as to achieve a sense of reality far greater than that produced by the ordinary means is undoubted. But, then, which reality is it, the superficial or the profound? We have to consider the quality of Miriam Henderson's consciousness, and the extent to which Miss Richardson is able to reveal it. We have to decide whether the flying helter-skelter resolves itself by degrees into a perceptible whole. When we are in a position to make up our minds we cannot deny a slight sense of disappointment. Having sacrificed not merely 'hims and hers', but so many seductive graces of wit and style for the prospect of some new revelation or greater intensity, we still find ourselves distressingly near the surface. Things look much the same as ever. It is certainly a very vivid surface. The consciousness of Miriam takes the reflection of a dentist's room to perfection. Her senses of touch, sight and hearing are all excessively acute. But sensations, impressions, ideas and emotions glance off her, unrelated and unquestioned, without shedding quite as much light as we had hoped into the hidden depths. We find ourselves in the dentist's room, in the street, in the lodging-house bedroom frequently and convincingly; but never, or only for a tantalizing second, in the reality which underlies these appearances. In particular, the figures of other people on whom Miriam casts her capricious light are vivid enough, but their sayings and doings never reach that degree of significance which we, perhaps unreasonably, expect. The old method seems sometimes the more profound and economical of the two. But it must be admitted that we are exacting. We want to be rid of realism, to penetrate without its help into the regions beneath it, and further require that Miss Richardson shall fashion this new material into something which has the shapeliness of the old accepted forms. We are asking too much; but the extent of our asking proves that *The Tunnel* is better in its failure than most books in their success.

Romance and the heart

Review of *The Grand Tour* by Romer Wilson, and *Revolving Lights* by Dorothy Richardson (*TLS*, 19 May 1923)

... There is no one word, such as romance or realism, to cover, even roughly, the works of Miss Dorothy Richardson. Their chief characteristic, if an intermittent student be qualified to speak, is one for which we still seek a name. She has invented, or, if she has not invented, developed and applied to her own uses, a sentence which we might call the psychological sentence of the feminine gender. It is of a more elastic fibre than the old, capable of stretching to the extreme, of suspending the frailest particles, of enveloping the vaguest shapes. Other writers of the opposite sex have used sentences of this description and stretched them to the extreme. But there is a difference. Miss Richardson has fashioned her sentence consciously, in order that it may descend to the depths and investigate the crannies of Miriam Henderson's consciousness. It is a woman's sentence, but only in the sense that it is used to describe a woman's mind by a writer who is neither proud nor afraid of anything that she may discover in the psychology of her sex. And therefore we feel that the trophies that Miss Richardson brings to the surface, however we may dispute their size, are undoubtedly genuine. Her discoveries are concerned with states of being and not with states of doing. Miriam is aware of 'life itself'; of the atmosphere of the table rather than of the table; of the silence rather than of the sound. Therefore she adds an element to her perception of things which has not been noticed before, or, if noticed, has been guiltily suppressed. A man might fall dead at her feet (it is not likely), and Miriam might feel that a violet-coloured ray of light was an important element in her consciousness of the tragedy. If she felt it, she would say it. Therefore, in reading *Revolving Lights* we are often made uncomfortable by feeling that the accent upon the emotions has shifted. What was emphatic is smoothed away. What was important to Maggie Tulliver no longer matters to Miriam Henderson. At first, we are ready to say that nothing is important to Miriam Henderson. That is the way we generally retaliate when an artist tells us that the heart is not, as we should like it to be, a stationary body, but a body which moves perpetually, and is thus always standing in a new relation to the emotions which are the same. Chaucer, Donne, Dickens – each if you read him, shows this change of the heart. That is what Miss Richardson is doing on an infinitely smaller scale. Miriam Henderson is pointing to her heart and saying she feels a pain on her right, and not on her left. She points too didactically. Her pain, compared with Maggie Tulliver's, is a very little pain. But, be that as it may, here we have both Miss Wilson and Miss Richardson proving that the novel is not hung upon a nail and festooned with glory, but, on the contrary, walks the high road, alive and alert, and brushes shoulders with real men and women.

5

Woman's word

Annie Leclerc

Annie Leclerc, Parole de femme *(1974), extracts translated by Claire Duchen. Reprinted from Claire Duchen*, French Connections *(London: Hutchinson 1987).*

Nothing exists that has not been made by man – not thought, not language, not words. Even now, there is nothing that has not been made by man, not even me: especially not me.

We have to invent everything anew. Things made by man are not just stupid, deceitful and oppressive. More than anything else, they are sad, sad enough to kill us with boredom and despair.

We have to invent a woman's word. But not 'of' woman, 'about' woman, in the way that man's language speaks 'of' woman. Any woman who wants to use a language that is specifically her own, cannot avoid this extraordinary, urgent task: we must invent woman.

It is crazy, I know. But it is the only thing that keeps me sane.

Whose voice is speaking these words? Whose voice has always spoken? Deafening tumult of important voices; and not one a woman's voice. I haven't forgotten the names of the great talkers. Plato, Aristotle and Montaigne, Marx and Freud and Nietzsche. I know them because I've lived among them and among them alone. These strong voices are also those who have reduced me the most effectively to silence. It is these superb speakers who, more than any others, have forced me into silence.

Whose voice do we hear in those great, wise books we find in libraries? Who speaks in the Capitol? Who speaks in the temple? Who speaks in the law-courts and whose voice is it that we hear in laws? Men's.

The world is man's word. Man is the word of the world.

No, no, I'm not making any demands. I am not tempted by the dignity of Man's status; it amuses me. When I consider Man, I am only playing.

And I say to myself: Man? What is Man? Man is what man brings into the world. We made children, they made Man.

They turned the specific into the universal. And the universal looks just like the specific.

Universality became their favourite ploy. One voice for all. With one voice, only one can speak. Man.

All I want is my voice.

You let me speak, yes, but I don't want your voice. I want my own voice, I don't trust yours any more.

It is no longer enough to speak *about* myself for me to find a voice that is my own. Woman's literature: feminine literature, very feminine, with its exquisite feminine sensitivity. Man's literature is not masculine, with its exquisite masculine sensitivity. A man speaks in the name of Man. A woman in the name of women. But as it is man who has set out the 'truth' about us all, the truth about women, it is still man who speaks through woman's mouth.

The whole of feminine literature has been whispered to women in man's language. The whole range, all the melodies, of femininity, have already been played out.

Is it possible to invent anything new?

We have to invent: otherwise we'll perish.

This stupid, military, evil-smelling world marches on alone towards its destruction. Man's voice is a fabric full of holes, torn, frayed; a burned out voice.

However wide we open our eyes, however far we stretch our ears, from now on, the summits from where laws are made, male summits with all their sacred values, are lost in the thick fog of indifference and boredom. Which is when women open their mouths and begin to speak. From now on, no man's voice will come to cover up the multiple, vigorous voices of women.

But we still aren't there. In fact we won't get there unless woman manages to weave a fabric, whole and new, made of a voice springing from within herself. Because the voice can be new, but the words worn out. Watch out woman, pay attention to your words.

Let me say first of all where all this comes from. It comes from me, woman, from my woman's belly. It began in my belly, with small, slight, signs, hardly audible, when I was pregnant. I began to listen to this timid voice which had no words.

Who could tell me, could I ever express (and what words would I use), to speak of the extraordinary joy of pregnancy, the immense, terrible joy of childbirth.

That is how I first learned that my woman's body was the site of Dionysian celebrations of life.

So then I looked at men. For man, there is only one celebration of sexuality: intercourse. He doesn't want to hear about the others, the multiple celebrations of my body.

And this one celebration of his, he wants it all for himself. He demands that my necessary presence remain discreet and totally devoted to his pleasure.

Well it's too bad for him, but I must talk about the pleasures of my body, no, not those of my soul, my virtue or my feminine sensitivity, but the pleasures of my woman's belly, my woman's vagina, my woman's breasts, luxuriant pleasures that you can't even imagine.

I must talk about it, because only by talking about it will a new language be born, a woman's word.

I have to reveal everything that you have so determinedly hidden, because it was with that repression that all the others began. Everything that was ours, you converted to dirt, pain, duty, bitchiness, small-mindedness, servitude.

Once you had silenced us, you could do whatever you wanted with us, turn us into maid, goddess, plaything, mother hen, *femme fatale*. The only thing you demand really insistently is our silence: in fact, you could hardly demand anything more; beyond silence, you would have to demand our death.

It is our silence and the triumphant sound of your voice that authorized the theft of our labour, the rape of our bodies, and all our silent slavery, our silent martyrdom. How can it be that we are now coming out of our coma, and that our tongues, though still sticky with respect for your values, are loosening up, slowly?

You had proclaimed the universality of your language. Very good for asserting your power, but not so good for keeping it.

We listen, convinced, to those who say 'All men are born free and remain equal in their rights.'

And slowly we discover that the person who has nothing, has the right to nothing. Not to equality, nor to freedom. And we end up by demanding the letter of the law. Equality. Freedom.

My body flows with the vast rhythmic pulsation of life. My body experiences a cycle of changes. Its perception of time is cyclical, but never closed or repetitive.

Men, as far as I can judge, have a linear perception of time. From their birth to their death, the segment of time they occupy is straight. Nothing in their flesh is aware of time's curves. Their eyes, their pulse, neglect the seasons. They can only see History, they fight only for History. Their sexuality is linear: their penis becomes erect, stretches, ejaculates and becomes limp. That which makes them live kills them. They escape death only by a new life that in turn, kills them again.

My body speaks to me of another sense of time, another adventure. Thirteen times a year, I experience the cyclical changes of my body. Sometimes my body is completely forgotten. Not thinking about its pains or its pleasures, I come, I go, I work, I speak and my body is an abstraction. Sometimes, my body is there, present.

Ten, twelve days before my period, my breasts swell, become hardened. This seems, in my case, to follow ovulation, fertility. I can't say that this is always so, because other women say they experience this during their period or just before.

The nipple is tender, bright red, very sensitive. The slightest contact makes it harder. You say, friends say to each other, 'My breasts are sore.' Especially if you are worried that your period is late, and you are looking for any hopeful signs, you weigh your breasts in your hands, feel them, press them with anxious care, trying to force them to admit that they hurt, you say, you repeat, oh yes, they are sore. But it's not that. They don't hurt, it's just that we can feel them. They are alive, aroused, open to pain but not sore. They are also open to caresses, much more so than usual; continually caressable, strangely open to pleasure. When my period is due, my breasts are loving, avid, sensitive.

I haven't finished talking about my body yet. For it experiences still more wonders. Just because you aren't involved with them, does it mean that I must hide them under a hideous mask of pain and suffering? Do I have to feel bad because I take pleasure in experiences you can't know, to the point of denying myself this pleasure too?

You have poisoned my life. For centuries. Deprived of my body, I only knew how to live through you. Badly, hardly living. Slaving away, enduring, being silent and being pretty. My body there for work and for pleasing you; never for my own pleasure. My body, never my own, for me. Mouth sewn up, face made up. Vagina open when you want it, closed up with Tampax. Scoured, scraped, made hygienic, deodorized, and re-odorized with rose-smelling perfume, it's too much, it's stifling me, I need my own body. That is what I mean by living.

You could say, well what are women complaining about since you say there are so many possibilities for them to be happy? It is because these possibilities that we have here and now are merely an anticipation of what could be possible in a radically different society, in which woman's status would also be changed. As would the way in which she is perceived by others.

I'm not saying to women, be happy; but only, do you know that you are capable of happiness?

But we have to understand everything that denies women's happiness – and which is not only her economic, sexual and familial oppression.

We know full well, because it is glaringly obvious, that women are denied happiness because they are overburdened with domestic tasks and with anxieties that postpone their pleasure in life indefinitely, almost until her death. When does a woman really have the chance to take pleasure in herself, in man, in the sun, in the rain, the wind, in children, in the seasons, even in the home, when she is constantly harassed by the need to take care of – the housework, the dishes, the washing, the shopping, the ironing, the cooking?

When can she even glimpse the possibility of happiness when, already rushed off her feet, she adds the hardship and humiliation of a badly-paid job? We can't pretend that we don't know about all this, because it can't be hidden, we can *see it*.

But do we know enough about what else denies a woman happiness, maybe even more radically? Do we know the extent of a tyranny we can't see – we can't see it because we can see neither the person exercising it nor how it operates, nor exactly on what it operates?

Do we understand that, excluded from her body, kept in ignorance about the pleasures it contains, it is the ability to experience happiness that is missing?

If women are so politically apathetic, so persistently conservative, is it not also because they are incapable of imagining what their pleasure in living could be?

The only bodily pleasure they are aware of missing is the one which they see men indulge in, more often and better than they do: a properly sexual pleasure. But is their imagination so limited that they can't think of other pleasures? Are they so shortsighted that they can't see the source of their problems? Are they too humble, too lazy? If only they learned to find in themselves those joys from which the world is cut off, would their struggle not acquire a new vigour and a new, indispensable rigour? If only they knew that, if man made this world which is an oppressive world, it is up to women to prepare the coming of a different world, which would at last be a world of life.

Women will not be liberated as long as they do not also want to be liberating, by denouncing and by fighting *all* oppression, those that come from man, from power, from work, but also those that come from themselves and operate on themselves, on others, and particularly on their children: dis-incarnated women, de-sexualized women, disinfected, disaffected, glossy magazine women, puppet women, but also women who are men's accomplices, accomplices of the strong man, the husband, boss, cop, and also jealous women, capricious and vengeful, bourgeois women, mean women, finally and above all, women the dragon of the family, women martyrs of devotion, voracious mother-hens, possessive and murderous mothers, odious step-mothers.

As long as we are somehow in complicity with man's oppressions, as long as we perpetuate them on to our children, turning them into vigorous oppressors or into docile victims, we will never, never be free.

6

Women's exile

Interview with Luce Irigaray

Translated by Couze Venn

Reprinted from Ideology and Consciousness, *vol.I (1977).*

What are now the most important problems, are they those concerned with feminine sexuality or with linguistics?

They are certainly the questions posed by feminine sexuality. For these questions involve at the same time psychoanalysis, philosophy, ideology and politics, and constitute at the present time some of the most important considerations for their interpretation.

That doesn't mean that I've abandoned linguistics. The question of language is closely allied to that of feminine sexuality. For I do not think that language is universal, or neutral with regard to the differences between the sexes. In the face of language, constructed and maintained by men only, I raise the question of the specificity of a feminine language: of a language which would be adequate for the body, sex and the imagination (imaginary) of the woman. A language which presents itself as universal, and which is in fact produced by men only, is this not what maintains the alienation and exploitation of women in and by society?

We shall come back to that. But could you, to start with, clarify the reasons that led you to write your book Speculum?

I wrote this book from my experience of psychoanalysis; to start with from the point of view of the patient being analysed – i.e. from the couch side of the fence – then as analyst. Gradually, I came to think that the discourse carried on by psychoanalysis about female sexuality was mistaken. It seemed to me to be impossible to fit those women who were undergoing analysis with me into these schemas and theories. For that would be to impose on them a concept of sexuality and of sexual difference which slotted them into the existing society and ideology, but by subjecting them to a law which completely repressed their desire.

That does not mean that what psychoanalysis describes, including the question of female sexuality, is false. But the state of things that it describes is presented by psychoanalysis as a universal and immutable norm, instead of interpreting it as an historically determined state.

It seems to me that one of the most important ideas in your book is that it is impossible to compare men and women within a symmetrical frame.

In any case, it is not simply a comparison which is the basis of psychoanalytic discourse – nor in the whole history of philosophy – since the feminine is in fact defined in it as nothing other than the complement, the other side, or the negative side, of the masculine; thus, the female sex is described as a lack, a 'hole'. Freud, and psychoanalysts following him maintain that the only desire on the part of the woman, when she discovers she has 'no sex', is to have a penis, i.e. *the only sexual organ which is recognized and valued.*

It might seem extraordinary that such theories could have been upheld. At the same time, that is easily understood: as long as power is only in the hands of the male, the 'other' – woman – can only appear as a lack or a negative. To say that the sex of the woman is an absence of sex, and that she can only have one desire: to possess a penis, is not, again, a simple comparison. It's an attempt which constitutes the female sex as the complement and the opposite necessary to the economy of the male sex. It is thus a complete misunderstanding of the specificity of the female, and a refusal, or rather an inability to recognize its existence and autonomy.

Already during Freud's lifetime, Karen Horney, Melanie Klein, Ernest Jones had questioned the concept of female sexuality. But these critiques did not fundamentally question the Freudian system. Any account of female sexuality which can be reduced to local and specific questions, in the end only serves to perpetuate the system. So long as one does not question the overall functioning of the psychoanalytic discourse and even of all theoretical discourse – even unconsciously – one only guarantees the continuation of the existing system. It is for that reason that in *Speculum*, I re-examine philosophy from Plato to Hegel, i.e. the history of western thought, of which Freud only represents a further development and a consequence. For the status of female sexuality in analytical theory is only the symptom of a much more general functioning of the discourse held historically by the so-called patriarchal ideology.

It is not a matter of naively accusing Freud, as if he were a 'bastard'. Freud's discourse represents the symptom of a particular social and cultural economy, which has been maintained in the west at least since the Greeks.

What we have to question is the system of representation, the discursive system at work in this socio-cultural functioning. And, in this respect, what Freud demonstrates is quite useful. When he argues – for example, and according to a still organistic argument – that women's sex is a 'lack', that castration for her amounts to her perceiving that she has no sex, he describes rigorously the consequence of our socio-cultural system. Lacan, using a linguistic schema, concludes likewise, and repeats the same process, when he writes that woman is a lack in the discourse, that she cannot articulate herself, but she does not 'exist', etc.

In some sense, this is not false. Can female sexuality articulate itself, even minimally, within an Aristotelian type of logic? No. Within this logic, which dominates our most everyday statements – while speaking, at this moment, we are still observing its rules, female sexuality cannot articulate itself, unless precisely as an 'undertone', a 'lack', in discourse. But why would this situation be unchanging? Why can one not transcend that logic? To speak outside of it?

How could you describe this language of the female?

It is obviously very difficult. First of all I would say it has nothing to do with the syntax which we have used for centuries, namely, that constructed according to the following organization: subject, predicate, or; subject, verb, object. For female sexuality is not unifiable, it cannot be subsumed under the concept of subject. Which brings into question all the syntactical norms. . . .

Meaning?

I think we must go back to the question not of the anatomy but of the morphology of female sex. In fact, it can be shown that all western discourse presents a certain isomorphism with the masculine sex: the privilege of unity, form of the self, of the visible, of the specularizable, of the erection (which is the becoming in a form). Now this morphologic does not correspond to the female sex: there is not 'a' female sex. The 'no sex' that has been assigned to the woman can mean that she does not have 'a sex', and that her sex is not visible, or identifiable, or representable in a definite form. There is indeed a visible exterior of the female sex, but that sex is also 'interior'. Besides, the sexual functioning of the woman can in no way lend itself to the privilege of the form: rather what the female sex enjoys is not having its own form.

When one says, or believes that this sex is a 'hole', it is a way of indicating that it cannot represent itself in either the dominant discourse or 'imaginary'. Thus I have tried to find what the specific modes of functioning of the female sex and 'imaginary' could be. Instead of, first of all, stopping at the 'parts' of this sex, such as they are defined in masculine parameters: the vagina or the home of the penis, the mechanism for producing children, or even, breasts (which can be willy-nilly, represented metaphorically as phallic), I'm trying to say that the female sex would be, above all, made up of '*two lips*'. These two lips of the female sex make it once and for all a return to unity, because they are always at least *two*, and that one can never determine of these two, which is one, which is the other: they are continually interchanging. They are neither identifiable nor separable one from the other. Besides, instead of that being the visible or the form which constitutes the dominant criteria, it is the *touch* which for the female sex seems to me primordial: *these 'two lips' are always joined in an embrace.*

When Freud maintains that the little girl discovers that compared with the little boy she has 'no sex', and that this 'castration' will completely arrest her in her auto-eroticism, that statement makes no sense, other than culturally. Indeed, nothing can prevent the woman from being permanently in auto-eroticism since she is all the time embracing herself within herself – without even requiring hands, instrument, and without it being visible. This continuity of feminine auto-eroticism is interrupted, however, by a kind of process which could be described as rape: by maintaining to women that they 'need' a penis, by instructing them that they are nothing by themselves, that they are not female without the penis. That is when they are exiled from their auto-eroticism, which, by the way, prevents them from having a 'desire' for the male sex.

You may perhaps be able to see that when one starts from the 'two lips' of the female sex, the dominant discourse finds itself baffled: there can no longer be a unity in the subject, for instance. There will always therefore be a plurality in feminine language. And it will not even be the Freudian 'pun' i.e., a superimposed hierarchy of meaning, but the fact that at each moment there is always for women 'at least two' meanings, without one being able to decide which meaning prevails, which is 'on top' or 'underneath', which 'conscious' or 'repressed'. Truly it would rather be the whole of feminine language which is still in the repressed form.

For, a feminine language would undo the unique meaning, the proper meaning of words, of nouns: which still regulates all discourse. In order for there to be a proper meaning, there must indeed be a unity somewhere. But if feminine language cannot be brought back to any unity, it cannot be simply described or defined: there is no feminine metalanguage. The masculine can partly look at itself, speculate about itself, represent itself and describe itself for what it is, whilst the feminine can try to speak to itself through a new language, but cannot describe itself from outside or in formal terms, except by identifying itself with the masculine, thus by losing itself.

I have the impression that you are describing a kind of process within language which is in some way similar to what Freud describes in the development of genitality, which in fact constitutes a process of unification. Masculine language would follow a similar development. Am I right?

You could say so. But one must above all think that there is an older complicity between the values recognized in discourse, and those admitted for sexuality. These values are in fact the same. They have a specific 'translation' when it's a matter of sexuality. Thus, to place genitality in a privileged position amounts in fact to according a privileged status to the values which unify, but also the values of production, the values of 'making', and with the aim of bringing to light something visible and which would be the proof of the efficiency of 'making' – in this case the child. But all these determinations of a 'good' sexuality are not an invention of Freud. Here again, he describes and normalizes, in the name of psychoanalytic science, the effect of social and cultural norms in sexuality.

That the criteria for a valid sexuality should be the same as those of a valid discourse, and that the criteria should be acceptable for a masculine sexuality should not be surprising. It is men who determined those criteria for evaluation. By contrast, women, left outside any active participation in the elaboration of socio-cultural norms, have been submitted to 'laws' which owed nothing to them.

Thus, the idea has been introduced in women's imagination that their pleasure lies in 'producing' children: which amounts to bending them to the values of production, even before they have had an occasion to examine their pleasure.

Besides, since a specific feminine sexuality could have been a bother for the socio-cultural order, by not corresponding to the proclaimed values – for instance, it has been said that women had no desire, no 'libido', and that they were very often 'frigid' through a 'natural' inferiority. Yet, in all those so-called 'truths', one must above all understand that female sexuality poses a problem for the dominant values, and that the issue has been, until now, repressed or censored, including by psychoanalysts.

Consider one example: the problem of the orgasm for women. Many women believe they are 'frigid', and they are often told this is so. When a women tells me that she is 'frigid', I laugh, and tell her I don't know what it means. She laughs too, which brings about a release, and above all a loss of guilt towards a 'frigidity' for which she feels responsible, and which means, first of all, that she has been moulded into models of male sexual 'techniques' which do not at all correspond to her sexuality – namely, the teleology of the orgasm. There is no privilege of the orgasmic unity for women: she does not enjoy just *one* orgasm, nor necessarily a determined orgasm, in only one definite and definitive manner. The teleological model is, to repeat, possible for a man – even if he thus loses pleasure – but not for a woman. The pleasure of the woman is always multiple, and not of course uniquely genital. When she begins to contract on the edge of a genital orgasm, she effectively loses the world of her pleasure.

You are active in the Women's Liberation Movement?

Yes.

Could you say something about your work in the Movement of Liberation?

Before trying to give an answer, I would like to make two things clear.

The first is that I cannot tell you everything about what the Liberation Movement does. To pick up again what I was telling you previously regarding the language of woman: what is happening in the movement cannot be glossed over, described, related 'from outside'. The second thing is that I prefer to speak in the plural about *movements of liberation of women*. Indeed, in the women's struggle today there is a great number of groups and tendencies; thus to speak of them as *a* Movement runs the risk of introducing hierarchies among them, or of leading to claims of orthodoxy.

Let us come back to my work: I am trying first of all, as I briefly indicated earlier, to re-examine the masculine 'imaginary', to interpret how it has reduced us to silence, to mutism, and I am trying, from that perspective, at the same time, to find a possible space for the feminine imaginary.

But it's obviously not a simple 'individual' task. Of course, what I say or write derives from my own experience, but that experience is not uniquely 'personal': a long history has placed all women in the same sexual, social and cultural situation.

Whatever may be the inequalities between women, they all suffer, even unconsciously, the same oppression, the same exploitation of their body, the same denial of their desire. That's why it is very important for women to unite, and to unite 'among themselves'. So that they may begin to escape from the places, the roles, the gestures which have been assigned and taught to them by the society of men. So that they may love each other, whilst men have organized 'de facto' a rivalry between women. To discover another form of social existence than that which has always been imposed upon them. The first step in the movements of liberation is to enable every women to become 'conscious' that what she has felt in her own experience, which is a condition shared by all women, which makes it possible for *that experience to become politicized*. But, what is meant here by 'politicize'? There is not, not yet, a 'politics for women', at least in the wider sense. And if it were to exist some day, it would be very different from the politics instituted by men. For the issues raised by the exploitation of women's bodies go beyond the issues, the schemas, and, of course, the parties of the politics we know and which have up to now been practised. That obviously does not prevent political parties from wanting to recuperate the problem of women, by allowing them a little place in their ranks, in order to bring them into line (once more. . .) with their 'programme', with which they mostly have nothing to do, in the sense that it does not take into account their *specific exploitation*. Indeed, the exploitation of women is not a *regional* problem situated inside politics, and which would only involve a 'section' of the population, or a 'part' of the social 'body'. When women want to escape from exploitation, they do not simply destroy a

few 'prejudices': they upset the whole set of the dominant values –
economic, social, moral, sexual. They challenge every theory, every
thought, every existing language, in that these are monopolized by men
only. They question the *very foundation of our social and cultural order*,
the organization of which has been prescribed by the patriarchal system.
The patriarchal foundation of our social mode of existence is, in fact,
guided by the present political system, even if it is 'left wing'. Indeed up
till now, Marxism has paid little attention to the problem of the specific
exploitation of women, and women's struggles seem, more frequently,
to upset Marxists. And yet these struggles could be interpreted with the
help of the schemas for analysing social exploitation which are precisely
those at work in the elaboration of left-wing political programmes. But
one would have to go further in the analysis of exploitation and
demonstrate how the social mode of existence itself, 'socialité' in
general, exploits women. But no political perspective has as yet
examined its relation to phallocratic power.

In concrete terms, this means that women must continue to struggle
for equal pay, for social rights, against discrimination at work, in
education, etc. But that is not enough: women who are simply 'equal' to
men would be 'like them', and therefore not women. Once more, the
sexual difference would be cancelled, misunderstood and glossed over.
One must invent, among women, new forms of organization, new forms
of struggle, new challenges. The various movements of liberation have
already started to do so, and a women's 'Internationale' is emerging.
But here also one must create anew: the institution, hierarchies,
authority – i.e., the existing forms of political systems – belong to men's
world, not ours.

That explains some of the difficulties experienced by the liberation
movements. If women allow themselves to be caught in the trap of
power-seeking, in the game of authority, if they allow themselves to be
contaminated by the 'paranoid' mode of functioning of male politics,
they no longer have anything to say or to do *as women*. That is why in
France one of the tasks now is to try to bring together the various
tendencies in the Movement around a certain number of clearly defined
themes and specific action: *viz.*, rape, abortion, the challenging of the
privilege of the father's name in the case of judicial decisions regarding
the 'ownership of children', the equal participation of women in the
decision-making processes of the state, etc. All this ought not to blind us
to the fact that it is in order to establish their difference that women are
claiming their rights.

Personally, I refuse to be limited by the boundaries of just one group in the Women's Liberation Movement. Especially if it becomes ensnared in the exercise of power, if it pretends to determine women's 'truths', legislate on what it means to be a woman, and condemn women who may have immediate objectives different from its own. I think the most important aim is to make visible the exploitation common to all women and to discover the struggles which every woman should engage in, wherever she is: i.e., depending on her country, her occupation, her class, and her sexual estate – i.e., the most immediately unbearable of her modes of oppression.

Let us come back a minute to linguistics. What role has it played in France for psychoanalysis? With respect to Freud, does it seem that psychoanalysis today has changed its frame of reference and its scientific metalanguage?

It is Jacques Lacan who has undertaken this 'translation' of the economy of the unconscious and of the 'subject' into a theory of language and mathematical model. This is due to the influence of people like de Saussure, Roman Jakobson, Claude Lévi-Strauss, etc., i.e., to the importance of structuralism in France. Jacques Lacan – taking up the elements of a theory of language existing in embryonic form in Freud – has carried out an enormous task, whose influence in France is extremely strong.

However, there was, I think, one further step to take: to question linguistic theory itself, *viz.*, structuralism, and, more generally, any formalism. Lacan does not quarrel with the formal schemas to which he moulds the unconscious, nor the assumptions of universality of the models he uses. Thus, for him, the universal character of a 'langue', or even a language, seems to be self-evident. 'The unconscious is structured like a language', he claims repeatedly. Obviously, but which? And if that language is unique, and always the same – for men and women – Lacan can only lead back to a traditional position concerning the feminine.

In fact, there is lacking in Lacan a theory of enunciation which would be sufficiently complex, and which would allow him to account for the effect of sexual difference on the production of language. It is true that that theory of expression is still rather sketchy in linguistics. But I think there is in Lacan a taste for formalism which leads him to neglect what already exists in that line. In other words, Lacan interprets the unconscious by forcing it into certain existing theoretical models, while one should rather question these models from the point of view of the unconscious.

Anyway, one discovers here the question of the criteria of universality which dominate the whole of western thought, and thus psychoanalysis. When one defines the unconscious in terms of universal characteristics, one does not wonder whether these characteristics are valid for women also. I do not think that women, in fact, have an unconscious operating in the same way as that of men. Even the fact that women possess an unconscious is not self-evident. It is possible that one has been imposed on them. But to say that women's sexuality is naturally subject to processes of repression, sublimation, etc., that's very doubtful. I would rather frame the following question: are women not, partly, the unconscious? That is, is there not in what has been historically constituted as the 'unconscious', some censored, repressed element of the feminine? Certain functional criteria attributed to the unconscious, like non-contradiction, contiguity, etc., are, I think, close to female sexuality and language.

When psychoanalysis asserts that the Oedipus complex is an 'immutable' structure, 'universal', that seems to me to be ahistorical, and, indeed, naive. Why should what is effectively universal in the patriarchal system be so in an altogether different kind of society?

Psychoanalysts, like philosophers don't seem able to rethink their system. They do not see it as one historical construct among others, as an ideological 'symptom'. Does the claim that the Oedipus complex is an *a priori* universal truth not prevent psychoanalysis from functioning? When the psychoanalyst (male or female) listens, there ought not to exist, strictly speaking, *a priori* truths. The discourse/statement of the person being analysed, its transfer, cannot be forced, in advance, into a unique and definitive interpretation. When the psychoanalyst acts in this way, does she not subject those being analysed, and the analysts, to an obsessional and paranoid culture? Look at most analysts and those analysed: they think they have reached the last word, the 'truth', regarding their psyche and their sexuality. If they would keep it to themselves at least! But they preach to others; everywhere and ceaselessly.

Once again, I think that psychoanalysis is an historical event, and even an historical 'symptom'. But psychoanalysts fail to see that they are a product of history.

And yet, you are still a psychoanalyst?

Yes, because I believe the analytical framework is still effective, because people ask me for analysis, and because there is still a lot to understand about the unconscious. But the fact that a good many of the psychic mechanisms discovered by Freud (such as repetition, death wish, *après-coup*, sublimation, displacement, etc.), operate in *our culture* does not imply that they will always do so, nor that they should be 'normalized'.

Are you still using the Freudian concepts like the energy model of the libido, and the topological model (id, ego, super-ego)?

I think it would be better to state the problem in rather different terms. Freudian concepts are on the whole connected to the model provided by thermodynamics. And it is this model that one should suspect, by questioning whether it is universally adequate for the female, or even the male. Molecular biology today helps one to doubt the generality and exclusivity of the thermodynamic model as it applies to living organisms. To remain within the thermodynamic framework would amount partly to value death over life. Further, western thought has been dominated by the physics and the mechanics of solid matter, whereas the feminine refers much more to a mechanics of fluids, which has barely been elaborated. This misunderstanding of the specificity of an economy of fluids has an effect even on the representation of male sexuality itself; why, for instance, has such little emphasis been placed on the fluidity of the sperm? It has always been considered as being used to make solids, *viz.*, children.

Psychoanalysis maintains also that there is no feminine libido, without noticing that in the model of psychic economy which it is using, that libido cannot exist. For it is quite false to say that there is no specific female desire. It is a specific social and cultural structure which deprives women of their desire and of the possibility of their expressing it, *viz.*, because language and the systems of representation cannot 'translate' that desire. According to this, women are effectively totally lost, 'outside of themselves', and they no longer know what they themselves want because they submit, through the fear of being left on the shelf, to the existing order. What makes them 'passive' traps them in the roles described by 'femininity', in which their desire loses itself – which does not mean that they have none.

When J. Lacan bemoans: 'I beg them on my knees to tell me what they want and they tell me nothing', why does he not hear what is at issue here? It is because he situates himself in the functioning of language and of desire in which women cannot say anything, and in which he cannot hear them, even if they were to begin to speak to him. Lacan, to repeat, has done some very important theoretical work. But what limits him is his phallocratic power: he cannot bear that someone else speaks anything but *his truth* as he describes it. And it is up to him to describe what is the pleasure of the woman, not a woman! If a woman tries to express her pleasure – which, obviously, challenges his male point of view – he excludes her, because she upsets his system. Thus, soon after *Speculum* was published, I was sacked from the university where I was teaching. I was teaching a course in the Department of Psychoanalysis of Vincennes University, and J. Lacan and the Paris Freudian School expelled me. The meaning of this expulsion is clear: only men may say what female pleasure consists of. Women are not allowed to speak, otherwise they challenge the monopoly of discourse and of theory exerted by men.

One always finds the same question: that of the so-called universality of language and of the existing culture. What is its foundation? C. Lévi-Strauss explains that it is the exchange of women among men which characterizes the passage from the natural to the social order. What does that express concerning the exploitation of women's bodies? If women's bodies must act as the form of exchange between men, it means that women ensure the foundation of the symbolic order, without ever gaining access to it, and so without being paid in a symbolic form for that task. It is their silence, their silent bodies – but yet productive – which regulates the smooth exchange between men, and the social mechanism in general.

One can always, from this 'grounding' of the social order, examine Marxism. When Marx speaks of the exchange value of commodities, one could use his analysis to speculate whether the constitution of not only a specific society, but society in general, is not grounded – in the patriarchal system – on the fact that women act as commodities exchanged between men or groups of men.

One could equally, from that perspective, question psychoanalysis: in what way have hysterical women – including their so-called frigidity – helped to found (psycho) analytical theory? In what way do they continue to sustain that theory and to facilitate the exchange between male theorists in (psycho) analytical communities?

Do you not have the impression that this status of women as exchange commodity is beginning to change?

It's a very important question. I would like to answer that this might appear so, but that fundamentally this is not the case. Let us consider a simple and obvious example: it is still the man who generally chooses 'his' women. For centuries men have been polygamous – without anybody bothering to ask women if they liked it. But when today a woman tries to be polyandrous, this creates such enormous problems of interaction with men that it can only be sustained with difficulty. This has to do with the fact that it is male fantasms which dominate the sexual scene, not those of women. Women are caught up at the cross-road of male fantasms: this means, among other things, that a man desires a woman in terms of the fantasies of another man for her. But this should remain implicit, as that which guarantees, provided it remains hidden, the functioning of masculine desire. As for the specific language describing women's fantasms and which would express their desire and their image of themselves, it is still repressed, censored, and layered by sado-masochist fantasies induced by the dominant sexual framework.

When one examines what is presented as 'female fantasies' by magazines, sexology books, pornography, etc., one only finds, in fact, induced images, and not an 'imaginary' which would correspond to the specificity of female sexuality. There are nothing but rapes, violence, penetrations described as breaking and entering, female orgasms functioning as the proof of male power, an over-evaluation of the size of male sex, etc.: thus representations of the effect on women of male desire, and symptoms of the way in which women are subjected to this desire's economy. They are never, or rarely, fantasms which correspond to the self-eroticism of women. This female language of fantasm, which would be quite different, and could not be represented or circumscribed within a framework dominated by sight, is arrested, censored by the status which women have as objects of exchange, as commodity.

Don't you think that the dynamics of capitalism constitute an important factor in changing the exchange system? In a traditional society women function as direct means of exchange between men. But in advanced capitalism, that structure is no longer so definite: women are no longer tied to the family, to domestic life, in the same way as before.

Whatever be the evolution and the changes that have happened, women continue, on the whole, to reproduce and bring up children, make the food, and service men. Thus, they still ensure the social basis which enables exchange between men. From the moment that a man has a family, when 'his' wife reproduces and maintains through her work the life, desire, of the man, we have a form in which the appropriation of women's bodies is perpetuated, as a condition for the reproduction of the social order. Further, a man always takes 'his' woman from another man, against whom, in one way or another, he compares his phallic power and prestige. It is true that all of this has been somewhat displaced at the level of the *fantasmatique*, but only in some way.

In the present system, it is a fact that women maintain the productive forces of society. By producing children, by reproducing the labour force, they continue to mediate the exchange between men. In other words, women's bodies constitute the infrastructure of our society: *they reproduce the forces of production without being recognized as a force of production.*

Suppose there were a general strike by women. That is perhaps the only thing that would radically threaten capitalism – the free enterprise as well as the state capitalism of 'socialist' countries. And I mean a strike by all women, not just working women. I cannot imagine how the social order could manage, its reproduction would come to a halt.

I know that such a general strike is a utopia. But the idea does demonstrate the extent to which women's work constitutes the unrecognized infrastructure of our social systems.

And if one were to doubt that women still have the status of an object of exchange between men only it is sufficient to look at the difficulties they have in attending women's meetings: they have to find 'excuses'. And in order to maintain an effective social life with women, a woman must invent another form of society to get away from the networks of exchange and appropriation controlled by men. The ruling society, in any case, defends itself against women's movements by using aggression or by deriding them.

You have done research on the language of madness, of schizophrenia and of anxiety. What connection is there between this work and what you have just described?

These researches have made it possible for me to realize that sexual differences become embedded in language. To ignore that the male does not produce language in a universal mode but according to his sex, would amount to wiping out the difference between the sexes. In other words, there is a *dynamics of statements* which is different according to sex. Also, there are specific linguistic disturbances according to sexual differences: the way anxiety or psychosis is expressed differs with sex. This is most often forgotten in nosological models, as well as psycho-analytical models, which negate the difference between the sexes. For instance, one speaks of schizophrenia as if it were a nosological entity in which sexual differences do not matter. But I have recorded the statements of a large number of schizophrenics; I have used this 'corpus' to compare the language of ten male and ten female subjects. The results indicate quite a difference: men have an ability for syntactic modification, for 'metalanguage' which women do not have. A woman in a state of madness does not have, for some reason, the means for elaborating a delirium. Instead of language being the medium of expression of the delirium, the latter remains within the body itself. The dominant element in feminine schizophrenia is corporal pain, the feeling of deformation or transformation of organs, etc. Thus, in this case also, women do not manage to articulate their madness: they suffer it directly in their body, without being able to transpose it in some different mode.

I believe that this does not apply to only those women shut up in hospitals, or in a 'sickness' recognized by society. Nearly all women are in some state of madness: shut up in their bodies, in their silence and their 'home'. This kind of imprisonment means that they live their madness without it being noticed. This is perhaps why feminine madness is less explicit and, above all, less socially disruptive.

In psychiatric hospitals in Norway there are more women than men suffering from chronic schizophrenia, and their cases are more acute.

It seems to me that that is relevant to what I have just said: one can attempt some kind of therapy with someone who after all has some relation with language, and one can fit someone back into society who already has a social role, someone for whom society makes a valuable place and function. Whilst it is much more difficult to attempt a therapy for women schizophrenics. Schizophrenia being a form of autism, women would need to have a social and cultural possibility for coming out of autism. There are of course exceptions, as in the case of Mary Barnes who became a painter. But not all women can take up painting, writing or drama, etc. One would probably have to produce therapies which would be more corporal, invent new forms of therapy in 'woman's language', and form women's groups which make up micro-societies in which schizophrenics could become integrated. But, above all, one would need to modify the social status of women, and make sure that society does not control them without their being able to participate effectively in it. In this case also, one can see the liberation movements as enabling women to bring about a society which is appropriate for them.

Could you indicate, to conclude, the cause of these difficulties which women schizophrenics experience, and which, at a more general level, every woman experiences.

I think that the social system, at all the levels of its functioning, is such that women are totally 'censored' in their carnal relationship with their mothers and other women. Indeed, Freud, in his own way, did see this. According to him, as soon as she realizes her castration, the little girl turns away from her mother, because the latter does not possess the valued sex which she thought she had. Then, Freud says, the little girl 'hates' her mother – and thus herself and all other women. According to him, she develops 'a penis envy': the only worthwhile value for her is that of the male sex.

Freud describes this process in terms which can be criticized, and, importantly by describing it as normal and inevitable, which recalls the arguments I've already made. But the fact remains: the relationship of women to their mothers and to other women – thus towards themselves – are subject to total narcissistic 'black-out'; these relationships are completely devalued. Indeed, I have never come across a woman who does not suffer from the problem of not being able to resolve in harmony, in the present system, her relationship with her mother and with other women. Psychoanalysis has totally mythologized and 'censored' the positive value of these relationships. And it neglects, or transforms into guilt, the consequences of the narcissistic distress which the little girl suffers because of the devaluation of her relationship with her mother, and her own sex.

Everything happens as if there were a necessary break between the earliest investments, the earliest desires, the first narcissism of a little girl, and those of a 'normal' adult woman. In the place of those who would be in a position of continuity with her 'pre-history', she has, imposed on her, a language, fantasms, a desire which does not 'belong' to her and which establishes a break with her auto-eroticism. That kind of *schizo* which every woman experiences, in our socio-cultural system, only leaves her with nothing more than somatizations, corporal pains, mutism, or mimetism with which to express herself: saying and doing 'like men'.

Do you not think that that break is lived by men also?

It's not at all the same. For men, the first object of love is also the mother. But, in a way, she remains the last object: he does not change – in a love relationship with a woman, a man always looks for his mother. Besides, this is often the drama of love relations: he looks too much for her. Does a woman, in a relationship with a man, also discover her mother?

No.

This is serious. You are not in exile: you remain in continuous relation with your first object, with your first love, with your first attachments. If you displace them, it would be according to your laws: the language, the culture that you have made.

A woman, if she cannot in one way or another recuperate her first object, i.e., the possibility of keeping her earliest libidinal attachments by displacing them, is always exiled from herself. Yet, it is very difficult for her to find in her relationship with men the means for overcoming that loss of the first relationship with the mother's body. It may be that some men are more maternal than others. But, this remains difficult because men – besides not having either the body or the sex of the mother – have become culturally distanced from their bodies.

Historically, they have chosen sex and language against or in spite of the body. The depositories of the body are women. That is, men can find the body in women and also the primal substance – but women cannot find this in men. It would be necessary for women to be recognized as bodies with sexual attribute(s), desiring and uttering, and for men to rediscover the materiality of their bodies. There should no longer be this separation: sex/language on the one hand, body/matter on the other. Then, perhaps, another history would be possible....

Part Two

'NAMING' AND REPRESENTATION

Introduction

This part deals, essentially, with the issue of 'sexist language'. It opens with a theoretical debate: Dale Spender's view that 'man made language' and that language, Whorf-style, constructs a sexist universe, is contested by Maria Black and Rosalind Coward. Black and Coward argue that to speak of 'language' being sexist is both inaccurate and unhelpful. Inaccurate, because 'language' for linguists is a decontextualized system in which it is not obligatory to be sexist: sexism enters into the choices speakers and writers make in their use of the system in particular contexts, and into the way certain choices become conventionalized, inscribed in authoritarian practices like prescriptive grammar, which have little to do with the structure of language *per se*. (I think it is fair to comment here that many linguists would dispute this rather strong position. The relation between institutionalized rules in languages such as English and the grammatical system described by scientific linguists is a complicated issue: at what point, for instance, does an originally prescriptive rule like the generic masculine pronoun become acknowledged as part of the core system of English grammar?)

Black and Coward further argue that we should not be aiming, as many reformers have in effect aimed, at a sex-neutral discourse which refers equally to men and women. Rather the problem is to make men *gendered*: that is, to represent them as male and not simply as human, the norm, with women represented as 'the sex'.

Having posed these alternatives – sexist language or sexist discourse? – we may go on to consider the construction and deconstruction of sexism in two specific areas, vocabulary and grammar. In her paper 'The semantic derogation of women', Muriel Schulz shows how words associated with women have developed in ways not paralleled for words associated with men. Schulz puts forward a somewhat biologistic argument as to why this happens: men are envious of women's biological superiority and so feel a need to represent them as inferior (that they are able to do this is a consequence of their social dominance). It could be argued that things are not so simple. Men are not the only agents of semantic derogation, for the ideology that derogates women is subscribed to by many speakers and writers of both sexes. Some commentators would regard semantic derogation as a reflex of social power structures rather than a sort of masculine neurosis which men's power permits them to enshrine in language.

In contrast, it is perfectly clear that the recording of meanings in dictionaries *has* been carried out mainly by men, and some of the consequences are pointed out by Cheris Kramarae and Paula Treichler in their introduction to *A Feminist Dictionary*. Kramarae and Treichler are critical of traditional lexicography, and in this piece they explain their own quite different (rather than merely opposite) objectives in dictionary-making.

Finally in this selection of writings on vocabulary we have a contrasting piece taken from a work of imaginative fiction. In her fantasy novel *Native Tongue* Suzette Hadin Elgin throws into relief what *is* by describing what could be. Adopting a Whorfian perspective, she imagines women bringing about massive changes to their repressive and misogynist society (without a drop of blood being spilt!) by inventing a language, Láadan, that encodes their perceptions as women. The experiences for which a culture has a lexical item rather than a circumlocution are arguably foregrounded and thus easier to grasp: Láadan surprises by foregrounding experiences for which English does not have separate lexical items. It is an interesting exercise to try and think up other 'encodings' on a similar pattern.

The last section of this part deals with sexist grammar in English – what feminists have labelled 'he/man' language. Tillie Olsen states what many people perceive as the problem: women are excluded from discourse about 'man'. The other pieces reprinted here are directed towards two common responses to the problem – first, that it is 'natural', and second that it is trivial. Ann Bodine's paper 'Androcentrism in prescriptive grammar' shows how the generic masculine was for many years just a variant among others. Its status as a norm of correctness was established historically using arguments which were not purely linguistic, and which made effective use of ideas about the relative importance of the two sexes in society. Masculine was deemed 'the worthier gender' in life *and therefore* in grammar.

Finally, a very different kind of piece, Douglas Hofstadter's satirical 'A person paper'. The genre being satirized here is the conservative essay on the lamentable state of the language (Hofstadter's special target is the US columnist William Safire). The satirical technique is both unusual and disturbing: an extended analogy between racist and sexist insult. This helps us to see that whether readers perceive *man* as referring to men only is not the only significant issue. The symbolic offensiveness of Hofstadter's language is intolerable applying to Black people: 'One small step for a white; one giant leap for whitekind' has overtones of racial supremacy which most people find not merely unacceptable but horrifying in its implications. Douglas Hofstadter implicitly poses the question, why should women be any less offended?

7

Extracts from *Man Made Language*

Dale Spender

Reprinted from Dale Spender Man Made Language *(London: Routledge & Kegan Paul 1980)*

'The objects and events of the world do not present themselves to us ready classified', states James Britton (1975). 'The categories into which they are divided are the categories into which *we divide them*' (p. 23). My question which arises from this statement is not whether it is an accurate assessment, for I readily accept that language is a powerful determinant of reality, but who is the WE to whom James Britton refers? Who are these people who 'make the world' and what are the principles behind their division, organization, and classification?

Although not explicitly stated, Britton is referring to males. It is men who have made the world which women must inhabit, and if women are to begin to make their own world, it is necessary that they understand some of the ways in which such *creation* is accomplished. This means exploring the relationship of language and reality.

Susanne Langer (1976) has pointed out that human beings are symbolizing creatures (it is, perhaps, our capacity to symbolize that differentiates us from other species), and we are constantly engaged in the process of producing symbols as a means of categorizing and organizing our world. But it would be foolish to have complete faith in the system of order we have constructed because it is, from the outset, imperfect, only ever serving as an approximation. Yet it seems that we are foolish: we do 'trust' the world order we have created with our symbols and we frequently allow these representations to beguile us into accepting some of the most bizarre rules for making sense of the world. It is our capacity to symbolize and the use (or misuse) we make of the symbols we construct that constitutes the area of language, thought, and reality.

It is because we can be seduced by language that a debate has been waged for many years on the relationship of language, thought, and reality. On the one hand, there is considerable evidence that not all human beings are led to the same view of the world by the same physical evidence and on the other hand, is the explanation – namely the Sapir–Whorf hypothesis – that this is because of language. It is language which determines the limits of our world, which constructs our reality.

One of the tantalizing questions which has confronted everyone from philosophers to politicians is the extent to which human beings can 'grasp things as they really are'; yet in many ways this is an absurd question that could arise only in a mono-dimensional reality which subscribed to the concept of there being only *one* way that 'things' can be. Even if there were only one way, it is unlikely that as human beings we would be able to grasp that 'pure', 'objective' form, for all we have available is symbols, which have their own inherent limitations, and these symbols and representations are already circumscribed by the limitations of our own language.

Language is *not* neutral. It is not merely a vehicle which carries ideas. It is itself a shaper of ideas, it is the programme for mental activity (Whorf 1976). In this context it is nothing short of ludicrous to conceive of human beings as capable of grasping things as they really are, of being impartial recorders of their world. For they themselves, or some of them, at least, have created or constructed that world and they have reflected themselves within it.

Human beings cannot impartially describe the universe because in order to describe it they must first have a classification system. But, paradoxically, once they have that classification system, once they have a language, *they can see only certain arbitrary things*.

Such an understanding is not confined to linguistics. The sciences of physiology and biology have also helped to substantiate – sometimes inadvertently – the false nature of impartiality or objectivity. Evidence gathered from these disciplines demonstrates that we ourselves come into the process of organizing and describing the universe. Unfortunately for those advocates of the human capacity to 'grasp things as they really are' there is one basic flaw in their argument – they have failed to take into account that the brain can neither see nor hear:

To speak metaphorically, the brain is quite blind and deaf, it has no direct contact with light or sound, but instead has to acquire all its information about the state of the outside world in the form of pulses of bio-electrical activity pumped along bundles of nerve fibres from the external surface of the body, its interface with the environment.

(F. Smith 1971: 82)

The brain too, has to interpret: it too can only deal in symbols and never know the 'real' thing. And the programme for encoding and decoding those symbols, for translating and calculating, is set up by the language which we possess. What we *see* in the world around us depends in a large part on the principles we have encoded in our language:

> each of us has *to learn to see*. The growth of every human being is a slow process of learning 'the rules of seeing', without which we could not in any ordinary sense see the world around us. There is no reality of familiar shapes, colours and sounds to which we merely open our eyes. The information that we receive through our senses from the material world around us has to be interpreted according to certain human rules, before what we ordinarily call 'reality' forms.
>
> (Williams 1975: 33)

When one principle that has been encoded in our language (and thought) is that of sexism, the implications for 'reality' can readily be seen. So too can the implications for 'objectivity', because 'scientific method' has been frequently accepted as being 'above' fallible human processes and, because its truths have been paraded as incontestable, many individuals have had little confidence in their own experience when this has clashed with prevailing scientific 'truths'.

It is not just feminists who have come to challenge some of the accepted notions about the impartiality of science and who have focused on the relationship of language, thought, and reality – although there are distinctive and additional features of the feminist approach which I will discuss later. There is new interest in such areas as the philosophy or sociology of science in which the question of 'objectivity' is being taken up, and where old answers are being viewed as inadequate and false (Chalmers 1978: Kuhn 1972). That science is a dogma, just as were the feudal, clerical, and market dogmas which preceded it, that is open to query and to challenge (Young 1975: 3), is not a traditional evaluation of scientific method, but it is an evaluation that is becoming increasingly more popular. That reason, objectivity and empiricism have been used to justify 'science' in a way that revelation, divine inspiration, and mythology have been used to justify 'religion', is a factor which has not been explored: yet the parallels exist. It has been just as heretical or crazy to challenge one dogma as it was in the past to challenge the other.

But this is changing. Alan Chalmers (1978), for example, tackles some of the misapprehensions that are held about science and scientific method, whereby the naming of something as 'science' has implied 'some kind of merit, or special kind of reliability' (p. xiii). He, too, takes up some of the issues of language, thought, and reality when he readily demonstrates (partly by use of a diagram, p. 22) that not all human beings – scientists included – are led to the same view of the world by the same physical evidence, for what observers see when they view an object or event 'is not determined solely by the images on their retinas but depends also on the experience, knowledge, expectations and general inner state of the observer' (p. 24), which, as Chalmers illustrates, may very often be culturally specific and which I would argue is largely determined by language, which is the means of ordering and structuring experiences, knowledge, expectations, and inner states.

Chalmers is intent on discrediting the premise that science *begins* with observation and he convincingly points out that this is a fallacy: contrary to the belief of the 'purity' of empiricism, he indicates that 'theory precedes observation' (p. 27) and the types of theories which are culturally available play a substantial role in determining what the observers – empirical scientists among them – can *see*.

When there are a sexist language and sexist theories culturally available, the observation of reality is also likely to be sexist. It is by this means that sexism can be perpetuated and reinforced as new objects and events, new data, have sexist interpretations projected upon them. Science is no more free of this bias than any other explanatory activity.

It is this recognition that human beings are part of the process of constructing reality and knowledge which has led Dwight Bolinger (1975) to 'reinterpret' our past and to assert that our history can validly be viewed *not* as the progressive intuiting of nature but as exteriorizing a way of looking at things as they are circumscribed by our language. Once certain categories are constructed within the language, we proceed to organize the world according to those categories. We even fail to see evidence which is not consistent with those categories.

This makes language a paradox for human beings: it is both a creative and an inhibiting vehicle. On the one hand, it offers immense freedom for it allows us to 'create' the world we live in; that so many different cultures have created so many different 'worlds' is testimony to this enormous and varied capacity (Berger and Luckmann 1972, have categorized this aspect of language as 'world openness', p. 69). But, on the other hand, we are restricted by that creation, limited to its confines, and, it appears, we resist, fear and dread any modifications to the structures we have initially created, even though they are 'arbitrary', approximate ones. It is this which constitutes a language *trap*.

It could be said that out of nowhere we invented sexism, we created the arbitrary and approximate categories of male-as-norm and female as deviant. A most original, imaginative creation. But, having constructed these categories in our language and thought patterns, we have now been trapped for we are most reluctant to organize the world any other – less arbitrary or imperfect – way. Indeed, it could even be argued that the trap which we have made is so pervasive that we cannot envisage a world constructed on any other lines.

It is, however, at this point that feminist insights into language, thought and reality are differentiated. While it could be said that we invented sexism from out of nowhere and utilized the principle in encoding reality, I doubt that feminists would make such a statement. While it could be argued that it was mere accident that 'object-ivity' and the 'scientific method' came to acquire their meritorious[1] status and while such a discussion could occur without reference to gender, I also doubt whether feminists would completely accept such an explanation. The distinctive and additional feature of feminist analysis of language, thought, and reality is that feminists assert that we did *not* create these categories or the means of legitimating them. To return to James Britton's statement at the beginning of this chapter, I would reiterate that it has been the dominant group – in this case, males – who have created the world, invented the categories, constructed sexism and its justification, and developed a language trap which is in their interest.

Given that language is such an influential force in shaping our world, it is obvious that those who have the power to make the symbols and their meanings are in a privileged and highly advantageous position. They have, at least, the potential to order the world to suit their own ends, the potential to construct a language, a reality, a body of know-ledge in which they are the central figures, the potential to legitimate their own primacy, and to create a system of beliefs which is beyond challenge (so that their superiority is 'natural' and 'objectively' tested). The group which has the power to ordain the structure of language, thought, and reality has the potential to create a world in which they are the central figures, while those who are not of their group are peripheral and therefore may be exploited.

In the patriarchal order this potential has been realized.

Males, as the dominant group, have produced language, thought, and reality. Historically it has been the structures, the categories, and the meanings which have been invented by males – though not of course by *all* males – and they have then been validated by reference to other males. In this process women have played little or no part.

***

In order to live in the world, we must *name* it. Names are essential for the construction of reality for without a name it is difficult to accept the existence of an object, an event, a feeling. Naming is the means whereby we attempt to order and structure the chaos and flux of existence which would otherwise be an undifferentiated mass. By assigning names we impose a pattern and a meaning which allows us to manipulate the world.

But names are human products, the outcome of partial human vision and there is not a one-to-one correspondence between the names we possess and the material world they are designed to represent. We are dependent on names, but we are mistaken if we do not appreciate that they are imperfect and often misleading: one of the reasons that people are not led to the same view of the universe by the same physical evidence is that their vision is shaped by the different names they employ to classify that physical evidence.

Naming, however, is not a neutral or random process. It is an application of principles already in use, an extension of existing 'rules' (Sapir 1970) and of the act of naming. Benjamin Whorf has stated that it is

> no act of unfettered imagination, even in the wildest flights of nonsense, but a strict use of already patterned materials. If asked to invent forms not already prefigured in the patternment of his [*sic*] language, the speaker is negative in the same manner as if asked to make fried eggs without eggs.

(1976: 256)

Names which cannot draw on past meanings are meaningless. New names, then, have their origins in the perspective of those doing the naming rather than in the object or event that is being named, and that perspective is the product of the prefigured patterns of language and thought. New names systematically subscribe to old beliefs, they are locked into principles that already exist, and there seems no way out of this even if those principles are inadequate or false.

All naming is of necessity biased and the process of naming is one of encoding that bias, of making a selection of what to emphasize and what to overlook on the basis of a 'strict use of already patterned materials'. Theoretically, if *all* members of a society were to provide names and these were to be legitimated, then a variety of biases could be available; the speakers of a language could 'choose', within the circumscribed limits of their own culture. Practically, however, difficulty arises when one group holds a monopoly on naming and is able to enforce its own particular bias on everyone, including those who do not share its view of the world. When one group holds a monopoly on naming, its bias is embedded in the names it supplies and these 'new' names help to maintain and strengthen its initial bias.

It is relatively easy to see how this is done. John Archer (1978) has documented this process at work in the construction of knowledge about sex roles, and he quotes one example of the work of Witkin *et al.* (1962). Witkin and his colleagues wanted to find out whether there were sex differences in the perception of a stimulus in a surrounding field and they designed an experiment where the subjects could either *separate* the stimulus (an embedded figure) from the surrounding field or else they could see the *whole*, they could see the stimulus as part of the surrounding field.

In many of these experiments Witkin and his colleagues found that females were more likely to see the stimulus and surrounding field as a whole while males were more likely to separate the stimulus from its context.

Witkin of course was obliged to name this phenomenon and he did so in accordance with the principles already encoded in the language. He took the existing patterns of male as positive and female as negative, and objectively devised his labels. He named the behaviour of males as *field independence*, thereby perpetuating and strengthening the image of male supremacy; he named the female behaviour as *field dependence* and thereby perpetuated and strengthened the image of female inferiority.

It is important to note that these names do not have their origins in the events: they are the product of Witkin's subjective view. There is nothing inherently dependent or independent in seeing something as a whole, or dividing it into parts. Witkin has coined names which are consistent with the patriarchal order and in the process he has extended and reinforced that order.

There are alternatives. With my particular bias I could well have named this same behaviour as positive for females and negative for males. I could have described the female response as *context awareness* and the male response as *context blindness*, and though these names would be just as valid as those which Witkin provided they would no doubt have been seen as *political* precisely because they do not adhere to the strict (sexist) rules by which the names of our language have traditionally been coined.

From this it can be seen that those who have the power to name the world are in a position to influence reality. Again, if more than one set of names were available, users of the language could elect to use those names which best reflected their interests; they could choose whether to call males field independent or context blind, and the existence of such a choice would minimize the falseness which is inherent in but one or other of the terms. But because it has been males who have named the world, no such choice exists and the falseness of the partial names they have supplied goes unchecked.

Notes

1 At this point I consulted *The Concise Oxford English Dictionary* to find out if the word I wanted was meritorious or meretricious. Obviously it is meritorious: meretricious (the closest entry to my feeling for meritricious) is defined as 'of, befitting a harlot'. Now where does that one come from!

References

Archer, J. (1978) 'Biological explanations of sex-role stereotypes: conceptual, social and semantic issues', in J. Chetwynd and O. Hartnett (eds), *The Sex Role System*, London: Routledge & Kegan Paul

Berger, P. and Luckmann, T. (1972) *The Social Construction of Reality*, Harmondsworth: Penguin.

Bolinger, D. (1975) *Aspects of Language*, New York: Harcourt Brace Jovanovich.

Britton, J. (1975) *Language and Learning*, Harmondsworth: Penguin.

Chalmers, A. (1978) *What is This Thing Called Science?* Milton Keynes: Open University Press.

Kuhn, T. (1972) *The Structure of Scientific Revolutions*, Chicago: Chicago University Press (2nd edn).

Langer, S. (1976) *Philosophy in a New Key*, Cambridge, Mass.: Harvard University Press (3rd edn).

Sapir, E. (1970) *Selected Writings in Culture, Language and Personality*, ed. D. Mandelbaum, Berkeley: University of California Press.

Smith, F. (1971) *Understanding Reading*, New York: Holt Rinehart & Winston.

Whorf, B. L. (1976) *Language, Thought and Reality*, ed. J. B. Carroll, Cambridge, Mass.: MIT Press.

Williams, R. (1975) *The Long Revolution*, Harmondsworth: Penguin.
Witkin, H. A. *et al.* (1962) *Psychological Differentiation*, New York: Wiley.
Young, M. F. D. (ed.) (1975) *Knowledge and Control: New Directions for the Sociology of Education*, London: Collier-Macmillan.

8

Linguistic, social and sexual relations: a review of Dale Spender's *Man Made Language*

Maria Black and Rosalind Coward

Reprinted from Screen Education *no. 39 (Summer 1981). Copyright the Society for Education in Film and Television, 29 Old Compton Street, London W1V 5PL.*

Dale Spender's book, *Man Made Language*,[1] is the latest, and probably the most widely read, in a long series of books and papers about the categorization and positioning of women in language. The debates around language are, and have been, crucial to feminist theoretical and political practices. At the theoretical level, they have focused attention on ideology, gender identification, and sexual difference not as 'ideas' or 'attitudes' but as material practices with their own mode of organization and specific effects on other social practices. At the political level, objections to linguistic expressions that demean and exclude women have been an important means of introducing and sustaining feminist positions and concerns in political groups. We do not, therefore, dispute the importance of Dale Spender's work, and we welcome the data she has made available. Some aspects of her analysis, however, and some of the conclusions she reaches raise several questions, particularly since Dale Spender's approach seems to reproduce many of the problems inherent in previous discussions of language and class. The purpose of this paper is a reconsideration of some of these issues. The paper is divided into three main sections. In the first, we examine the assumptions that underlie her notion of 'man-made', and the problems that these assumptions give rise to. In the second, we discuss her notion of language, and try to show that a distinction between language as a system and discourse is necessary to the development of feminist theory. Finally, we attempt to provide the beginnings of an alternative analysis, and discuss some of the implications of this shift.

Man-made

Women's subordination in language, Dale Spender argues, lies in women's negative relation to language. The effect of subordination attached to women's relation to language cannot be overruled by the construction of new and positive terms, for 'the problem lies not in the words but in the semantic rule which governs their positive or negative connotations' (p. 29). Intentionally or otherwise, men 'have formulated a semantic rule which posits them as central and positive as the norm, and they have classified the world from that standpoint, constructing a symbolic system which represents patriarchal order' (p. 58).

Dale Spender's notion of women's negative relation to language is drawn from discussions of ideology and language which have taken place within socialist feminism. This tendency attempted to look at the specificity of women's oppression as it occurred in systems of representation as well as in social practices. It remained within an account of the social structure which did not neglect class antagonisms. Language was recognized as having an active role in the construction of social definitions and the possibility of subject positions. Dale Spender, however, has disregarded the context in which these ideas emerged and the function which they fulfilled. In attempting to foreground 'sexism' in language she disregards the developments which had taken place around issues of language and ideology within socialism.

At certain moments, Dale Spender also argues for the importance of language in constructing notions of sexuality and playing an active role in the construction of reality. At the next moment, language is reduced to being an instrument of expression, simply reflecting the 'interests' of given social groups, i.e. men and women. Language constructs the positions of men and women, but men pre-exist language and use it to perpetuate their interests. Dale Spender's arguments to some extent reproduce those made within a version of Marxism indifferent to any questions of ideology and its effectivity within the social formation. Society is seen as structured around two dominant classes with antagonistic interests. These dominant classes are sometimes argued to have different relations to language. In Dale Spender's account, class division is replaced by sex division. Although in the first half of her book Dale Spender discusses the suspect nature of research designed to prove that women speak differently from men, she then goes on to hegemonize all instances of sexism in language under the idea of women's negative relation to language. Thus, grammatical prescriptions, sexist idioms, the effect of the sex of the speaker are all encompassed as essentially the same phenomena, produced by the different relation which men and women have to language. Dale Spender explains the dominance of the 'male semantic rule' as an effect of the dominance of male definitions or meanings. Men, like the ruling class in some Marxist arguments, have the power to define reality, and the rules of language reflect men's meanings. Women, like the working class, are deprived of power; they are always defined by male language and unable to promote their own. Dale Spender does not suggest that women speak a different language, and in this respect her ideas are not unlike Harold Rosen's.[2] Rosen took Bernstein to task for setting up a model of two dominant modes of speech, to the denigration of 'non-standard English'. But he also assumed a separate 'reality' for the two classes: the one defines reality, the other produces its own meanings in its own dialect.

In a similar way, Dale Spender suggests that male meanings are now dominant; women's definitions can hardly be heard. Childbirth, for example, is defined by men as the ultimately satisfying experience for a woman. All references to pain and fear are obliterated. Women's accounts, she argues, would not conceal the pain and the difficulties. This understanding of language is problematic, assuming as it does that 'meanings' derive from clear-cut groups, generated by their different social experiences. The division between these groups is simply assumed; all empirical data of speech acts and utterances is then forced to fit these divisions. This position assumes that 'meanings' are derived from experience. Meanings reflect the individual's experience of reality and are simply expressed in language. The communality of 'meanings', i.e., group meanings, is seen as an effect of groupings of individuals with structurally similar experiences. Serious reservations can be raised to this position. One is that it reduces language to being an instrument through which reality is expressed. This contradicts assertions that language has a material existence and effectivity. To stress that language is not an instrument expressing the meanings of pre-existent groups is to argue, on the contrary, that meaning derives from the relationships between linguistic entities. This relationship is socially constrained but is not an expression of a social order that pre-exists language. Language participates in the social and has an active role in the construction of subject positions.

This leads on to our second reservation, which is that notions of class or group meanings have proved very blunt instruments for the investigation of the production and circulation of attitudes. To assume pre-given groups gives us no real purchase on how ideologies participate in the production of groups and secure identification with the subject positions produced there. We can see the limitations of this approach by taking Dale Spender's own example of childbirth. There are women prepared to testify to the simultaneous pain and pleasure of childbirth. Indeed feminists have themselves been at the forefront of attempts to restore dignity to the ways in which childbirth has been seen. It has been feminists recently who have insisted on the significance of motherhood and the need to fight against belittling treatment of pregnant women and mothers. Debates around the introduction of anaesthetics in childbirth in the nineteenth century clearly show that suffering and pain in childbirth were seen by men as necessary states in the moral life of women. It is easy to produce evidence from men about the horror of childbirth, and the disgust and fear at exposure to such pain. What this indicates is that 'meanings' do not accrue exclusively to pre-existing groups, but are produced in definite ideologies. The problem is not male definitions of childbirth but systematic representations about childbirth where women are deprived of control of the forms in which childbirth can occur. Here what needs to be challenged is professional male hierarchies, alienating medical practices, and the policies around, and the ideological treatment of, childbirth and childcare. Another reservation derives from this. It relates to the notion of power at play. This assumes that one group literally has power over the other. This is a simplistic analysis of the workings of power. In a society structured along a series of unequal divisions, there are clearly a number of groups who have power in relation to other groups: whites, men, managers. The forms of domination and subordination are by no means always identical. A woman can be subordinated as a woman and be actively racist. It is rarely a case of direct, literal coercion with one clearly identifiable ruling group responsible for all the forms of domination found in the society. Marxist discussions around the term ideology emerged precisely to investigate the fact that social practices and systems of representation appeared to work without any direct coercion. Moreover, ideologies did not seem to correspond in any direct sense with given interest groups.

These discussions within Marxism, to which we will return, themselves had implications for the conceptualization of the relationship between systems of representation and interest groups. Systems of representation are seen as producing the possibilities and positions for the subject rather than being the product of any individual or group meaning. All meaning is recognized to be social and could not properly be understood as the instrument of expression. From such a perspective, experience and identity cannot be seen as the origin of meaning but its outcome. The discussion of ideology within Marxism was at first envisaged as refining ways of understanding how equilibrium was maintained between two unequal classes. However, the more it has been considered the more it has been a challenge to the whole way in which Marxism has conceived of society as structured by the antagonistic interests of two monolithic classes. Dale Spender, however, in ignoring any of these considerations, has returned to an unreclaimed version of Marxism, as a matter of intersubjective domination; different groups have different experiences; language is expressive of the meanings available to these two radically different groups. She thereby contradicts her claim that language has an active role to play in the construction of social reality, and reduces it to being the expression of something pre-existent and independent of language.

Which language?

If we are to develop an adequate analysis of sexism in language, it is important to specify what we mean by 'language'. We can't simply assume that we are dealing with a transparent and homogeneous phenomenon: some explicit theoretical distinctions are necessary. Dale Spender rejects many of the theoretical distinctions of linguistics, but does not provide an alternative specification of her theoretical object. She employs the term 'language' to cover a variety of different phenomena – anything and everything that has to do with words. We are left, therefore, either with a theoretically useless, common-sense notion of 'language', or with the undifferentiated empiricist notions that underlie much of the sex-language research.

Language, as the object of linguistic theory, is a system of rules and representations (Saussure's *langue*, Chomsky's *grammar*), considered independently of its users and uses in context. The distinction was not drawn because of some implicit sexism, racism or classism as Dale Spender appears to suggest. Linguistic theory had to construct its own theoretical object to move away from the notion of language of prescriptive grammar, and those forms of empiricist investigation where everything observable or given in 'verbal behaviour' was considered as theoretically relevant. Dale Spender claims that any general distinction of this kind is bound to produce 'inadequacies and inaccuracies' without making explicit what these are, nor detailing how 'the definitions of what constitutes "proper linguistic study" have (conveniently?) acted as obstacles in pursuing feminist based questions' (p. 29). She seems to favour and adopt a sociolinguistic framework for her analysis. But sociolinguistics has not really 'collapsed the traditional dichotomy'. Sociolinguistic analysis is often carried out at such a level of generality that the specific properties of linguistic systems are not an issue: theoretical distinctions can thus be obscured. At best, sociolinguistics presupposes, or explicitly makes use of, theoretical concepts which could not have been developed without such a dichotomy. Dale Spender gives the impression that sociolinguistics is somehow more progressive than linguistics. This partly reflects the kneejerk approach of some sections of the Left to theoretical and semi-theoretical disciplines. Any discipline that mentions class, sex, or race has to be better than one that does not. Contrary to Dale Spender's suggestion, the 'widespread belief that there was something *wrong* with the language of Blacks and the working class' does not originate in linguistic theory. It has far more to do with prescriptive grammar and related educational and cultural practices. Theoretical linguists would openly deride any claim that, for example, the existence of glottal stops in Cockney is an indication of slovenliness, cultural deprivation, or 'restricted code'. Linguistically speaking, glottalization is such a complex process that its theoretical description has required major changes in phonological theory. The theoretical notion of 'grammatical' does not correspond to the prescriptive notion of 'correct English'. A grammatical structure is simply one that is generated by the rules of the grammar. For instance, the sentence – The man the feminist Dale inspired challenged became aphasic – is perfectly grammatical in so far as the syntactic rules of English predict it as a possible structure of the language. But it hardly corresponds to the common-sense notion of 'good English'. Most of the sex–language research that Dale Spender rightly criticizes is far more rooted in sociolinguistics and social psychology than in linguistic theory. The work of linguists like Robin Lakoff was the product of a linguistic approach which questioned, and eventually abandoned, precisely the distinction between linguistic systems, their users, and uses in context.[3] Some general notion of language as a 'social product', or a reflection of society, usually serves as a starting point for sociolinguistic analysis. If groups of speakers have particular positions in society, their language then ought to correspond to, or reflect, their social situation.

Hence the search for evidence of linguistic sex differences and/or the 'inferiority' of women's language.

One of the fundamental claims of linguistic theory is that linguistic systems are not homogeneous.[4] They consist of quite distinct sets of rules and representations. Three main levels of linguistic representation are usually identified: phonology, syntax and semantics – roughly, sounds, structures and meaning. The theoretical concepts used to specify phonological, syntactic and semantic representations are different, and there is no necessary one-to-one correspondence between the categories involved on each level. For instance, the domain of application of phonological rules can be a string defined in terms of phonological symbols and boundaries, while the domain of syntactic rules is a structure defined in terms of syntactic categories and relations. If we accept that language, in this sense, is not homogeneous, then it is more appropriate to evaluate the effects of the distinction between a system and its users or uses in context in relation to each of these 'subsystems'. Similarly, claims about the 'man-made' nature of language can be usefully broken down into claims about the nature and effects of phonological, syntactic, and semantic representations. The concepts and distinctions of theoretical linguistics are not sacrosanct. But, unless we direct our criticisms to specific concepts, analyse their effects, and show explicitly how they 'have acted as obstacles' to feminist analysis, we will not be able to identify our theoretical enemies and develop alternatives. Generalized accusations of sexism do not amount to an argument.

Sexist syntax

Although Dale Spender makes no claims about phonology, she argues that syntax, as well as semantics, is 'man-made' (cf. ch. 5). However, the 'evidence' she produces in support of her claim is at best irrelevant, and at worst misleading. Her evidence falls into two categories: the statements of various prescriptive grammarians and the use of *man/he*. The pronouncements of prescriptive grammarians are interesting material for the analysis of ideological discourses which undoubtedly have effects on educational policies and practices. But they do *not* constitute evidence of the structural and systematic properties of syntactic structure. Dale Spender appears to have no conception of syntax as distinct from prescriptive grammar, as it is evident from her astonishing statement that 'the structure of the language is more concrete and readily traced' than its 'semantic base'. Syntax is hardly that, though grammarians' statements may well be, as they are couched in the apparently obvious, common-sense terms that are so typical of ideological discourses. For instance, one of the prescriptive 'rules' Dale Spender mentions requires that the male term be placed before the female term in conjoined phrases like *men and women, husband and wife*. This is not a syntactic rule, but merely an ideological pronouncement, since it does not express any general *syntactic* property of co-ordinate structures. While all co-ordinate structures in English are constrained in other ways (for example, only syntactic categories of the same type can be conjoined), there is no *ordering* restriction. Thus, *women and men*, or *wife and husband* are as syntactically well-formed as a *sandwich and a cake*, or *very tired and depressed* instead of *a cake and a sandwich, depressed and very tired*. We do not need to change the syntax of the language once we distinguish clearly between prescriptive grammar and syntax. It is to our advantage to do so: we can then challenge and expose more effectively the grammarians' prescriptions. It is unfortunate, therefore, that Dale Spender's 'syntactic' evidence has been taken quite so seriously by other feminists, particularly since this sort of 'evidence' often triggers 'consensus' explanations of language: 'As Dale Spender points out, our rules of grammar are not based on any consensus of female and male opinion, but on the dictates of individual men' (Anna Coote 1981).[5] One wonders how, without already having a language, the patriarchs around the linguistic conference table managed to communicate to each other their plans about such a complex and sophisticated system. Did they draw pictures, or did they have syntax-free language? The question is not 'how did men make syntax?'; the issue here is how did certain idioms and stereotypical phrases like *men and women* arise, and why are idioms often a central component of ideological discourses where they function *as if* they were required by the structure of language, the organization of society or 'human nature'.

The only other issue Dale Spender discusses under the heading of syntax is the use of *man/he*. Her discussion makes clear that what she is talking about is the gender of the referent of both noun and pronoun. Reference has little to do with syntax; the relationship between a word and its referent, or possible referents, is not determined or constrained by syntactic factors. Therefore, 'this use of *man* and *he* as terms to denote a male, but on occasion to encompass a female' may well be sexist, but is *not* 'an example of sexist linguistic structure'. Structure does not come into it, and we cannot use 'structure', 'symbol', or 'word' interchangeably as Dale Spender does. Structural conditions do affect relations between a pronoun and its antecedent – for example, in (1) *John/Mary* and *he/she* can be co-referential on one interpretation

1 $\left\{ \begin{array}{c} John \\ Mary \end{array} \right\}$ said that $\left\{ \begin{array}{c} he \\ she \end{array} \right\}$ was leaving

but not in (2)

2 $\left\{ \begin{array}{c} He \\ She \end{array} \right\}$ said that $\left\{ \begin{array}{c} John \\ Mary \end{array} \right\}$ was leaving.

However, structural constraints on pronoun–antecedent relations are quite independent of gender. What probably underlies Dale Spender's treatment of pronoun gender as a syntactic phenomenon is the nebulous notion from school-book grammar that pronouns are 'grammatical words' and thus have something to do with syntax. But, in that case, Dale Spender's unified account of *man/he* would be wrong, as nouns are not 'grammatical words' and should be treated quite differently.

So the whole discussion of sexism and language is really a discussion of sexism and semantics, or sexism and some other level of representation which may not be specifiable within the framework of theoretical linguistics as it stands.

Sexist meaning

The issue of *man/he* could be incorporated into Dale Spender's analysis of 'meaning'. In fact, it is not clear why she does not consider it as an instance of one of her 'semantic rules'. Her data and observations about meaning are essentially the same as those of previous feminist analyses (cf. Miller and Swift 1979),[6] but she attempts to generalize them and give them some theoretical status. That is where the problems start: both her general approach to 'meaning' and the specific 'semantic rules' she puts forward are problematic. Her use of the terms 'meaning' and 'semantic' is as unclear as that of 'language'. As we have already seen, Dale Spender leaves us suspended between two interpretations of meaning, neither of which can advance feminist theory. Either everything is reducible to meaning, or meaning is a sort of experiential or mental entity that exists independently of language. Dale Spender's approach is fraught with problems and contradictions which are not explicitly recognized, and makes use of terms that we do not know how to interpret. As a consequence we do not know how seriously to take some of her claims.

For theoretical linguistics, the meaning of an expression is determined by the relations of paraphrase, synonymy, antonymy, entailment, and contradiction which that expression has with other expressions in the system. 'Meaning' is therefore a purely linguistic phenomenon, a product or effect of systematic relationships between expressions. The theoretical concept of meaning does not include any feelings, images or connotations which may be associated with particular expressions, nor is the semantic status of an expression evaluated in terms of what is plausible, usual or likely to happen 'outside' language.[7] Thus, Dale Spender's claim that 'it is a semantic contradiction to formulate representations of women's autonomy or strength' is patently false on the most common interpretation of 'semantic contradiction', since it would imply that

Sue's friends are all strong and independent women

is as semantically peculiar as

Sue killed Tom and Tom is alive and kicking.

But we are not given any other interpretation of 'semantic contradiction' that might lead to different predictions. Dale Spender claims that 'one semantic rule which we can see in operation in the language is that of the male as the norm'. This rule is complemented by, and sometimes subsumed under, a second general semantic rule: '...*any* symbol which is associated with the female must assume negative (and frequently sexual – which is also significant) connotations' (p. 29). Dale Spender stresses that 'it is not just a question of elimination or addition of words...for the problem lies not in the words but in the semantic rule which governs their positive or negative connotations..., and any strategies which are predicated on the removal of sexist words are unable to deal with this phenomenon' (p. 29). These rules play a central role in Dale Spender's analysis, so both their formulation and their implications have to be taken seriously.

There is clearly a problem with those analyses which focus on the meaning of single words such as *Man* and *he*. Feminists have often argued that *Man* does not mean 'human being' but 'male human being'; such claims are usually backed up by sentences like (1–2).

1 *Man's* vital interests are food, shelter, and access to females.
2 *Man* is the only primate that *commits rape.*

If *Man* is genuinely inclusive, (1–2) ought to be semantically anomalous, or at least have the same status as

3 *Man*, unlike other mammals, has difficulties in *giving birth.*

But utterances like (1–2) are commonly produced and readily accepted by many speakers, while utterances like (3) are not. Hence feminists have concluded that, contrary to the claims of semanticians and lexicographers, *Man* only means 'male'. This argument, however, is problematic because it would force us to conclude that there are no general terms referring to both men and women. That is, many apparently non-gender specific terms that bear no resemblance to the exclusively masculine *man*, occur in utterances where the same pattern of exclusive reference exemplified by (1–2) is also found, for example,

4 *People* will give up *their wives* but not power.
5 *Americans* of higher status have less chance of having a fat *wife.*
6 Young *people* should be out interfering with the local *maidens* (based on *The Times* June 1981).
7 *Drivers* – belt the *wife* and kids. Keep them safe. [*sic!*] (Road Safety sign).

The feminist argument thus has to be extended to a variety of words other than *Man*. Dale Spender's analysis in terms of general 'semantic rules' is presumably an attempt to overcome this problem and go beyond the meaning of individual words. Her first rule expresses the claim that the 'exclusion of women' from the language is a general phenomenon and not restricted to *Man/he*. Similarly, her second rule is an attempt to unify different manifestations of the semantic pejoration of women. But Dale Spender's 'semantic rules' raise a number of other problems. First of all, both rules are much *too general.* There are cases where non-specific terms do include, for example,

8 *People* don't like being ill, but *women* put up with *it* better than men.
9 I met several *Americans* this summer and the most interesting of *them* were *a journalist* and *her daughter.*

or sometimes refer exclusively to women, for example,

10 The *consumer* will not know that *she* is buying foreign eggs.

11 A $\left\{ \begin{array}{c} nurse \\ speech\ therapist \end{array} \right\}$'s first duty is to *her* patients.

Similarly, there are cases where the generalization expressed by the second rule that '*any* symbol associated with the female' has pejorative and/or sexual connotations does not hold at all, for example,

12 My $\left\{ \begin{array}{c} sister \\ daughter \\ aunt \end{array} \right\}$ took (her) *grandmother* out for lunch.

13 The new *headmistress* introduced herself to the pupils' *mothers*.

or cases where one female term has pejorative connotations but another, fairly similar term does not, for example, compare (14) and (15)

14 We have not spoken to the *female* who lives upstairs.

15 We have not spoken to the $\left\{ \begin{array}{c} woman \\ girl \end{array} \right\}$ who lives upstairs.

Dale Spender's rules do not always apply and, therefore, cannot be formulated as general 'semantic rules'. Linguistic rules are either totally general (i.e. apply in all contexts), or have specifiable conditions of application. These conditions usually are expressed in purely linguistic terms: they make reference only to phonological, syntactic or logical structures and relations; furthermore, the set of conditions cannot be an ad hoc list of cases where a rule just happens not to apply. There must be some theoretically principled way of grouping together sets of conditions on the basis of shared properties. None of these requirements are met by Dale Spender's analysis; she does not say anything about the nature of the conditions that constrain the application of her rules, and whether the many cases where they do not apply have anything in common. If Dale Spender's rules cannot be reformulated and their conditions of application stated explicitly, the generalizations embodied in them have to be brought into question. We cannot assume that a generalization is valid simply because there are examples to back it up: we have to deal with the counter-examples as well. Though there clearly are general patterns to be understood and explained, and this lends intuitive plausibility to Dale Spender's account, it is far from clear that all the relevant phenomena can be unified and adequately described in terms of two semantic rules of this kind.

There are other reasons to doubt the validity of Dale Spender's analysis. The statement of her second rule involves terms like 'pejorative' which have no general, systematic interpretation. Linguistic rules simply specify the structural properties of sentences, and the concepts used in their formulation have stable and identifiable interpretations across and within linguistic systems. But Dale Spender's second rule is quite different. First of all, we are not dealing with sentences, since the same phonological, syntactic, and logical structure – the same *sentence* – can be used to produce, or be interpreted as, different *utterances* with distinct connotations. For instance, both (16) and (17) may or may not have pejorative connotations depending on the speaker–hearers involved and on the context:

16 John is talking to that *woman* again.
17 He really behaved like a *man*.

Dale Spender's rules are not 'semantic rules' in the standard theoretical sense, but, if anything, principles of utterance-production and interpretation. If so, we have to ask whether these principles apply in all contexts, and whether terms like 'pejorative' are to be understood from the point of view of whoever produces the utterances, or those who interpret it, or both. Many examples like (16) and (17), for instance, may be produced but not interpreted as having pejorative connotations, and vice-versa. Precisely where the relationship between what is said and who says it becomes crucial, Dale Spender is strangely quiet about it. This is not surprising as she does not have the concepts to grasp such a relationship. She either relies on a hopelessly vague notion of language so that every speaker–hearer in each context has to be assigned a different 'language' – with a resulting theoretical Babel. Or she falls back on the concepts of linguistic theory which are relevant only to linguistic systems and sentences, without making explicit how they are to be reinterpreted for the purposes of utterance production and interpretation in context. We plainly need different concepts: the phenomena feminists are concerned with have to little to do with linguistic systems. As we have seen, language, as a system of phonological, syntactic, and logical structures and rules, is not inherently sexist or 'man-made' in Dale Spender's sense. Linguistic systems, however, serve as the basis for the production and interpretation of sets of related utterances – discourses – which effect and sustain the different categorizations and positions of women and men. It is on these *discourses*, and not on language in general or linguistic systems, that feminist analyses have to focus.

Unfortunately, there is no ready-made theoretical framework that feminists can simply take over and apply to the analysis of the relevant phenomena. The theories of discourse or 'pragmatics' developed within modern linguistics have little to offer to feminist analysis.[8] On these approaches, examples such as (1) to (11) would probably be handled by reference to social conditions and assumptions, which are simply 'reflected' in language. Words like *people, Americans,* or *nurse* are assumed to function semantically as non-gender specific terms; their varying gender references are explained in terms of 'extra-linguistic' assumptions about who has power, higher status, or is most likely to be a nurse in our society. There are several problems with this kind of approach. It lumps together a whole variety of factors under the common heading of 'social assumptions', 'encyclopedic knowledge', or whatever other term is used. Everything is displaced outside discourse which is then reduced to a mere reflection of reality or society. Both what discourse 'reflects', and the subjects of discourse, as rational, intentional and gendered individuals, are constituted independently of discourse. We are then faced with the same paradox we have already discussed in relation to Dale Spender's analysis: what discourses are supposed to construct and organize turns out to be the cause and origin of these discourses.

In spite of these problems, some approaches within pragmatic theory might be able to handle utterances involving terms that presuppose particular social and sexual relations (cf. examples 4–7, 11–12); it is not clear, however, that a similar account can be given of the fact that women are often not treated as 'human' on a par with men. Why is it often possible to use general categories such as *Man, human,* or *people* to refer exclusively to males, sometimes to both females and males, but rarely to females alone? The difference in acceptability between utterances like (1–2), on the one hand, and (3), on the other, has to be explained, as well as the existence of utterances like

18 This thieving gang consists of three *people* from Latin America, and *a woman* (BBC Radio 4 News).[9]
19 Normal *people* do not go around raping and murdering women.
20 Well, it is only *human* nature (heard at the time of the Yorkshire Ripper's killings).

In contra-position with these utterances, the following would sound distinctly odd:

21 This thieving gang consists of three *people* from Latin America and a *man*.

22 The committee was appointed to review...the problems of special groups...the handicapped, ethnic groups, Aboriginals and *men* (adapted from Naked Ape,[10] The *Guardian* June 1981).

23 You can't argue with Jane's typically *human* $\left\{ \begin{array}{c} logic \\ notions \end{array} \right\}$.

What we have here appears to be some systematic patterning of masculine and feminine referents in relation to general categories of humanity. This is what Dale Spender took to be a general rule of language. We have argued that language cannot be understood in general in this way. In other words, we have to make a distinction between what Pecheux and his colleagues call the *linguistic base* (the object of linguistic theory), and *discursive processes*.[11] The phenomena in question have to be understood by reference to discursive regularities. We have to ask how gendered meaning is produced in particular utterances, how these utterances are produced and sustained in relation to other utterances.

Discursive formations

In what precedes we have seen how it is impossible to consider meaning outside its production through a particular organization of words into utterances. The meaning of a given utterance is fixed through the arrangement of words, and through the relationship of this utterance to other utterances that have already been made. This implies that it is the discursive organization which speaks the subject, rather than static meanings originating from a group experience. This, however, does not solve the problem of understanding the denigration of women in language, and what relation this has to the social order and the relations between the sexes. We need to understand how the cultural codes of the already-said are understood, put into circulation, and are effective within society. It is for this reason that we see a need to continue discussions around ideology and language already initiated within Marxism. Many socialist feminists adhered to the term as a way of exploring sexual construction and its effects as 'relatively autonomous', but not completely separate from economic structures. But there were two main reasons why socialist feminist theory ran aground before consolidating this exploration. On one hand, the way in which Marxism was taken up as an intellectual discipline as well as political theory was as an explanation of the causal links between various aspects of the social formation. As we know, this all too frequently suggested the ultimate determination by economic class antagonisms. Frequently this was accompanied by a political subordination of so-called 'ideological struggles'. As taken up by socialist feminists Marxism often appeared as the promise of 'the explanation' of the articulation between sex and class. Yet the explanation has never been delivered because there is no *causal* determination. If sexual subordination is relatively autonomous from the economic mode of production, where does it arise if not in some earlier and fundamental division between men and women? If that is the case, then how does this earlier form articulate with class divisions? As their model or cause? If so, what happens to the challenge to the 'naturalness' of class division which Marxism is supposed to deliver? On the other hand, some of the impetus to explore the concept of ideology was almost instantly undermined by a theoretical critique of its generalizing and universalizing claims. It has been argued that the concept of ideology presupposes a model of society and human consciousness where social reality is transmitted directly into ideological representations; it has equally been suggested that what this delivers is a dogmatic description of 'reality' which ultimately denies effectivity to the 'discursive level'.[12] For this reason, attention has been concentrated on 'discursive formations', a strategic attention designed to suspend generalizations about the relationship between social formation and activities of the human mind. Foucault (1972, p. 29) summarizes this attention as one designed to grasp the forms of regularities in utterances and statements. The aim is to explore

> Relations between statements (even if the author is unaware of them; even if the statements do not have the same author; even if the authors were unaware of each other's existence); relations between groups of statements thus established (even if these groups do not concern the same, or even adjacent fields; even if they do not possess the same formal level; even if they are not the locus of assignable exchanges); relations between statements and groups of statements and events of a quite different kind (technical, economic, social, political). To reveal in all its purity the space in which discursive

events are deployed is not to undertake to re-establish it in an isolation that nothing could overcome; it is not to close it upon itself; it is to leave oneself free to describe the interplay of relations within it and outside it.[13]

Some would perhaps like to argue that the dismissal of the term ideology has been somewhat premature. It is possible, for example, to imagine that ideologies might be examined as systems of representation without assuming that they necessarily reflect a principle governing the social structure.

Whatever term becomes the focus of discussion, the point of the argument is the same. Language and the meanings produced therein are not expressive of any simple social division be it class, sex or whatever. If we do not want to reduce language to a simple instrument or effect of a class or sex position but to see it as something productive of the positions we can occupy, then we have to develop these insights of recent discussions of ideology. These see discourses as determinate forms of social practice with their own conditions of existence in other social practices (for example political/economic or scientific) and in social relations, and as having definite effects with regard to those practices and relations. It still seems necessary, in the face of numerous misreadings, to insist that this is not about absenting language from the social formation; on the contrary, it is to insist that language has a material existence. It defines our possibilities and limitations, it constitutes our subjectivities. The insistence on starting where Marxist feminist debates left off comes from no sentimental or unexamined commitment to Marxism or socialism. Far from it, it comes from the fact that discussions of ideology and language arose from precisely the desire not to offer reductive explanations of the social formation. These reductive explanations always ended by denying the subordination of women through sexual and ideological as well as economic and political practices. Indeed, it was exactly this work which emphasized that there were organizations of meaning in language and representational practices which actively participated in the subordination of women. These could in no way be 'explained' by the existence of class divisions. In other words, we are suggesting that we cannot solve the problem of the ways in which representation and language participate in the construction of denigratory attitudes and activities towards women by returning to forms of analysis which reduce language to the expression of pre-existent group positions.

127

The statement, that we should pay attention to discursive unities, their conditions of existence, and their effects with regard to other practices, is thought by some to avoid analysis. Always insisting on complexity and non-reductionism, it appears not to offer any immediately graspable explanation. We have already outlined why there are pressing reasons to persevere rather than look for easy solutions. To some extent discussions within Marxism have demonstrated anyway that the search for causal explanations understood as 'generative' principles is an unrewarding task which always reduces explanations to dogmatic assertions. In addition, we have argued that the idea of generative principles always reduces accounts of ideology and language to expressions of pre-existent groups.

Ungendered man, endangered species

We argue that there are very distinct advantages in insisting that society is not reducible to generating principles reflected in all social practices. We can see this by re-examining the case on which *Man Made Language* rests, that is, that there is a male 'semantic rule' expressed in man being the norm for humanity, and women being defined negatively or pejoratively. First, there is the problem of how this rule is supposed to have arisen. On the one hand, it is suggested that until now, patriarchy has been in dominance. Male definitions have always dominated because men have always dominated. On the other hand, there is the curious effect of Dale Spender's examination of etymological changes. She suggests that certain words have been devalued through the acquisition of sexual connotations to the female term. Thus, *mistress, hostess, dame* are all presented as words which were somehow, once upon a time, more equal than they are now. This leads us again to express very real reservations with how linguistic data is being interpreted. Etymological data is clearly vital (witness the suggestive use made of it by Miller and Swift in *Words and Women*), but taken in isolation from other changes and uses in the language it can produce a very distorted picture. For example, *mistress* had been in use quite early as a specifically sexual term meaning 'sweetheart'. In addition, the disappearance of *mistress* as head of the household surely could not be separated from the appearance of another term, that of *housewife*, bearing witness to very definite transformations of households and conceptions of women's place in them. Language does not simply reflect its past history nor its current function. Linguistic value has to be understood in relation to other aspects of the overall structure of language. We have to understand not just histories of words, but the relationship of terms to other terms, the relationship between terms in statements, the relationship between statements. This is at the crux of our disagreement with Dale Spender. We do not accept a theory of social organization which posits a 'reality' – patriarchy, capitalism, or whatever – which is simply reflected in language, either as history or function. Instead we see definite discursive constructions with definite conditions of existence which are *effective with regard to other practices*. This suggests a different approach to linguistic phenomena which refuses to start either from a purely historical or a purely functional approach. We can see the difference by re-examining Dale Spender's 'semantic rules'. The two rules are often conflated into a single generalization: language defines women as 'negative'; the term 'negative' means that women are excluded from the meaning or reference of general terms as well as being defined pejoratively. We would like to suggest that this conflation is misleading, and that we are dealing with quite different phenomena which have to be analysed separately. We have already argued that women's exclusion as representatives of generalized humanity is not the product of any 'semantic rule'; there is nothing impossible or even improbable about a sentence like *She was so wretched she looked hardly human*. Women, in other words, can represent humanity and share in the general attributes which the human is said to possess as distinct from the animals. Frequently, however, a term which refers to the human species, i.e., *mankind*, excludes women. It is clear that the attributes of exclusion in the term *mankind* do not come from its relation to the term *man*, a point we have made in connection with terms like *people*, *Americans*, etc. (cf. examples (4) to (7)). Perhaps this phenomenon could be understood not in terms of the hidden male gender of general terms, but the fact that the attributes of the male can in fact disappear into a 'non-gendered' subject. Women, on the other hand, never appear as non-gendered subjects. Women are precisely *defined*, never as general representatives of human or all people, but as specifically feminine, and frequently sexual, categories: whore, slag, mother, virgin, housewife. The term 'negative' cannot be understood as synonymous with 'pejorative'. Women are not the norm, but this does not mean that they are *not defined*. The curious feature is exactly the excess of (sexual) definitions and categories for women. A similar profusion is not found for men, whose differentiation from one another comes not through sexual attributes and status, but primarily through occupation, or attributes of general humanity, for example, decent, kind, honest, strong. Men remain men and women become specific categories in relation to men and to other categories. Prince Charles and Lady Diana Spencer disappeared into the church and emerged as *man and wife*. Being a man is an entitlement not to *masculine* attributes but to *non-gendered* subjectivity. We suggest that it is this which gives a certain discursive regularity to the appearance of gender in language. The conditions of existence of this discursive regularity might be looked for in the development of discourses on citizenship, law, anthropology and sexuality.

The development of the state in western capitalism has been understood as producing a political discursive which suppresses reference to different groups and conflicts of interest. Here the classic Marxist understanding of the state may be helpful. The emergence of the state is seen as the point of regulation of class interests at a supra-individual level. Thus, the particularity of the interests of individuals (or in Marx/Engels's case, individuals and their families (!)) is guaranteed by the abstraction of generalized interests, that is, the abstraction characteristic of the political level. Leaving aside critiques of Marxism for the way in which the political level is often reduced to being the expression of the interests of a given group, this outline of the state is a useful starting point. It indicates the necessary emergence of a distinct representation of a generalized political subject who represents all people and in whose representation all conflict is suppressed. The modern state emerged in the disintegration of the relatively diffused hierarchy of the feudal state. Previously, political responsibilities and rights were derived from particular status given in a very definite hierarchy. The capitalist state, however, increasingly addressed its political representations to a generalized 'citizen' – sexless, classless, a citizen of the world. As is well known, the development of these political representations was to some extent accompanied by the emergence of distinctive legal forms whereby feudal status gave way to conceptions of the rights of the free individual. This modern state and its political representations emerged not just in a rigidly divided class society, but in a literally patriarchal society. The representation of the general citizen and the rights of the free individual did not obscure class divisions, but obscured the fact that political representation was the right of certain groups of property-owning men to represent their families.

In the nineteenth century, feminists began to challenge women's political exclusion, and simultaneously to seek employment in certain

professions which themselves were coming under the increasing intervention of the state – the law, medicine, education, etc. The challenge of
the feminists caused the ideology of citizenship to become explicit;
women were not included as *persons*.[14] Numerous legal judgments were
produced during the second half of the nineteenth century excluding
women from certain employment and from political and legal
representations. Citizenship, based on the notion of the rights of the
person, did not include women. It is no coincidence either that this
period saw a consolidation of definitions of women around their
sexuality. The judgments made were frequently supported by statements
on women's appropriate 'sphere of influence'. Men had public
responsibilities, women had private ones. Men were masters of the
realm of the state. Women ruled supreme in the home. This was the
period when, according to Foucault, there was increasing development
of state activity.[15] In England, the period around 1880–1900 saw
unprecedented state activity, intervening in housing, health, education,
etc. It has been suggested that this period was especially witness to an
intensification of intervention around sexuality concerned with the
production of a new conception of the family, loosely policed by the
state but able to solve wider social crises. It is clearly the case that the
same period saw an unparalleled 'scientific' investigation of sexuality,
whose outcome was the appearance of definite categories like
'homosexual'.[16] Finally, this was also the period where the popular
definitions of 'mankind among the other animals' were consolidated.
Discussions around the specific attributes of 'humanity' themselves
emerged in the disintegration of the political theory based on ideas of the
male as sovereign power within his home, a microcosm of the sovereign
power of the king. While this theoretical approach was overthrown in
the nineteenth century, it left its mark on theories of the nature of
society. Investigations were profoundly 'androcentric', assuming that
the political subject of any given society was the male. These comments
are merely a number of hints at the conditions which have contributed
to the possibility of men assuming a non-gendered subjectivity while
women are always defined and categorized. Perhaps, it might be
suggested that this tentative interpretation does not greatly alter the
conclusions of Dale Spender. However, our different interpretation and
approach has very different political implications.

Dale Spender ultimately sees feminism as a politics of 'making new
meaning':

From providing an alternative individual meaning for motherhood, to constructing a collective understanding of the domestic labour debate, women must take every opportunity to encode their own meanings and to validate the meanings encoded by other women.

We do not see the problem as one of the suppression of female meanings, nor do we see the solution as simply validating everything produced by women, as the expression of pre-existent feminine values. We see one of the major political problems confronting feminism to be the need to force men to recognize themselves as *men*. The discursive formation which allows men to represent themselves as non-gendered and to define women constantly according to their sexual status is a discursive formation with very definite effects. It allows men to deny the effect of their gendered subjectivity on women. It is not a question of men secretly believing that masculine is the norm. What is available to them is a discourse where gender and sexual identity appears to be absent. Thus, Paul Hirst can make the following comment: 'I dispute that there is anything so definite as there being a category of man. I don't recognise myself as a man.'[17] It is precisely this refusal to recognize the effects of masculinity which constitutes the problem for women. The women's movement takes its existence from the fact that however differently we are constituted in different practices and discourses, women are constantly and inescapably constructed *as women*. There is a discourse available to men which allows them to represent themselves as people, humanity, mankind. This discourse, by its very existence, excludes and marginalizes women by making women the sex. Our aim is not just to validate the new meanings of women but to confront men with their maleness. This is not just about masculine behaviour, but about discursive practices. It is about making men take responsibility for being men. Men are sustained at the centre of the stage precisely because they can be 'people' and do not have to represent their masculinity to themselves. They need never see themselves or their maleness as a problem. Our understanding of the effects of discursive practices leads us to suggest that men can never be displaced from the centre until they can be forced to recognize themselves as men and to take responsibility for this.

Notes

1 D. Spender, *Man Made Language* (London: Routledge and Kegan Paul 1980).

2 H. Rosen, *Language and Class: A Critical Look at the Theories of Basil Bernstein* (Bristol: Falling Wall Press 1972).

3 This is the approach that has become known as 'generative semantics'.

4 For an introductory discussion of this claim and of the different levels of linguistic representation, see N. V. Smith and D. Wilson, *Modern Linguistics* (Harmondsworth: Penguin 1979).

5 A. Coote, 'The nature of man talk', *New Statesman* (2 January 1981).

6 C. Miller and K. Swift, *Words and Women* (Harmondsworth: Penguin 1979).

7 The term 'semantics' also covers the study of the logical form of sentences, and the properties of 'logical operators' such as negation, disjunction, conjunction, etc. In the rest of the paper, we have used the term 'logical' to indicate this aspect of linguistic structure.

8 For a general and more detailed critique of the distinction between semantics and pragmatics see M. Pecheux, (1975) *Les Verités de La Palice* (Paris: Maspero 1975). (English translation: *Language, Semantics and Ideology*, (London: Macmillan, 1983)).

9 The context made clear that the woman was also from Latin America.

10 Naked Ape was a long-running column feature in the *Guardian* which reprinted examples of outrageous sexism sent in by readers.

11 See note 8 and R. Woods, 'Discourse analysis: the work of M. Pecheux', *Ideology and Consciousness* 2 (Autumn 1977).

12 P. Q. Hirst, *On Law and Ideology* (London: Macmillan 1980).

13 M. Foucault, *Archaeology of Knowledge* (London: Tavistock 1972).

14 A. Sachs and J. H. Wilson, *Sexism and the Law: A Study of Male Belief and Judicial Bias* (Oxford: Martin Robertson 1978).

15 M. Foucault, *History of Sexuality* (London: Allen Lane 1978).

16 J. Weeks, *Sex and Society* (London: Longman 1981).

17 *Leveller* (30 May–12 June 1981).

9

The semantic derogation of woman

Muriel R. Schulz

Reprinted from B. Thorne and N. Henley (eds), Language and sex: difference and dominance *(Rowley, Mass.: Newbury House 1975).*

The question of whether or not language affects the thought and culture of the people who use it remains to be answered. Even if we were to agree that it does, we would have difficulty calculating the extent to which the language we use influences our society. There is no doubt, on the other hand, that a language reflects the thoughts, attitudes, and culture of the people who make it and use it. A rich vocabulary on a given subject reveals an area of concern of the society whose language is being studied. The choice between positive and negative terms for any given concept (as, for example, in the choice between *freedom fighter* and *terrorist*) reveals the presence or absence of prejudicial feelings toward the subject. The presence of taboo reveals underlying fears and superstitions of a society. The occurrence of euphemism (*passed away*) or dysphemism (*croaked*) reveals areas which the society finds distasteful or alarming. To this extent, at least, analysis of a language tells us a great deal about the interests, achievements, obsessions, hopes, fears, and prejudices of the people who created the language.

Who are the people who created English? Largely men – at least until the present generation. Stuart Flexner (1960: xii) points out that it is mostly males who create and use slang, and he explains why. A woman's life has been largely restricted to the home and family, while men have lived in a larger world, belonged to many sub-groups, and had acquaintances who belonged to many other sub-groups. That men are the primary creators and users of the English language generally follows from the primary role they have traditionally played in English-speaking cultures. They have created our art, literature, science, philosophy, and education, as well as the language which describes and manipulates these areas of culture.

An analysis of the language used by men to discuss and describe women reveals something about male attitudes, fears, and prejudices concerning the female sex. Again and again in the history of the language, one finds that a perfectly innocent term designating a girl or woman may begin with totally neutral or even positive connotations, but that gradually it acquires negative implications, at first perhaps only slightly disparaging, but after a period of time becoming abusive and ending as a sexual slur.

That disparagement gravitates more toward terms for women than for men is evident from some matched pairs designating males and females. Compare, for example, the connotations of *bachelor* with those of *spinster* or *old maid*. Or compare the innocuousness of *warlock* with the insinuations of *witch*. *Geezer* 'an eccentric, queer old man'[1] and *codger* 'a mildly derogatory, affectionate term for an old man' carry little of the opprobrium of such corresponding terms for old women as *trot*, *hen*, *heifer*, *warhorse*, *crone*, *hag*, *beldam*, and *frump*. Furthermore, if terms designating men are used to denote a woman, there is usually no affront. On the other hand, use a term generally applied to women to designate a man, and you have probably delivered an insult. You may call a woman a *bachelor* without implying abuse, but if you call a man a *spinster* or an *old maid*, you are saying that he is 'a prim, nervous person who frets over inconsequential details'. If you speak of a woman as being a *warlock*, you may be corrected; if you say a man is a *witch*, he is presumed to have a vile temper. Or call a woman an *old man* and you have simply made an error of identification. Call a man an *old woman* or a *granny* and you have insulted him.

The term used to denote a semantic change whereby a word acquires debased or obscene reference is *pejoration*, and its opposite is *amelioration*. It is the purpose of this paper to study the pejoration of terms designating women in English and to trace the pattern whereby virtually every originally neutral word for women has at some point in its existence acquired debased connotations or obscene reference, or both.

The mildest form of debasement is a democratic levelling, whereby a word once reserved for persons in high places is generalized to refer to people in all levels of society. Even this mild form of derogation is more likely to occur with titles of women than with titles of men. *Lord*, for example, is still reserved as a title for deities and certain Englishmen, but any woman may call herself a *lady*. Only a few are entitled to be called *Baronet* and only a few wish to be called *Dame*, since as a general term, *dame* is opprobrious. Although *governor* degenerated briefly in nineteenth-century Cockney slang, the term still refers to men who 'exercise a sovereign authority in a colony, territory, or state'. A *governess*, on the other hand, is chiefly 'a nursemaid', operating in a realm much diminished from that of Queen Elizabeth I, who was acknowledged to be 'the supreme majesty and governess of all persons' (*OED*). We might conceivably, and without affront, call the Queen's Equerry a *courtier*, but would we dare refer to her lady-in-waiting as a *courtesan*? *Sir*, and *Master* seem to have come down through time as titles of courtesy without taint. However, *Madam*, *Miss*, and *Mistress* have all derogated, becoming euphemisms respectively for 'a mistress of a brothel', 'a prostitute', and 'a woman with whom a man habitually fornicates'.

The latter titles illustrate the most frequent course followed by pejorated terms designating women. In their downhill slide, they slip past respectable women and settle upon prostitutes and mistresses. When *abbey*, *academy*, and *nunnery* became euphemisms for 'brothel', *abbess* acquired the meaning 'keeper of a brothel', *academician*, 'a harlot', and *nun*, 'a courtesan'. (Here, at last, one male title also pejorated. *Abbot* at the same time came to mean 'the husband, or preferred male of a brothel keeper'.) Although technically *queen* has withstood pejoration in English (*princess* has not), a thinly veiled homonym has existed side-by-side with it since Anglo-Saxon times. The *queen* is 'the consort of the king' or 'a female sovereign', whereas *quean* means 'prostitute'. Spelling has kept the two terms apart visually (both derived from the same Old English root, *cwen* 'woman'), but as homonyms they have long provided writers with material for puns. Thus, in *Piers Plowman* (IX, 46) we are told that in the grave one cannot tell 'a knight from a knave, or a quean from a queen', and Byron calls Catherine the Great 'the Queen of queans' (*Don Juan*, Canto 6, stanza xcvi).

Female kinship terms have also been subject to a kind of derogation which leaves the corresponding male terms untouched. *Wife* was used as a euphemism for 'a mistress' in the fifteenth century, as was *squaw* in America during the Second World War. *Niece* has been used as a euphemism for 'a priest's illegitimate daughter or concubine', and surely Humbert Humbert was not the first man to hide his mistress behind the locution, *daughter*. Browning uses *cousin* as an evasive term for Lucrezia's lover in 'Andrea del Sarto' (1.200). As a term for a woman, it was cant for 'a strumpet or trull' in the nineteenth century.

And *aunt* was generalized first to mean 'an old woman' and then 'a bawd or a prostitute'. It is the latter meaning which Shakespeare draws upon in the lines: 'Summer songs for me and my aunts/As we lie tumbling in the hay' (*Winter's Tale*, IV, 3, 11–12). Even *mother* was used as a term for 'a bawd' and *sister* as a term for 'a disguised whore' in the seventeenth century.

Terms for domestics are also more subject to pejoration if they denote females. *Hussy* derives from Old English *huswif* 'housewife' and at one time meant simply 'the female head of the house'. Its degeneration was gradual. It declined in reference to mean 'a rustic, rude woman'; then it was used as an opprobrious epithet for women in general; and finally it referred to 'a lewd, brazen woman or a prostitute'. In their original employment, a *laundress* made beds, a *needlewoman* came in to sew, a *spinster* tended the spinning wheel, and a *nurse* cared for the sick. But all apparently acquired secondary duties in some households, because all became euphemisms for 'a mistress' or 'a prostitute' at some time during their existence.

One generally looks in vain for the operation of a similar pejoration of terms referring to men. *King, prince, father, brother, uncle, nephew, footman, yeoman,* or *squire*, for example, have failed to undergo the derogation found in the history of their corresponding feminine designations. Words indicating the station, relationship, or occupation of men have remained untainted over the years. Those identifying women have repeatedly suffered the indignity of degeneration, many of them becoming sexually abusive. It is clearly not the women themselves who have coined and used these terms as epithets for each other. One sees today that it is men who describe and discuss women in sexual terms and insult them with sexual slurs, and the wealth of derogatory terms for women reveals something of their hostility.

If the derogation of terms denoting women marks out an area of our culture found contemptible by men, the terms they use as endearments should tell us who or what they esteem. Strangely enough, in English the endearments men use for women have been just as susceptible to pejoration as have the terms identifying the supposedly beloved object itself.[2] *Dolly, Kitty, Biddy, Gill* (or *Jill*), and *Polly* all began as pet names derived from nicknames. All underwent derogation and eventually acquired the meaning of 'a slattern', 'a mistress', or 'a prostitute'. *Jug* and *Pug*, both originally terms of endearment, degenerated to apply contemptuously to 'a mistress or a whore'. *Mopsy*, a term of endearment still found in Beatrix Potter's *Peter Rabbit*, for centuries also meant 'a

slatternly, untidy woman'. *Mouse* began as a playful endearment, but
came to mean 'a harlot, especially one arrested for brawling or assault'.
Even *sweetheart* meant 'one loved illicitly' in the seventeenth century,
although it has ameliorated since. Duncan MacDougald (1961: 594)
describes the course all of these endearments seem to have followed:

> 'Tart', referring to a small pie or pastry, was first applied to a young
> woman as a term of endearment, next to young women who were
> sexually desirable, then to women who were careless in their morals,
> and finally – more recently – to women of the street.

If endearments for young girls have undergone pejoration, so have
terms denoting girls and young women. *Doll* 'a small-scale figure of a
human being' referred first to 'a young woman with a pretty babyish
face', then became an insulting epithet for women generally, and finally
acquired the meaning of 'a paramour'. *Minx* originally meant 'a pert,
young girl', and this meaning exists today, despite its pejoration to 'a
lewd or wanton woman; a harlot'. *Nymph* and *nymphet* both referred to
beautiful young girls, or women. *Nymph* became a euphemism in such
phrases as 'nymph of the pave' and 'nymph of darkness', while *nymphet*
acquired the derogated meaning of 'a sexually precocious girl; a loose
young woman'. *Peach* is an enduring metaphor for 'a luscious,
attractive girl or woman', but around 1900 it, too, degenerated to mean
'a promiscuous woman'. *Broad* was originally used with no offensive
connotations for 'a young woman or a girl' (Wentworth and Flexner
1960), but it acquired the suggestion of 'a promiscuous woman' or 'a
prostitute'. *Floozie*, first 'an attractive but uncultivated girl', pejorated
to mean 'an undisciplined, promiscuous, flirtatious young woman;
cynical, calculating'. *Girl*, itself, has a long history of specialization and
pejoration. It meant originally 'a child of either sex'; then it was
specialized to mean 'a female child'; later it meant 'a serving girl or
maidservant'; and eventually it acquired the meanings 'a prostitute', 'a
mistress', or 'the female sex – or that part of it given to unchastity'.
Today *girl* has ameliorated (but *girlie* has sexual undertones), and we
can call a female child, a *sweetheart*, or even a woman a *girl* without
insult (although the emcee who jollies along the middle-aged 'girls' in
the audience is plainly talking down to them).

That emcee has a problem, though. There just aren't many terms in
English for middle-aged or older women,[3] and those which have
occurred have inevitably taken on unpleasant connotations. Even a
relatively innocuous term like *dowager* is stigmatized. *Beldam* is worse.

Formed by combining the English usage of *dam* 'mother' with *bel* indicating the relationship of a grandparent, it simply meant 'grandmother' in its earliest usage. It was later generalized to refer to any 'woman of advanced age', and, as so frequently happens with words indicating 'old woman', it pejorated to signify 'a loathsome old woman; a hag'. *Hag*, itself, originally meant simply 'a witch' and was later generalized as a derisive term for 'an ugly old woman', often with the implication of viciousness or maliciousness. Julia Stanley (1973) records it as a synonym for 'a prostitute'. *Bat* followed the opposite course. Originally a metaphor for 'prostitute' (a 'night bird'), it has become a generalized form of abuse meaning simply 'an unpleasant woman, unattractive'. It still bears the taint of its earlier metaphoric use, however, and is banned on TV as an epithet for a woman (Wentworth and Flexner 1960). *Bag* meant 'a middle-aged or elderly slattern' or 'a pregnant woman' before it came to mean 'a slatternly prostitute' or 'a part-time prostitute' in the late nineteenth century. In the US it has ameliorated slightly and refers (still derisively) to 'an unattractive, ugly girl; an old shrew'.

To be fat and sloppy is just as unforgivable in a woman as is being old, and the language has many terms designating such a person (are there any designating slovenly men?) – terms which have undergone pejoration and acquired sexual overtones at one time or another.[4] A *cow* 'a clumsy, obese, coarse, or otherwise unpleasant person' became specialized to refer chiefly to women and then acquired the additional sense of 'a degraded woman' and eventually 'a prostitute'. *Drab* (also occurring as *drap*) originally referred to 'a dirty, untidy woman', but was further pejorated to refer to 'a harlot or prostitute'. Both *slut* and *slattern* were first used to designate 'a person, especially a woman, who is negligent of his appearance'. Both acquired the more derogatory meaning 'a woman of loose character or a prostitute', and both are currently polysemantic, meaning concurrently 'a sloppy woman' or 'a prostitute'. *Trollop*, another word for 'an unkempt woman', extended to mean 'a loose woman', and eventually 'a hedge whore'. *Mab*, first 'a slattern' and then 'a woman of loose character' seems to have withstood the third logical step of degeneration in England. In the US, however, it is used as an epithet for 'a prostitute' as well.

Horse metaphors used to denote women have also undergone sexual derogation. *Harridan*, 'a worn-out horse' seems to have originally been used as a metaphor for 'a gaunt woman', then 'a disagreeable old woman', and later 'a decayed strumpet' or 'a half-whore, half-bawd'. A *jade* was originally 'a broken-down, vicious or worthless horse', or else such a man, as is illustrated in the lines from *The Taming of the Shrew*: 'Gremio: What! This gentleman will outtalk us all./Lucentio: Sir. Give him head. I know he'll prove a jade' (I, 2, 249). It became a contemptuous epithet for women, however, and was eventually another synonym for 'whore'. A *hackney* (or *hack*) was first 'a common riding horse, often available for hire'. Its meaning was extended to encompass, with derogatory connotations, anyone who hires himself out (hence *hack writer*), but when used for women it acquired sexual overtones as a metaphor for 'a woman who hires out as a prostitute' or for 'a bawd'. A *tit* referred either to 'a small horse' or 'a small girl', but degenerated to mean 'a harlot'. There is in all of these horse metaphors, perhaps, the sense of a woman as being a *mount*, a term used indifferently for 'a wife' or 'a mistress' in the nineteenth century.[5]

All these terms originated as positive designations for women and gradually degenerated to become negative in the milder instances and abusive in the extremes. A degeneration of endearments into insulting terms for men has not occurred. Words denoting boys and young men have failed to undergo the pejoration so common with terms for women. *Boy, youth, stripling, lad, fellow, puppy*, and *whelp*, for example, have been spared denigration. As for terms for slovenly, obese, or elderly men, the language has managed with very few of them. A similar sexual difference is evident in terms which originated as words denoting either sex. Often, when they began to undergo pejoration they specialized to refer solely to women in derogatory terms. Later they frequently underwent further degeneration and became sexual terms of abuse. *Whore* is a well-known example of the process. Latin *carus* 'dear' is a derivative of the same Indo-European root. It was probably at one time a polite term (Bloomfield 1933: 401). Originally it seems to have referred to 'a lover of either sex', but eventually it specialized to refer solely to women. Later it degenerated to meaning 'a prostitute', and it became a term occurring only in 'coarse, abusive speech' (*OED*). A *harlot* was originally 'a fellow of either sex', referring more to men than women in Middle English and characterizing them as 'riffraff'. It degenerated further and Shakespeare's *harlot King* (*Winter's Tale* II, 3, 4) was characterized as 'lewd'. However, after Elizabethan times the word was specialized for women only, meaning first 'a disreputable woman' and later, specifically, 'a prostitute'. *Bawd*, similarly, originally referred to a 'go-between or panderer of either sex', but after 1700 it was used only for women, either as 'a keeper of a brothel' or 'a prostitute'.

Wench, 'a child of either sex', had sufficient prestige to appear in *Piers Plowman* in the phrase *Goddes Wench* 'the Virgin Mary' (1. 336). Later it was specialized to refer to 'a rustic or working woman'. As do so many terms referring to rustics, male or female (compare *villain, boor, peasant, churl,* for example), the term degenerated. Then it acquired sexual undertones, coming to refer first to 'a lewd woman' and finally to 'a wanton'. *Wench* has been rehabilitated and has lost its stigma. Today it can be used to refer to a woman without suggesting wantonness. Another term which specialized to refer to women, then degenerated to the point of abusiveness, and later ameliorated is *cat.* Originally it was a term of contempt for 'any human being who scratches like a cat'. Later it was specialized to refer to 'a spiteful, backbiting woman' (a usage which survives). For a period it meant 'a prostitute', but this sexual taint was lost in the nineteenth century, and only the less denigrating (but still pejorative) sense of 'spiteful woman' remains.

A comparison of the metaphors *cat* and *dog* illustrates the difference evident in many terms designating male and female humans. The term for the female is more likely to become pejorative, more likely to acquire sexual suggestions, and less likely to be transferable to a male. *Cat* originally meant 'any spiteful person', but specialized to refer only to women. It remains an abusive term for women. *Dog* is only 'sometimes used contemptuously for males'. More frequently it is used 'in half-serious chiding' (Farmer and Henley 1965) as in *He's a sly dog,* or to mean 'a gay, jovial, gallant fellow' (*OED*), as in *Oh, you're a clever dog!* However, *dog* has recently been transferred to women, and it occurs in totally negative contexts, meaning either 'a woman inferior in looks, character, or accomplishments' or 'a prostitute'. Or compare the use of *bitch.* It is an abusive term when applied to a woman, meaning either 'a malicious, spiteful, domineering woman' or 'a lewd or immoral woman'. When applied to a man it is 'less opprobrious and somewhat whimsical – like the modern use of *dog*' (*OED*). *Pig,* applied contemptuously to men, means 'a person who in some way behaves like a pig'. When applied to a woman, it means 'a woman who has sloppy morals'. *Sow* is not transferable to men. It is an abusive metaphor for 'a fat, slovenly woman', which in the US has acquired the additional sense of 'a promiscuous young woman or a prostitute'.

Robin Lakoff (1973) has pointed out that metaphors and labels are likely to have wide reference when applied to men, whereas metaphors for women are likely to be narrower and to include sexual reference. She uses as an example the term *professional*. If you say that a man is a *professional*, you suggest that he is a member of one of the respected professions. If you call a woman a *professional*, you imply that she follows 'the oldest profession'. In a similar way, if you call a man a *tramp* you simply communicate that he is 'a drifter'. Call a woman a *tramp* and you imply that she is 'a prostitute'. Historically, terms like *game, natural, jay, plover*, and *Jude* have meant merely 'simpleton or dupe' when applied to men, but 'loose woman or prostitute' when applied to women. A male *pirate* is 'one who infringes on the rights of others or commits robbery on the high seas', whereas a female *pirate* is 'an adultress who chases other women's men'.[6]

What is the cause of the degeneration of terms designating women? Stephen Ullman (1967: 231–2) suggests three origins for pejoration: association with a contaminating concept, euphemism, and prejudice. As for the first possibility, there is some evidence that contamination is a factor. Men tend to think of women in sexual terms whatever the context, and consequently any term denoting women carries sexual suggestiveness to the male speaker. The subtle operation of this kind of contamination is seen in the fortunes of such words as *female, lady*, and *woman. Woman* was avoided in the last century, probably as a Victorian sexual taboo, since it had acquired the meaning 'paramour or mistress' or the sense of intercourse with women when used in plural, as in *Wine, Women, and Song*. It was replaced by *female*, but this term also came to be considered degrading and indelicate. Freyer (1963: 69) tells that 'When the Vassar Female College was founded in 1861, Mrs Sarah Josepha Hale, editor of *Godey's Lady's Book*, spent six years in securing the removal of the offending adjective from the college sign.' The *OED* recorded *female* as a synonym 'avoided by writers', and the *Third* identifies it as a disparaging term when used for women. It was replaced in the nineteenth century by *lady*, which Mencken (1963: 350) called 'the English euphemism-of-all-work'. *Lady* also vulgarized, however, and by the time Mencken wrote, it was already being replaced by *woman*, newly rehabilitated. Even so neutral a term as *person*, when it was used as a substitute for *woman*, suffered contamination which Greenough and Kittredge found amusing (1901: 326):

> It has been more or less employed as a substitute for *woman* by those who did not wish to countenance the vulgar abuse of *lady* and yet shrank from giving offense. The result has been to give a comically slighting connotation to one of the most innocent words imaginable.

Despite this repeated contamination of terms designating women, we cannot accept the belief that there is a quality inherent in the concept of *woman* which taints any word associated with it. Indeed, the facts argue against this interpretation. Women are generally acknowledged to be – for whatever reasons – the more continent of the two sexes, the least promiscuous, and the more monogamous. Nevertheless, the largest category of words designating humans in sexual terms are those for women – especially for loose women. I have located roughly a thousand words and phrases describing women in sexually derogatory ways.[7] There is nothing approaching this multitude for describing men. Farmer and Henley (1965), for example, have over 500 terms (in English alone) which are synonyms for *prostitute*. They have only sixty-five synonyms for *whoremonger*.

As for the second possibility, one must acknowledge that many terms for 'women of the night' have arisen from euphemism – a reluctance to name the profession outright. The majority of terms, however, are dysphemistic, not euphemistic. For example, the bulk of terms cited by Farmer and Henley (1965) as synonyms for *prostitute* are clearly derogatory: *broadtail, carrion, cleaver, cocktail, flagger, guttersnipe, mutton, moonlighter, omnibus, pinchprick, tail trader, tickletail, twofer,* and *underwear* are just a few.

The third possibility – prejudice – is the most likely source for pejorative terms for women. They illustrate what Gordon Allport calls (1954: 179) 'the labels of primary potency' with which an in-group stereotypes an out-group. Certain symbols, identifying a member of an out-group, blind the prejudiced speaker to any qualities the minority person may have which contradict the stereotype.

> Most people are unaware of this basic law of language – that every label applied to a given person refers properly only to one aspect of his nature. You may correctly say that a certain person is *human, a philanthropist, a Chinese, a physician, an athlete.* A given person may be all of these but the chances are that *Chinese* stands out in your mind as the symbol of primary potency. Yet neither this nor any other classificatory label can refer to the whole of a man's nature.

Anti-feminism, he points out, contains the two basic ingredients of prejudice: denigration and gross overgeneralization (p. 34).

Derogatory terms for women illustrate both qualities which Allport attributes to prejudice. And what is the source or cause of the prejudice? Several writers have suggested that it is fear, based on a supposed threat to the power of the male. Fry (1972: 131) says of male humour: 'In man's jokes about sex can be found an answer as to why man is willing to forego to a large extent the satisfactions of a reality and equality relationship with his fellow mortal, woman. Part of this answer has to do with the question of control or power.' He theorizes that power becomes a question because the male is biologically inferior to the female in several respects. Girls mature earlier than boys physically, sexually, and intellectually. Boys are biologically frailer in their first years of life than girls. At the other end of their life span, they also prove to be weaker. More men have heart attacks, gout, lung cancer, diabetes, and other degenerative diseases than women. Finally, they deteriorate biologically and die earlier than women. Fry (1972: 133) continues: 'The jokes men tell about the relationships between the sexes – especially the frankly sexual jokes – reveal awareness and concern, even anxiety, about the general presence of these biologic disadvantages and frailties.'[8] Grotjahn (1972: 53) concurs that anxiety prompts man's hostility, but he believes the source is fear of sexual inadequacy. A woman knows the truth about his potency; he cannot lie to her. Yet her own performance remains a secret, a mystery to him. Thus, man's fear of woman is basically sexual, which is perhaps the reason why so many of the derogatory terms for women take on sexual connotations.

I began with the acknowledgement that we cannot tell the extent to which any language influences the people who use it. This is certainly true for most of what we call *language*. However, words which are highly charged with emotion, taboo, or distaste do not only reflect the culture which uses them. They teach and perpetuate the attitudes which created them. To make the name of God taboo is to perpetuate the mystery, power, and awesomeness of the divine. To surround a concept with euphemisms, as Americans have done with the idea of death, is to render the reality of the concept virtually invisible. And to brand a class of persons as obscene is to taint them to the users of the language. As Mariana Birnbaum (1971: 248) points out, prejudicial language 'always mirror[s] generalized tabloid thinking which contains prejudices and thus perpetuates discrimination'. This circularity in itself is justification for bringing such linguistic denigration of women to a conscious level. The semantic change discussed here, by which terms designating women routinely undergo pejoration, both reflects and perpetuates derogatory attitudes towards women. They should be abjured.

Notes

1 Citations are based upon, but are not necessarily direct quotations from, the *Oxford English Dictionary*, cited henceforth as *(OED)*, *Webster's Third International (Third)*, the *Dictionary of American Slang* (Wentworth and Flexner 1960), *Slang and its analogues* (Farmer and Henley 1965), *A Dictionary of Slang and Unconventional English* (Partridge 1961), and the *American Thesaurus of Slang* (Berrey and Van den Bark 1952). Sources are only indicated if the source is other than one of the above, or if the citation contains unusual information.

2 Endearments and terms for young women have undergone a similar pejoration in other languages, as well. Thass-Thienemann (1967: 336) cites *Metze* and *Dirne* from German, *fille* or *fille de joie* from French, *hêtaira* and *pallakis* or *pallakê* from Greek, and *puttana* from Italian as endearments which degenerated and became sexual slurs.

3 There are few terms for old people of either sex in English, 'senior citizen' being our current favourite euphemism. However, the few terms available to denote old men (*elder, oldster, codger, geezer, duffer*) are, as was mentioned above, less vituperative than are those denoting women.

4 C. S. Lewis (1961), in discussing four-letter words, makes a point which is perhaps applicable to the tendency these words have to acquire sexual implications. He argues, with evidence from Sheffield and Montaigne, that four-letter words are not used in order to provoke desire. In fact, they have little to do with sexual arousal. They are used rather to express force and vituperation.

5 Several bird names originating as metaphors for young girls have also become abusive epithets for them. *Columbine, quail, flapper, bird, chicken, hen*, and in the US *seagull* all began affectionately but acquired the meaning 'a prostitute'.

6 Several terms which originally applied to thieves, beggars, and their female accomplices have specialized and pejorated as terms for women: *Badger, doxy, moll* (from *Mary*), *mollisher*, and *bulker*, for example. *Blowse* reversed the process. Denoting first 'a prostitute', and then 'a beggar's trull', it finally ameliorated slightly to mean 'a slattern or a shrew'. Other terms which originally designated either sex but came to refer only to women with the sense of 'a prostitute' are *filth, morsel* (perhaps with the present sense of *piece*), *canary, rig*, and *rep*. The reverse has happened in a strange way with *fagot* (or *faggot*). It was first a term of abuse for women (sixteenth to nineteenth centuries) or a term for 'a dummy soldier'. Today it has transferred as an abusive term for 'a male homosexual'. Not all the terms specializing to women acquired sexual implications. *Potato* 'ugly face', *prig, prude, termagant*, and *vixen* were all used in a general sense first and only later narrowed to refer specifically to women.

7 I have restricted myself in this paper to terms which have undergone the process of pejoration or amelioration – terms which have not always been abusive. The majority of derogatory words for women, of course, were coined as dysphemisms and are, hence, outside the scope of my study. In Farmer and Henley (1965), the chief entry containing synonyms for 'prostitute' is *tart*, while for 'whoremonger' it is *mutton-monger*. There are, in addition to the English

synonyms, over 200 French phrases used to refer to women in a derogatory and sexual way, and another extended listing occurs under the entry *barrack-hack*. Stanley (1973) lists 200, and I found another 100, culled chiefly from Fryer (1963), Sagarin (1962), Berrey and Van den Bark (1952), Partridge (1961), and Wentworth and Flexner (1960).

8 Bettelheim and Janowitz (1950: 54–5) also cite anxiety as the source of prejudice. They argue that the prejudiced person 'seeks relief through prejudice, which serves to reduce anxiety because prejudice facilitates the discharge of hostility, and if hostility is discharged anxiety is reduced. Prejudice reduces anxiety because it suggests to the person that he is better than others, hence does not need to feel so anxious'.

References

Allport, Gordon W. (1954) *The Nature of Prejudice*, Cambridge, Mass.: Addison-Wesley.

Berrey, Lester V. and Van den Bark, Melvin (1952) *The American Thesaurus of Slang*, New York: Thomas Y. Crowell.

Bettelheim, Bruno and Janowitz, Morris (1950) *Dynamics of Prejudice*, New York: Harper & Row.

Birnbaum, Mariana D. (1971) 'On the language of prejudice', *Western Folklore* 30: 247–68.

Bloomfield, Leonard (1933) *Language*, New York: Henry Holt.

Farmer, J. S. and Henley, W. E. (1965) *Slang and its Analogues*, repr. of 7 vols. publ. 1890–1904, New York: Kraus Reprint Corp.

Flexner, Stuart, (1960) 'Preface' to Harold Wentworth and Stuart Flexner (eds) *Dictionary of American Slang*, New York: Thomas Y. Crowell.

Fry, William P. (1972) 'Psychodynamics of sexual humor: man's view of sex', *Medical Aspects of Human Sexuality* 6: 128–34.

Fryer, Peter (1963) *Mrs. Grundy: Studies in English Prudery*, London: Dennis Dobson.

Gove, Philip (ed.) (1971) *Webster's Third New International Dictionary*, Springfield, Mass.: G. & C. Merriam.

Greenough, James Bradstreet and Kittredge, George Lyman (1901) *Words and Their Ways in English Speech*, New York: Macmillan.

Grotjahn, Martin (1972) 'Sexuality and humor. Don't laugh!', *Psychology Today* 6: 51–53.

Lakoff, Robin (1973) 'Language and woman's place', *Language in Society* 2: 45–80.

Lewis, C. S. (1961) 'Four-letter words', *Critical Quarterly* 3: 118–22.

MacDougald, Duncan, Jr (1961) 'Language and sex', in Albert Ellis and Albert Abarbanel (eds) *The Encyclopedia of Sexual Behavior*, London: Hawthorne Books, vol. II.

Mencken, H. L. (1963) *The American Language. The Fourth Edition and the Two Supplements*, abridged and ed. by Raven I. McDavid, Jr, New York: Knopf.

Oxford English Dictionary (1933) Oxford: Clarendon Press.

Partridge, Eric, (ed.) (1961) *A Dictionary of Slang and Unconventional English*, 5th edn, New York: Macmillan.

Sagarin, Edward (1962) *The Anatomy of Dirty Words*, New York: Lyle Stuart.

Stanley, Julia (1973) 'The metaphors some people live by', unpublished mimeo.

Thass-Thienemann, Theodore (1967) *The Subconscious Language*, New York: Washington Square Press.

Ullman, Stephen, (1967) *Semantics. An Introduction to the Science of Meaning*, New York: Barnes & Noble.

Wentworth, Harold and Flexner, Stuart Berg (eds) (1960) *Dictionary of American Slang*, New York: Thomas Y. Crowell.

10

Words on a feminist dictionary

Cheris Kramarae and Paula Treichler

Reprinted from A Feminist Dictionary (*London: Pandora Press 1985*).

This is a word-book with several purposes: to document words, definitions, and conceptualizations that illustrate women's linguistic contributions; to illuminate forms of expression through which women have sought to describe, reflect upon, and theorize about women, language, and the world; to identify issues of language theory, research, usage, and institutionalized practice that bear on the relationship between women and language; to demonstrate ways in which women are seizing the language; to broaden knowledge of the feminist lexicon; and to stimulate research on women and language. Like many other dictionaries, it is a compendium of words arranged in alphabetical order together with definitions, quoted citations and illustrations, and other forms of commentary. Yet in some respects, it is different from what many people expect a 'dictionary' to be. In this introduction, we will briefly elaborate on our goals for this book in relation to those of other lexicographic projects by women and men and suggest what future dictionary-making might include. (See also the dictionary entries under AUTHORITY, DICTIONARY, LANGUAGE, and LEXICO-GRAPHER.)

Lexicography (the writing or compiling of dictionaries), as we note below, may have a variety of aims and encompass many different sorts of projects. Though *A Feminist Dictionary* shares some of the aims and characteristics of other dictionaries, several important points should be noted:

1 We recognize women as linguistically creative speakers – that is, as originators of spoken or written language forms. The identification, documentation, and celebration of *women's* words and definitions depart from traditional lexicographic practice. Though dictionary editors

claim (often militantly) to collect words and definitions from diverse sources, their criteria and procedures (both explicit and implicit) for identification and preservation nearly always preclude the gathering of women's definitions. Definitions for many dictionaries, for example, are constructed from usages found in works of the 'best authors'; though the equation has been challenged in recent years, this designation usually means 'male authors'. Similarly, one criterion for the inclusion in a dictionary of a 'new word' is the number of times it is found cited in print; given current cultural practices, not only are men's words more likely to be cited in the mainstream press, but also few dictionary editors seek out print media where women's words would predominate (such as feminist periodicals). Thus despite whatever usage practices may actually exist in the world, multiple mechanisms act to exclude women's usages from dictionaries.

Sexism is also at work. H. Lee Gershuny (1973), examining sentences in the *Random House Dictionary* that illustrated word usage, argued that a dictionary not merely reflects sexist social attitudes but acts in a variety of ways to preserve and recreate stereotypes as well – thus perpetuating notions of women as particular kinds of speakers (to illustrate usage for the word *nerves*, the *RHD* used 'Women with shrill voices get on his *nerves*'. As Meaghan Morris (1982) notes, a dictionary may also render women invisible; the Australian *Macquarie Dictionary* obliterates women's linguistic and political achievements through the way in which it constructs definitions and thus achieves what Morris calls 'code control': *sexism* is defined as 'the upholding or propagation of sexist attitudes', a *sexist attitude* as one which 'stereotypes a person according to gender or sexual preference, etc', and *feminism* as an 'advocacy of equal rights and opportunities for women'. As Morris points out, *sexism* was originally used by *women* attempting to construct a theory of patriarchy; the notion of stereotyping a 'person' by virtue of holding certain 'attitudes' obscures and almost makes nonsense of its original political meaning; by defining *feminism* in terms of its lowest common denominator, both current and historical distinctions among different feminist positions are eliminated. 'While it is true', writes Morris, 'that the usages accepted by the *Macquarie* are standard liberal currency today, the point is that the concepts developed by feminists are not even marginalised into second place, but rather omitted entirely' (p. 89). For another example, one might point to the *Doublespeak Dictionary* (William Lambdin 1979) which cites a small number of feminist linguistic innovations – largely, it would appear, to ridicule them; though one of the dictionary's stated aims is to identify deceptive, distorted, or ambiguous language, the nonsexist usage *him/her* (or her/him), designed to reduce the ambiguity of the so-called generic *he*, is castigated as a 'clumsy', 'legal', and 'neutered' style (pp. 109–10). Dictionaries are, in fact, a prime example of discourse in which the generic *he* has evidently seemed adequate to represent the whole of humankind.

In short, the systematic – even when inadvertent – exclusion of one sex replicates and preserves the linguistic and cultural rule of the other. The traditional focus on 'literary', 'newsworthy', or 'authoritative' sources obscures women's very existence as speaking subjects. Interestingly, women's documented reputation for speaking more 'correctly' than men do does not help them here; for they are interpreted to be mere receivers and transmitters of the code and hence incapable of making original contributions to the language. While men's definitions have been preserved in hundreds of dictionaries, this view of women's speech has excluded their words; in producing this dictionary, it is this view that we most wish to challenge and subvert. Accordingly, *A Feminist Dictionary* insists upon the significance of women as speaking subjects and documents their linguistic contributions.

2 We acknowledge the socio-political aspects of dictionary-making. While we see this dictionary as a balance to the weight of other dictionaries in men's favour, we have tried as well to be self-conscious and explicit about our decisions and procedures. A recurrent difficulty in creating a 'feminist' dictionary concerns *whose* feminism an entry represents. Our 1980s feminism has inevitably pulled us toward the material that seems most useful and enriching to us. Though citations from earlier periods perform the valuable task of making women's names and words visible and attesting to the existence of women's rebellious words through the years, we are especially aware as we make selections from archival materials that we may be disturbing somewhat the links between the words of our foresisters and their times. Forms of domination and the texture of feminist discussions have changed over the years in ways our selection process and the structure of the dictionary may obscure. The dictionary format can only hint at the complexities involved in feminist discussions.

As feminist lexicographers, we do not claim objectivity nor believe that simply by offering a dictionary of 'women's words' we can reverse the profound structural inequities of history and culture. The dictionary is also therefore a critique of current and past practices; collectively, the entries provide commentary on the institutionalized processes and politics through which some forms of language are privileged over others – how words get into print, why they go out of print, the politics of bibliography and archival storage, the politics of silence, of speech, of what can be said, of who can speak and who listen.

3 We preserve women's *own* words. *A Feminist Dictionary* is subtitled *In Our Own Words*. Though *our* words – as scholars and writers – figure in many of the entries, the core of the book lies in the verbatim citation of other women's words. These citations are intended not only to illustrate word usage or illuminate a particular perspective but also to encourage a reading of the original source in its entirety. As we initially talked about this project, we thought it might be a book of key words – that is, a set of short essays about words or concepts that have had special significance for feminism. But such synthesizing articles would have hidden the diversity we found as well as obscured both the problematics and pleasures of feminist talk and writing. We have tried to provide narrative entries at certain key points to create a framework for the book as a whole, but these are not forced on the reader; rather they are offered as background, interpretation, and allusion. Accordingly, entries take a variety of shapes including short aphorisms, longer citations, dialogues and trialogues, etymologies, and narrative text.

4 We are not seeking to set forth a linguistic norm for a given community of speakers. In practical terms, the fact that we forsake this traditional theoretical grounding for lexicography means that with few exceptions we do not specify 'part of speech' (noun, verb, etc.) nor label entries according to their linguistic status (obsolete, rare, visionary, neologism, etymologically incorrect, politically incorrect, etc.). The entry for HERSTORY, for example, labels it neither as a coinage (all words are coinages) nor as folklinguistics; such labels have meaning only in reference to a 'real' body of 'authorized' words, and as we have already noted there are many reasons why we should be dubious of this authorization process. At the same time, the dictionary draws words and definitions from such utopian works as Monique Wittig's and Sande Zeig's *Lesbian Peoples: Material for a Dictionary* (1976), Sally Miller Gearheart's *Wanderground* (1978), and Suzette Haden Elgin's *Native Tongue* (1984), thereby suggesting not only what is or has been but what might be.

5 Though *A Feminist Dictionary* is not intended to be a guide to women's intellectual thought, individual entries (see for example FARKSOO, GIRL, MARRIAGE, TRAFFIC IN WOMEN) are intended

to stimulate research or theoretical development; collectively, the dictionary's entries should work to illuminate many lines of feminist thinking and debate. At the same time, by tracing a word or idea through a series of cross-references, the reader may begin to explore a particular line of theoretical thinking and see links between particular words and ideas. Our dictionary does not spell out all those links nor attempt to fashion contemporary feminisms into a seemingly codified and interpreted body of thought. We hope that *A Feminist Dictionary* will be used as women work to name and analyse specific structural oppressions and work for revolutionary change.

A note on male dictionary-making

We have suggested ways in which *A Feminist Dictionary* is different from many other dictionaries. But it is also important to note that our project addresses many of the same theoretical questions and practical problems that other dictionary-makers have had to address. Further, the term *dictionary* itself encompasses projects of striking diversity – many of which, like this one, depart from the practices characteristic of the 'standard' American dictionary with its familiar claims to authority, comprehensiveness, legislative value, and scientific objectivity.

Under the rubric 'dictionary' go the *Oxford English Dictionary, Webster's Third International,* the *Random House Dictionary,* the *American Heritage Dictionary,* and other standard contributions to lexicography. But the term also includes a range of individual, often quirky, projects. These include Gustave Flaubert's *Dictionary of Accepted Ideas,* published in 1881 (see ACTRESS) and Ambrose Bierce's 1911 *The Devil's Dictionary* (see MUSH); even Raymond Williams's *Keywords* (1976) can in some sense be called a dictionary. A number of influential dictionaries explicate and analyse subsets of the lexicon: J. Laplanche and J.-B. Pontalis's *Dictionary of Psychoanalysis* (1973), Thomas Bottomore's *Dictionary of Marxist Thought* (1983), and Oswald Ducrot and Tzvetan Todorov's *Encyclopedic Dictionary of the Sciences of Language* are examples. There have also been hundreds of man-made dictionaries produced to explicate even more specialized subsets of the lexicon, virtually all oriented towards traditionally masculine occupations, interests, or values. Dictionaries vary as to organizational arrangement (some, like *Roget's Thesaurus* or David Wallechinsky and Irving Wallace's *The People's Almanac* (1975), are arranged by semantic category as opposed to alphabetical format, for example), purpose (some dictionaries are essentially glossaries of 'hard words'), accessibility, influence, and methodology (for example, whether the data are primarily qualitative or quantitative – the latter an important feature of linguistic atlases and many dialect dictionaries). Finally, dictionaries vary enormously in terms of resources. Some are products of one person alone in a room with books. In contrast, the *Oxford English Dictionary* took seventy years to complete. *Webster's Third* was estimated to have required 757 'editor years' and to have cost more than $3,500,000 to produce.

The 1612 Italian *Vocabolario degli Accademici della Crusca* was the first big dictionary of a modern standard language; based almost exclusively on citations from classical Florentine writers like Dante, it did not claim to describe or prescribe general speech norms but did establish the tradition of drawing meanings from the 'best authors'. The disjunction between spoken and written language continually complicates the task of specifying what a given language consists of. Many countries established academies, language boards, or commissions to legislate upon this question; in France, most notoriously, the Académie Française officially determines what *the code* is to be. Despite attempts to establish similar bodies as keepers of the code in Britain and the United States, a generally anti-authoritarian tradition has prevailed, with dictionaries – beginning with Samuel Johnson's very influential *Dictionary* of 1755 – taking on this codifying role. When the final volume of James Murray's *Oxford English Dictionary* was published in 1928 (seventy years after the British Philological Society initiated the project), the Oxford University Press expounded upon its 'superiority to all other English dictionaries, in accuracy and completeness.... [It] is the supreme authority, and without a rival' (K. M. Elisabeth Murray 1977: 312). Most other English and American dictionaries have been directed towards the documentation of existing language forms; a tradition of lexicographic positivism leads editors to claim 'scientific objectivity'. In contrast, dictionary editors in other languages have often inserted themselves much more forcefully into the codification process; one German lexicographer, for example, invented an elaborate system for labelling entries which among other things distinguished between obsolete words 'recently introduced by good writers or deserving re-introduction' and those 'incapable of re-introduction' (Ladislav Zgusta (ed.) 1980: 9).

In contemporary linguistics, attempts to define 'the lexicon' are linked to various theoretical questions: how is our internal knowledge of a language – its 'internalized norm' – to be externally and explicitly represented? What is the source of our knowledge of these norms (for example, introspection, experience, empirical research)? How do dictionary entries relate to each other and to objects in the world? What is the status of cultural knowledge in our understanding of the meaning of a word? What is the relation of word usage to conditions for speaking? How is it possible to represent anything in language when in representing or interpreting one text, we inevitably create another? These questions are relevant as we explore the relationship between women and language: how is a concept like *woman* to be explicitly specified in a definition? (see BLACK WOMEN, DICTIONARY, ETYMOLOGY, WHITE WOMEN, WOMAN, WOMEN OF COLOUR). Whose data will be used to formulate such a definition? (see OBJECTIVITY.) What kind of 'research' is deemed necessary (and by whom) for the construction of dictionary definitions? (See WOMEN AND LANGUAGE RESEARCH.) Whose purposes will particular definitions serve? (See LANGUAGE.) What consequences (for example, legal) might a given definition have for women in the 'real world'? (See RAPE, PROSTITUTION, WOMAN.) From what stance or perspective does one present 'new' definitions of women without inscribing authority and universality upon the definition by its very construction and publication? (See AUTHOR, AUTHORITY, DICTIONARY).

There is no doubt that the 'male' dictionaries, constructed almost entirely by men with male readers and users in mind, offer useful information about words and about the world. Yet their exclusion of women, together with their pervasive claims to authority, is profoundly disturbing. The authority inherent in dictionary-making, and the strange arrogance towards language it may generate, is explicitly articulated by some lexicographers:

> To me, making a dictionary has seemed much like building a sizable house singlehanded; and, having built it, wiring, plumbing, painting and furnishing it. Moreover, it takes about as long. But there can be no question that there is great satisfaction in the labor. When at last you survey the bundles of manuscript ready for the press you have the pardonable but, alas, fleeting illusion that now you know everything; that at last you are in the position to justify the ways of man to God.
>
> (J. A. Cuddon 1977)

Thus despite the immense achievements that some of these dictionaries represent and their unique contributions to scholarship, they have been created within the context of social arrangements where hostility towards and exclusion of women have thrived.

As H. Lee Gershuny (1977) has pointed out, the dictionary's significant role as the cultural authority for meaning and usage makes it an important site for feminist analysis. As the review above suggests, lexicography is a complex enterprise that encompasses many kinds of projects. It is all the more striking then that for women, no matter what the project, the ultimate outcome is the same: whether descriptive or prescriptive, authoritarian or democratic, massive or minimal, systematic or quixotic, these dictionaries have systematically excluded any notion of women as speakers, as linguistic innovators, or as definers of words. Women in their pages have been rendered invisible, reduced to stereotypes, ridiculed, trivialized, or demeaned. Whatever their intentions, then, dictionaries have functioned as linguistic legislators which perpetuate the stereotypes and prejudices of their writers and editors, who are almost exclusively male.

Women's dictionaries, feminist dictionaries

But there is another tradition. In 1892, Anna Julia Cooper in her essay 'The higher education of women' wrote:

In the very first year of our century, the year 1801, there appeared in Paris a book by Silvain Marechal, entitled 'Shall Woman Learn the Alphabet.' The book proposes a law prohibiting the alphabet to women, and quotes authorities weighty and various, to prove that the woman who knows the alphabet has already lost part of her womanliness. The author declares that woman can use the alphabet only as Molière predicted they would, in spelling out the verb *amo*; that they have no occasion to peruse Ovid's *Ars Amoris*, since that is already the ground and limit of their intuitive furnishing; that Madame Guion would have been far more adorable had she remained a beautiful ignoramus as nature made her; that Ruth, Naomi, the Spartan woman, the Amazons, Penelope, Andromache, Lucretia, Joan of Arc, Petrarch's Laura, the daughters of Charlemagne, could not spell their names; while Sappho, Aspasia, Madame de Maintenon, and Madame de Staël could read altogether too well for their good; finally, that if women were once permitted to read

Sophocles and work with logarithms, or to nibble at any side of the apple of knowledge, there would be an end forever to their sewing on buttons and embroidering slippers.

(Anna Julia Cooper 1892, in Bert James Loewenberg and Ruth Bogin (eds) 1976: 318)

But women were not to be kept from the alphabet. While N. H.'s *The Ladies Dictionary* (1694), was not a sisterly effort but a male effort which offered ladies some definitions of women's names and essays on topics such as love and religion, several eighteenth-century dictionaries suggested the growth of more genuine interest in women as readers; they were dedicated not only to 'scholars' but also to 'the Female sex' (Shirley Morahan 1981: 55). Women became writers as well. Elizabeth Elstob produced the first grammar of Anglo-Saxon in 1715; her dedication to the Princess of Wales noted that her royal highness had probably never before received a book written by a member of the female sex.

With the feminist movement, certainly by the time of Mary Wollstonecraft's *Vindication of the Rights of Women* in 1789, came increasing self-conscious attention to the meaning of words. Not only have feminists been concerned with women's access to words – through reading, education, writing, and publication – but also they write about how words like WOMAN, RIGHTS, JUSTICE, MARRIAGE, and EQUALITY are to be defined (see the dictionary entries under these words). They critique existing definitions (see WILL) and propose new ones (see HOME, CHIVALRY, WOMEN). They point to words and concepts in the cultural mainstream that undermine our ability even to articulate women's condition (see ANGEL); the so-called 'generic' use of *he* and *man* was challenged (for example, by Charlotte Carmichael Stopes 1908; and see entries under HE and MAN). They challenge existing language and originate new language (see -ESS, BIBLE, OBEY, PRAYER). With the organization of the suffrage movement, this engagement with language grew even more intense, with women beginning the process of reclaiming male-defined negative words about women (see RECLAMATION, SUFFRAGETTE). Suffragists and suffragettes published their own ABCs ('N is for NOW, Mr. Putoff, M.P., The day after no-time Will not do for me'). In 1941, Mary Ritter Beard undertook a feminist critique of the *Encyclopaedia Britannica*; though the editors who had commissioned the forty-two page report did not act on her suggestions, she recommended redefining many entries and adding material on the contributions and concerns of women (Ann J. Lane 1977).

In the modern feminist movement, beginning in the late 1960s, feminists have addressed language issues in relation to feminist theory, scholarship, action, and policy. A central problem is the relationship of women to a male-oriented symbolic system: what the writer Varda One called 'Manglish' in her language columns in the early 1970s and what Dale Spender identifies as 'man-made language' (1980). Examination of the processes of cultural authorization has led feminists to the institution where language and authority most dramatically intersect: the dictionary. Gershuny, mentioned above (p. 155), undertook a systematic study of the dictionary in the early 1970s. At the same time, Varda One's columns inspired the *New Feminist English Dictionary*, subtitled 'An intelligent woman's guide to dirty words' (1974). Ruth Todasco and her colleagues began their project as they 'sat around with an unabridged dictionary and started shouting out dirty words', a process that yielded six types of 'patriarchal epithets: Woman as Whore, as Whorish, as Body, as Animal, as -ess, and as -ette' (Ruth Todasco 1974). This demonstration of men's myths about women and their sexuality was drawn primarily from the established dictionaries of the English language which, Todasco wrote, 'are museum pieces of an archaic culture', but also a 'powerful reinforcing expression of men's prejudice against women'. Julia Penelope Stanley (1977) also used standard dictionaries and grammars to identify words designating males and females, pointing out both structural and political exclusions of females; Muriel Schulz (1975), examining pairs of words like dog and bitch, proposed a process that she called the SEMANTIC DEROGATION OF WOMEN to account for the repeated 'sliding' of the female term towards negative meanings, usually associated with sexuality or prostitution. Many other projects during the last fifteen years have sought to illuminate the implications for women of the received male standard and of the semantic and social space in which words and their meanings come to life.

A different approach is taken in the 'Woman's New Word Dictionary', an issue of a feminist journal edited by Midge Lennert and Norma Willson (1973). Feminist definitions replace man-made ones; *construction*, for example, is defined as 'a well-paying field of human endeavor not open to women', and *tipping* as 'a fantasy that allows our society to justify less than minimum wages for waitresses'. In the 1976 *Lesbian Peoples: Material for a Dictionary*, published first in French,

Monique Wittig and Sande Zeig offer their work as a corrective to what they call the 'lacunary' – the empty spaces of our history as represented by most dictionaries and fables. More recently Suzette Haden Elgin, a linguist, has created a women's language to incorporate women's concerns; the Láadan lexicon includes many words about, for example, the complexities of and feelings towards pregnancy, menstruation, the failure of published histories to record accomplishments of women, the varieties of love – concepts which exist at present only through lengthy explanations. (Begun in 1982, the Láadan language project is the subject of Elgin's 1984 science-fiction novel *Native Tongue*.) Other projects, similarly, seek not merely to challenge the male lexicon but to offer radical new interpretations of it, to change what the lexicon of the English language is to consist of and how it is organized, and in doing so to challenge the processes and institutions which create and codify language use. Thus Liz Mackie's 'Socialist Feminist Dictionary (59th edition)' defines CAREER WOMAN as

> an archaic term which correlates strongly with the meritocratic phase of British monopoly capitalism. It became obsolete in the twenty-first century when the entry of large numbers of women into the workforce reduced the working day, improved conditions at the workplace and eventually brought about universal 'part-time' working and shared childrearing.

> (Liz Mackie 1984: 8)

Thus a 'dictionary' is created not to authorize but to challenge and envision.

While different in scope and format, all these projects are companions to *A Feminist Dictionary* and signal the continuing and intense interest women have had in finding, creating, and using alternatives to male lexicographic traditions.

References

Cooper, A. J. (1892) 'The higher education of women', in B. J. Loewenberg and R. Bogin (eds) (1976) *Black Women in Nineteenth Century American Life*, Pennsylvania: State University Press.

Cuddon, J. A. (1977) *A Dictionary of Literary Terms*, New York: Doubleday.

Elgin, S. H. (1985) *Native Tongue*, London: Women's Press.

Gearheart, S. M. (1978) *The Wanderground*, Watertown, Mass.: Persephone Press.

Gershuny, H. Lee (1973) 'Sexist semantics', unpubl. dissertation.

——(1977) 'Sexism in the language of literature', in A. P. Nilsen, H. Bosmajian, H. L. Gershuny, and J. P. Stanley (eds) *Sexism in Language*, Urbana, Ill.: NCTE.

Lambdin, W. (1979) *Doublespeak Dictionary*, Los Angeles, Calif.: Pinnacle Books.

Lane, A. J. (1979) *Mary Ritter Beard: A Sourcebook*, New York: Schocken Books.

Lennert, M. and Willson (eds) (1973) *A Woman's New Word Dictionary*, Lomita, Calif.: 51% Publications.

Mackie, L. (1984) 'Socialist feminist dictionary, 59th edition', *Sourcream*, Vol. 4/5.

Morahan, S. (1981) *A Woman's Place: Rhetoric and Readings for Composing Yourself and Your Prose*, Albany, NY: SUNY Press.

Morris, M. (1982) 'A-mazing grace: notes on Mary Daly's poetics', *Intervention* 16, 70–92.

Murray, K. M. E. (1977) *Caught in the Web of Words: J. A. H. Murray and the Oxford English Dictionary*, Oxford: Oxford University Press.

Schulz, M. R. (1975) 'The semantic derogation of women', in B. Thorne and N. Henley (eds) *Language and Sex: Difference and Dominance*, Rowley, Mass.: Newbury House.

Stanley, J. P. (1977) 'Paradigmatic woman: the prostitute', in D. L. Shores and C. P. Hines (eds) *Papers in Language Variation*, Birmingham, University of Alabama Press.

Stopes, C. C. (1908) *The Sphere of 'Man' in Relation to that of 'Woman'*, London: T. Fisher Unwin.

Todasco, R. (ed.) (1973) *An Intelligent Woman's Guide to Dirty Words*, Chicago: Loop Center YWCA.

Wittig, M. and S. Zeig (1979) *Lesbian Peoples: Materials for a Dictionary*, New York: Avon.

Zgusta, L. (1980) *Theory and Method in Lexicography*, Columbia, SC: Hornbeam Press.

11

Extract from *Native Tongue*

Suzette Haden Elgin

Reprinted from Native Tongue *(London: Women's Press 1985).*

The linguistic term *lexical encoding* refers to the way that human beings choose a particular chunk of their world, external or internal, and assign that chunk a surface shape that will be its name; it refers to the process of word-making. When we women say 'Encoding', with a capital 'E', we mean something a little bit different. We mean the making of a name for a chunk of the world that so far as we know has never been chosen for naming before in any human language, and that has not just suddenly been made or found or dumped upon your culture. We mean naming a chunk that has been around a long time but has never before impressed anyone as sufficiently important to *deserve* its own name.

You can do ordinary lexical encoding systematically – for example, you could look at the words of an existing language and decide that you wanted counterparts for them in one of your native languages. Then it's just a matter of arranging sounds that are permitted and meaningful in that language to make the counterparts. But there is no way at all to search systematically for capital-E Encodings. They come to you out of nowhere and you realize that you have always needed them; but you can't go looking for them and they don't turn up as concrete entities neatly marked off for you and flashing NAME ME. They are therefore very precious.

(Chornyak Barren House, *Manual for Beginners*, p. 71)

Encodings in Láadan, a women's language

Appendix

From: A First Dictionary and Grammar of Láadan

A sampler from Láadan:

As is true in the translation from any language into another, many words of Láadan cannot be translated into English except by lengthy definitions. A miscellaneous sampling is given here to illustrate the situation; it consists mainly of samples from the 'ra-' prefixing forms of the language.

doóledosh: pain or loss which comes as a relief by virtue of ending the anticipation of its coming

doroledim: This word has no English equivalent whatsoever. Say you have an average woman. She has no control over her life. She has little or nothing in the way of a resource for being good to herself, even when it is necessary. She has family and animals and friends and associates that depend on her for sustenance of all kinds. She rarely has adequate sleep or rest; she has no time for herself, no space of her own, little or no money to buy things for herself, no opportunity to consider her own emotional needs. She is at the beck and call of others, because she has these responsibilities, and obligations, and does not choose to (or cannot) abandon them. For such a woman, the one and only thing she is likely to have a little control over for indulging her own self is FOOD. When such a woman overeats, the verb for that is 'doroledim'. (And then she feels guilty, because there are women whose children are starving and who do not have even THAT option for self-indulgence ...)

lowitheláad: to feel, as if directly, another's pain/grief/surprise/joy/ anger

núháam: to feel oneself cherished, cared for, nurtured by someone; to feel loving-kindness

óothanúthul: spiritual orphanhood; being utterly without a spiritual community or family

ráahedethi: to be unable to feel lowitheláad, above; to be empathically impaired

ráahedethilh: to be unwilling to feel lowitheláad, above; to be empathically impaired

ráahedethilh: to be musically or euphonically deprived

radama: to non-touch, to actively refrain from touching

radamalh: to non-touch with evil intent

radéela: non-garden, a place that has much flash and glitter and ornament, but no beauty

radíidin: non-holiday, a time allegedly a holiday but actually so much a burden because of work and preparations that it is a dreaded occasion; especially when there are too many guests and none of them help

radodelh: non-interface, a situation which has not one single point in common on which to base interaction, often used of personal relationships

raduth: to non-use, to deliberately deprive someone of any useful function in the world, as in enforced retirement or when a human being is kept as a plaything or a pet

rahéena: non-heart-sibling, one so entirely incompatible with another that there is no hope of ever achieving any kind of understanding or anything more than a truce, and no hope of ever making such a one understand why ... does not mean 'enemy'

rahobeth: non-neighbour, one who lives nearby but does not fulfil a neighbour's role; not necessarily pejorative

rahom: to non-teach, to deliberately fill students' minds with empty data or false information; can be used only of persons in a teacher/student relationship

ralaheb: something utterly spiceless, 'like warm spit', repulsively bland and blah

ralée-: non-meta (a prefix), something absurdly or dangerously narrow in scope or range

ralith: to deliberately refrain from thinking about something, to wall it off in one's mind by deliberate act

ralorolo: non-thunder, much talk and commotion from one (or more) with no real knowledge of what they're talking about or trying to do, something like 'hot air' but more so

ramime: to refrain from asking, out of courtesy or kindness

ramimelh: to refrain from asking, with evil intent; especially when it is clear that someone badly wants the other to ask

ranem: non-pearl, an ugly thing one builds layer by layer as an oyster does a pearl, such as a festering hatred to which one pays attention

ranl: non-cup, a hollow accomplishment, something one acquires or receives or accomplishes but empty of all satisfaction

rarilh: to deliberately refrain from recording; for example, the failure throughout history to record the accomplishments of women

rarulh: non-synergy, that which when combined only makes things worse, less efficient, etc.

rashida: non-game, a cruel 'playing' that is a game only for the dominant 'players' with the power to force others to participate

rathom: non-pillow, one who lures another to trust and rely on them but has no intention of following through, a 'lean on me so I can step aside and let you fall' person

rathóo: non-guest, someone who comes to visit knowing perfectly well that they are intruding and causing difficulty

raweshalh: non-gestalt, a collection of parts with no relationship other than coincidence, a perverse choice of items to call a set; especially when used as 'evidence'

sháadehul: growth through transcendence, either of a person, a non-human, or thing (for example, an organization, or a city, or a sect)

wohosheni: a word meaning the opposite of alienation; to feel joined to, part of someone or something without reservations or barriers

wonewith: to be socially dyslexic; uncomprehending of the social signals of others

12

Extract from *Silences*

Tillie Olsen

Reprinted from T. Olsen, Silences *(London: Virago 1980).*

Exclusion: language itself

'Language itself, all achievement, anything to do with the human [cast] in exclusively male terms.'

> But 'glory' doesn't mean 'a nice knockdown argument,' Alice objected.
>
> When *I* use a word, Humpty Dumpty said in a rather scornful tone, it means just what I choose it to mean – neither more nor less.
>
> The question is, said Alice, whether you can make words mean so many different things?
>
> The question is, said Humpty Dumpty, who is to be master – that's all.
>
> (Lewis Carroll, *Through the Looking Glass*)

It is the saturation – the never ceasing, lifelong saturation.
Man. The poet: he (his). The writer: he (his).
No, not simply a matter of 'correct usage'; our inherited language; i.e., *man*, a generic term, defined as including, subsuming, woman, the entire human race.

The perpetuating – by continued usage – entrenched, centuries-old oppressive power realities, early on incorporated into language: male rule; male ownership; our secondariness; our *exclusion*.

In reading Auden ('The poet is the father who begets the poem'), the effort having to be made in us somewhere to include ourselves as writer also. The reinforcement to the 'ground of departure' attitudes: 'a *real* writer has balls – is male...'.

The unconscious, conscious harm (as well, as ill), to a woman – when writing of writing or writers or of oneself as poet, as writer – of having to refer to oneself, and to one's activity, as masculine. As Willa Cather: 'usually the young writer must have *his* affair with the external material *he* covets...'. Or as Denise Levertov, from 'The Poet in the World' :

> He picks up crystal buttons from the ocean floor
> Gills of the mind pulse in unfathomed water.
>
> In the infinite dictionary he discovers
> gold grains of sand....
>
> Blind to what he does not yet need,
> he feels his way over broken glass
> to the one stone that fits his palm....

Why is it so hard for us? So difficult to, naturally, state our presence in the 'she' 'hers' belonging to us?

(Precision of language – the writer's special tool and task. Exact to meaning.

Man, he, mankind – *only* if meaning: exclusively male.

Humanity (two more syllables) when meaning the human race. (Ascent of Humanity, not 'Ascent of Man'.) The individual (not he); the human being (not man); humankind (not mankind) – if that is what is meant. To write naturally: the poet, she; the writer, she – if the reference is to self, if that is what is meant.

The awkwardness (and often ridicule) if we try now to be accurate. To say: she/he; her/him; or the ungrammatical 'they' when referring to both-sex poets, writers, or a writing activity.)

Marks of centuries-old entrenched power realities. Measure of the heaviness of our task no longer to abide by them – to find and raise our various truths into truthful language.

13

Androcentrism in prescriptive grammar: singular 'they', sex-indefinite 'he', and 'he or she'[1]

Ann Bodine

Reprinted from Language in Society *4 (1975). Cambridge: Cambridge University Press*

Abstract

This paper demonstrates that prior to the beginning of the prescriptive grammar movement in English, singular 'they' was both accepted and widespread. It is argued that the prescriptive grammarians' attack on singular 'they' was socially motivated, and the specific reasons for their attack are discussed. By analogy with socially motivated changes in second-person pronouns in a variety of European languages, it is suggested that third-person usage will be affected by the current feminist opposition to sex-indefinite 'he' – particularly since the well-established alternative, singular 'they', has remained widespread in spoken English throughout the two and a half centuries of its 'official' proscription. Finally, the implications of changes in third-person singular, sex-indefinite pronouns for several issues of general interest within linguistics are explored.

Introduction

There has always been a tension between the descriptive and prescriptive functions of grammar. Currently, descriptive grammar is dominant among theorists, but prescriptive grammar is taught in the schools and exercises a range of social effects. The relations between the beginning of prescriptive grammar in English and a variety of social issues were extensively explored in the early decades of the twentieth century, culminating in the work of McKnight (1928) and Leonard (1929).

Since 1930, interest has shifted elsewhere and new treatment of the subject has usually been restricted to summaries of earlier research, in textbooks for students of linguistics or English. A notable exception is Visser's monumental work (1963), which includes much new material on prescriptive grammar. More typical is Bloomfield and Newmark's comprehensive summary (1967: 288–325). Bloomfield and Newmark discuss prescriptive grammar as the linguistic manifestation of rationalism, of neo-classicism, and of status anxiety accompanying changes in class structure. They also trace the indirect contributions (through the rise of the vernacular) to the origins of prescriptive grammar by such diverse forces as nationalism and the anti-Latinism of the protestant revolution. These writers all see the inception of the prescriptive grammar movement as a whole as having significant social and psychological causes and consequences, but the specific choices of the prescriptive grammarians are rarely explored and are therefore treated as unmotivated and arbitrary.

This paper focuses on one small segment of the content of prescriptive grammar and explores the social factors behind the particular prescriptions and proscriptions that have been offered. Such an approach is suggested by Labov (1972: 64–5 n. 10), who has called for detailed investigation of a single prescribed form in order to better understand the mechanisms of change in prestige forms. The present investigation differs from the work of the 1920s not only because of its focus on the motivation behind *specific* prescriptions, but also because it deals with the issue of androcentrism, which in the 1920s was apparently not discussed with regard to language, despite the attention to sex roles which was generated by the suffragists.

Because of the social significance of personal reference, personal pronouns are particularly susceptible to modification in response to social and ideological change. Two phases of attention to English third-person singular sex-indefinite pronouns are explored here: first, the prescriptive grammarians' attack on singular 'they' and 'he or she', which began at the end of the eighteenth century and continues today; second, the current feminist attack on sex-indefinite 'he' which began in force about 1970. Changes and possible changes in English third person singular pronouns are then compared with changes in second person singular pronouns in a variety of European languages. Finally, implications of change in English third person singular pronouns for several important linguistic issues are considered.

Singular 'they', sex-indefinite 'he', and 'he or she'

There is a tradition among some grammarians to lament the fact that English has no sex-indefinite pronoun for third person singular and to state categorically that the only course open is to use 'he' in sex-indefinite contexts. Other grammarians omit the lamentations but state just as categorically that 'he' is the English sex-indefinite pronoun. This matter has taken a new turn recently with the insistence of many feminists that 'he' should not be used when the referent includes women, and that speakers of English should find some substitute. The reaction to this demand has ranged from agreement, to disagreement, to ridicule, to horror, but invariably the feminists' demand is viewed as an attempt to alter the English language.

In fact, the converse is true. Intentionally or not, the movement against sex-indefinite 'he' is actually a counter-reaction to an attempt by prescriptive grammarians to alter the language. English has always had other linguistic devices for referring to sex-indefinite referents, notably, the use of the singular 'they' (their, them)[2] as in sentences 1 to 3.

1 Anyone can do it if they try hard enough. (mixed-sex, distributive)
2 Who dropped their ticket? (sex unknown)
3 Either Mary or John should bring a schedule with them. (mixed-sex, disjunctive)

This usage came under attack by prescriptive grammarians. However, despite almost two centuries of vigorous attempts to analyse and regulate it out of existence, singular 'they' is alive and well. Its survival is all the more remarkable considering that the weight of virtually the entire educational and publishing establishment has been behind the attempt to eradicate it.

Figures 1 and 2 show two different analyses of the English pronominal system; only nominative case is given, since the accusative and possessive pronouns have the same semantic ranges. Figure 1 represents the reality of the language – the pronominal system as developed and used by speakers of English, who have been striving for communicative effectiveness under a variety of social and cognitive pressures. Figure 2 represents the construct of early English grammarians (Aickin 1693: part II, 9–10; Buchanan 1762: 102–3; Collyer 1735: 21–4; Gildon & Brighton 1711: 77; Greaves 1594: 13–14; Kirby 1746: 56, 80; Lane 1700: 29; Lowth 1762: 31–5; Murray 1795:

Figure 1 English pronouns according to usage (Two significant features of Figure 1 are the extension of 'you', which will not be discussed here, and the extension of 'they', which is the subject of this paper. Personal pronominal usages not included in Figure 1 are 'it' when used of a baby, second person plural 'ya'll' or 'you all', and impersonal 'one'.)

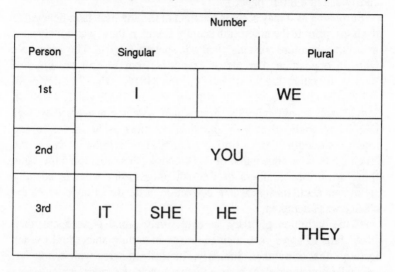

Figure 2 English pronouns according to traditional grammatical analysis

Person	Number		
	Singular		Plural
1st	I		WE
2nd	YOU		
3rd	IT	SHE	HE	THEY

29–31; Poole 1646: 7–8; Priestly 1761: 9–10; Saxon 1737: 48, 50; Wallis 1653: 97, 99; Ward 1765: 126, 349–52; Wharton 1654: 39–42), who were striving for tidy analysis under social and cognitive pressures peculiar to that small and unrepresentative subset of the English-speaking population. (One striking feature of Figure 1, the extension of the pronoun 'you' to first and third persons, falls outside the scope of this paper and is presented only so as not to falsify what, according to my best understanding, is the correct picture. This feature is to be considered in a future paper.)

Surprising as it may seem in the light of the attention later devoted to the issue, prior to the nineteenth century singular 'they' was widely used in written, therefore presumably also in spoken, English. This usage met with no opposition. Dozens of examples from several centuries of English literature are listed by Poutsma (1916: 310–12), McKnight (1925: 12–13; 1928: 197, 528–30), and Visser (1963: vol. I, 75–8). In formal analyses of the English pronominal system, however, 'they' was incorrectly analysed as only plural in meaning as in Figure 2, and nineteenth-century prescriptive grammarians tried to change the language to their conception of it. Of course, they attempted the same thing with vast numbers of English usages, but what is socially significant about this particular 'correction' is the direction in which the change was attempted.

If the definition of 'they' as exclusively plural is accepted, then 'they' fails to agree with a singular, sex-indefinite antecedent by one feature – that of number. Similarly, 'he' fails to agree with a singular, sex-indefinite antecedent by one feature – that of gender. A non-sexist 'correction' would have been to advocate 'he or she', but rather than encourage this usage the grammarians actually tried to eradicate it also, claiming 'he or she' is 'clumsy', 'pedantic', or 'unnecessary'. Significantly, they never attacked terms such as 'one or more' or 'person or persons', although the plural logically includes the singular more than the masculine includes the feminine. These two situations are linguistically analogous. In both cases the language user is confronted with an obligatory category, either number or sex, which is irrelevant to the message being transmitted. However, the two are not socially analogous, since number lacks social significance. Consequently, number and gender have received very different treatment by past and present prescriptive and descriptive grammarians of English. Of the three forms which existed in English for a sex-indefinite referent ('he or she', 'they', and 'he'), only one was selected as 'correct' while the other two were proscribed. Although the grammarians felt they were motivated by an interest in logic, accuracy, and elegance, the above analysis reveals that there is no rational, objective basis for their choice, and therefore the explanation must lie elsewhere. It would appear that their choice was dictated by an androcentric worldview; linguistically, human beings were to be considered male unless proven otherwise.

This principle has been resisted by speakers, and to a lesser extent by writers, of English. According to Leonard (1929: 225),

> [T]he minute attention to agreement, particularly of pronouns, had little effect on the writers of the period following; probably quite as many cases of reference of 'they' and 'their' to words like 'person' and 'one' and 'everybody' could be discovered in an equal number of pages of Jane Austen or Walter Scott and of Addison or Swift. And though the matter was brought to sharp focus and fully attended to by the critics of the succeeding period, there is good evidence that British usage is still about equally unfettered in the matter. The greater conservatism of American writers, as usual, has led them to follow this rule more carefully.

By 'conservatism' here Leonard does not mean avoidance of change and adherence to established pattern, since established pattern included singular 'they'. 'Conservatism' here means reliance on the authority of grammarians, which has been more characteristic of American writers and editors than of British writers and editors (McKnight 1925).

The advocacy by grammarians of English of the linguistic embodiment of an androcentric worldview was evident over two centuries before the invention of the proscription against singular 'they'. Wilson (1553) is one of the earliest to berate English language users who neglect to express linguistically the androcentric social order, for which Wilson claims the status of the 'natural' order.

> Some will set the Carte before the horse, as thus. My mother and my father are both at home, even as thoughe the good man of the house ware no breaches or that the graye Mare were the better Horse. And what thoughe it often so happeneth (God wotte the more pitte) yet in speaking at the leaste, let us kepe a natural order, and set the man before the woman for maners Sake.
>
> (Wilson 1560: 189; also in Mair edition 1909: 167)

Wilson elsewhere states the general principle to be followed with regard to the linguistic ordering of female and male as, 'the worthier is preferred and set before: As a man is sette before a woman' (1560: 234; also in Mair edition 1909: 208).

The same principle was repeated in the seventeenth century with reference to agreement of relative pronoun and antecedent.

The Relative agrees with the Antecedent in gender, number, and person.... The Relative shall agree in gender with the Antecedent of the more worthy gender: as, the King and the Queen whom I honor. The Masculine gender is more worthy than the Feminine.

(Poole 1646: 21)

Throughout the seventeenth and early eighteenth centuries English grammarians were sufficiently influenced by Latin grammar that the discussion of English syntax scarcely went beyond the Latin-derived Three Concords (subject and verb, substantive and adjective, relative pronoun and antecedent), with the above quotation from Poole being a restatement and discussion of the Third Concord. S. Saxon (1737) was among the first to enlarge upon the Three Concords, giving several distinct rules under each, as well as three additional Concords, each with their several rules, ending with a total of thirty-three distinct rules. But neither Poole nor S. Saxon, nor any grammarian of the intervening period whose work I have examined, specifically discusses agreement between personal pronouns and sex-indefinite antecedents. This is true despite the facts that, first, most of these grammarians include a version of the Third Concord among their syntactic rules and, second, until Ward (1765: 127) 'she, her, he, him' were often classed as relative pronouns. Thus, although androcentrism was present, it had not yet resulted in the proscription of singular 'they', which was still freely used along with 'he or she' and sex-indefinite 'he'.

Kirby (1746) continues the increase of syntactic rules, presenting eighty-eight rules, among which appears the earliest example I have found of the explicit advocacy of sex-indefinite 'he'. Rule 21: 'The masculine Person answers to the general Name, which comprehends both Male and Female; as Any Person, who knows what he says' (Kirby 1746: 117). Kirby has stopped referring to the masculine gender as the 'worthier' gender, but he substitutes the 'comprehensive' masculine for the 'worthy' masculine. One eighteenth-century grammarian explicitly denied the need for having an unmarked gender ('he'):

he must represent a male; *she* a female; and *it*, an object of no sex. ...But the plural *they* equally represents objects of all the three genders; for a plural object may consist of singular objects, some of which are masculine, others feminine, and others neuter; as, *a man and a woman and some iron were in the waggon, and they were all overturned....*

This frees the English, in a great measure, from the perplexity of such rules, as, 'The masculine gender is more worthy than the feminine....' These rules arise in the Latin and Greek, because the adjectives and possessive pronouns must agree, in grammatic gender, with the gender of the substantives to which they are applied; and when several substantives of different genders happen to denote a complex object, no one gender of an adjective or possessive pronoun, will suit those of such a series of substantives. And therefore neither the English adjectives, nor the plural personal, nor the plural possessive pronouns, have a distinction of gender.

(Ward 1765: 459–60)

The comprehensiveness and huge size (554 pages) of Ward's work make it unlikely that he overlooked prohibitions which were considered important by his contemporaries. Rather it would appear that Kirby's and Ward's contemporaries had not yet applied the concept of the preferential masculine to personal pronouns and that Kirby's Rule 21 is best viewed as an unusually early and very incipient form of the attack on singular 'they'.

Murray (1795) sets the tone for this attack, presenting the first 'false syntax' examples I have found for singular 'they':

RULE V. Pronouns must always agree with their antecedents, and the nouns for which they stand, in gender, number, and person, ...Of this rule there are many violations. '*Each* of the sexes should keep within *its* particular bounds, and content *themselves* with the advantages of *their* particular districts.' 'Can any one, on their entrance into the world, be fully secure that they shall not be deceived?' 'on *his* entrance,' and 'that *he* shall.' 'Let each esteem others better than themselves;' 'than *himself*'.

(Murray 1795: 95–6)

Later authors expanded their sections on the 'false syntax' of singular 'they' up to several pages.

This virtual explosion of condemnation of singular 'they' culminated in an Act of Parliament in 1850, which legally replaced 'he or she' with 'he'. The act clearly reveals a recognition that specification of both gender (for pronouns) and number (for pronouns and concrete nouns) is obligatory in English, even when such information is irrelevant to the communication. However, when the precision is unneeded it is disposed

173

of quite differently for number, which has no social significance, than for gender. Whereas unnecessary number is to be dispensed with by the arbitrary choice of either the singular *or* plural, unnecessary gender is to be dispensed with by the use of the masculine *only*.

An Act for shortening the language used in acts of Parliament...in all acts words importing the masculine gender shall be deemed and taken to include females, and the singular to include the plural, and the plural the singular, unless the contrary as to gender and number is expressly provided.

(cited in Evans and Evans 1957: 221).

Similarly, Kirby's Rule 21, cited above (p. 172), that the masculine comprehends both male and female, is immediately followed (Rule 22) by the *equation* of singular and plural, under certain circumstances, so that either may represent the other. Thus, in Rule 22 Kirby equates 'The Life of Men' and 'The Lives of Men' (1746: 117).

Thus, the 1850 Act of Parliament and Kirby's Rules 21–2 manifest their underlying androcentric values and worldview in two ways. First, linguistically analogous phenomena (number and gender) are handled very differently (singular *or* plural as generic vs masculine *only* as generic). Second, the precept just being established is itself violated in not allowing singular 'they', since if the plural 'shall be deemed and taken' to include the singular, then surely 'they' includes 'she' and 'he', and 'she or he'.

This special pleading for sex-indefinite 'he' was no less strong in America than in Britain, as may be seen in the following quotation from an American prescriptive grammarian.

Their is very commonly misused with reference to a singular noun. Even John Ruskin has written such a sentence as this: 'But if a *customer* wishes you to injure *their* foot or to disfigure it, you are to refuse *their* pleasure.' How Mr Ruskin could have written such a sentence as that (for plainly there is no slip of the pen or result of imperfect interlinear correction in it), or how, it having been written, it could be passed by an intelligent proof-reader, I cannot surmise. It is, perhaps, an exemplification of the straits to which we are driven by the lack of a pronoun of common gender meaning both he and she, his and her. But, admitting this lack, the fact remains that *his* is the representative pronoun, as *mankind* includes both men and women. Mr Ruskin might better have said, 'If a customer wishes you to injure his foot you are to refuse his pleasure.' To use 'his or her' in cases of this kind seems to me very finical and pedantic.

(White 1880: 416)

Another quotation from White shows his clear recognition of the social implications of grammar:

MARRY. – There has been not a little discussion as to the use of this word, chiefly in regard to public announcements of marriage. The usual mode of making the announcement is – Married, John Smith to Mary Jones; Some people having been dissatisfied with this form, we have seen, of late years, in certain quarters – Married, John Smith with Mary Jones; and in others – John Smith and Mary Jones. I have no hesitation in saying that all of these forms are incorrect. We know, indeed, what is meant by any one of them; but the same is true of hundreds and thousands of erroneous uses of language. Properly speaking, a man is not married to a woman, or married with her; nor are a man and a woman married with each other. The woman is married to the man. It is her name that is lost in his, not his in hers; she becomes a member of his family, not he of hers; it is her life that is merged, or supposed to be merged, in his, not his in hers; she follows his fortunes, and takes his station, not he hers. And thus, manifestly, she has been attached to him by a legal bond, not he to her; except, indeed, as all attachment is necessarily mutual. But, nevertheless, we do not speak of tying a ship to a boat, but a boat to a ship. And so long, at least, as man is the larger, the stronger, the more individually important, as long as woman generally lives in her husband's house and bears his name, – still more should she not bear his name, – it is the woman who is married to the man.

(1886: 139–40)

Steinbach cites White's writing as an example of 'the highly entertaining manner in which some rhetoricians teach accuracy of expression' (1930: 456). It might be more entertaining if it were definitely a thing of the past. However, as will be shown below (pp. 177–9) in the survey of present-day high school textbooks, it is not.

Although in the nineteenth and twentieth centuries the masculine gender was generally no longer championed as the 'worthier' gender, there has remained an underlying realization of the social implications of sex-indefinite 'he'. Fowler (1926) refers to the views of the scholar Whately, archbishop of Dublin in the early nineteenth century, concerning the use of singular (distributive) 'they': 'Archbishop Whately used to say that women were more liable than men to fall into this error, as they objected to identifying "everybody" with "him"' (p. 635). Fowler himself mentions, but dismisses with a joke, the possibility that the grammarians' invention and perpetuation of the proscription against singular 'they' constitutes a social injustice.

[The use of sex-indefinite 'he'] involves the convention (statutory in the interpretation of documents) that where the matter of sex is not conspicuous or important the masculine form shall be allowed to represent a person instead of a man, or say a man (homo) instead of a man (vir). Whether that convention, with *himself or herself* in the background for especial exactitudes, and paraphrase always possible in dubious cases, is an arrogant demand on the part of male England, everyone must decide for himself (or for himself or herself, or for themselves).

(Fowler 1926: 404)

Curme (1931: 552) considers the possibility that sex-indefinite 'he' is 'one sided', but then invokes 'the idea of the oneness of man and woman [which] is present to our feeling' as the basis for the generic use of the masculine. A linguist in Sterling A. Leonard's jury-based study[3] of current English usage rejects 'Each person should of course bear *his or her* share of the expense', on the basis that 'I prefer simply *his*. This seems to be a matter of pleasing the women' (cited in Leonard 1932: 103). Unlike these earlier commentators McCawley (1974: 103) sees no need to defend the equation of 'he' with 'person'. So unquestioningly does McCawley accept this equation that he claims that sex-indefinite 'he' carries no overtones of its primary, masculine meaning if it is used consistently in sex-indefinite contexts. On this basis McCawley further implies that the phrase 'he or she' is sexist in that it 'makes women a special category of beings' by mentioning them in addition to 'people' (i.e., 'he').

The changed social climate and the dispassionate tone in which textbooks are written today make it virtually impossible that any textbook writer in the second half of the twentieth century could make as explicitly androcentric a statement as, for instance, the tirade by White, the nineteenth-century American prescriptive grammarian quoted at length above (p. 175).

To determine how the issue is taught today I surveyed thirty-three of the school grammars now being used in American junior and senior high schools. Twenty-eight of these books (Blumenthal and Warriner 1964, grades 9, 10, 11, 12; Brooks and Warren 1958; Christ 1961, grades 7, 8, 9, 10; Conlin and Herman 1965, books 1, 2, 3; Greene, Loomis, Davis and Beidenharn 1965, grades 8, 9, 10; Haag 1965–8, books 1, 2, 3, 4; Roberts 1967; Rogers and Stewart 1967, grades 9, 10, 11, 12; Tressler, Christ and Starkey 1960, books 1, 2, 3, 4) condemn both 'he or she' and singular 'they', the former because it is clumsy and the latter because it is inaccurate. And then the pupils are taught to achieve both elegance of expression and accuracy by referring to women as 'he'. One of the modern textbook writers does show his awareness and approval of the hierarchy implied by the use of sex-indefinite 'he', when he tells children not to use 'he or she', which is 'awkward', but instead to follow the convention that 'grammatically, men are more important than women' (Roberts 1967: 355).

Most of the modern textbook writers, like most of the early prescriptive grammarians, give no such explicitly androcentric justification for prescribing sex-indefinite 'he', but instead argue that sex-indefinite 'he' is 'correct', whereas singular 'they' is 'inaccurate' and 'he or she' is 'awkward'. However, the line of argument developed in connection with the prescriptive grammarians is equally applicable here. That is, disagreement of number, as in the proscribed singular 'they', is no more 'inaccurate' than disagreement of gender, as in the unproscribed sex-indefinite 'he'. Similarly, the proscribed 'he or she' is no more 'clumsy' than the unproscribed 'one or more' and 'person or persons'. Thus, these writers appear to be the docile heirs to the androcentric tradition of the prescriptive grammarians, failing to confront, if not implicitly subscribing to, the androcentric motive.

The fact that the controversy over singular 'they' has anything to do with sex seems to have escaped the notice of today's textbook writers, or if they have noticed, they are not letting the kids in on it. Twenty-five of the above twenty-eight textbooks tell students that the reason 'they' is 'mistakenly' used for a singular antecedent is that the antecedent has a plural meaning. This is obviously an inadequate explanation, since 'they' is used for antecedents with both plural and singular meaning, as may be seen in the following sentences, collected by the author from the ordinary conversation of native speakers of American English holding bachelors, masters, and doctoral degrees.

4 Did everyone say they missed you like mad yesterday?
5 Somebody left their sweater.

6 Not one single child raised their hand.
7 When you call on a student, it's better if you can remember their name.

In 4, the antecedent of 'they' has a plural meaning, but the antecedents of 'they' in 5, 6, and 7 are clearly singular. Notice particularly 6 and 7. If the subjects were perceived as plural, surely the speakers would have said 'their hands' and 'their names' rather than 'their hand' and 'their name'.

Of all twenty-eight school grammars reviewed, only three gave children an adequate explanation of the use of 'they'. Although still condemning the use of 'they' in this manner, these three textbooks did give a socially and psychologically realistic assessment of why it is done. One of these realistic textbooks says, 'the pronoun *his* would apply equally to a man or to a woman. Nevertheless some people feel awkward about using *his* to refer to a woman and instead use *their*' (Blumenthal and Warriner 1964: 139). Blumenthal and Warriner then say this is unacceptable, at least in writing, and they also advise against the use of 'he or she' because it is 'clumsy'. The second of the realistic textbooks has more to say.

> English has a problem in that it has no common gender [in the third person singular].... The most awkward solution is to use both the masculine and the feminine pronoun: 'Everyone should raise his (or her) hand when he (or she) is ready.' We usually try to avoid this by following the convention that, grammatically, men are more important than women. For reference to mixed groups, we use just the pronoun *he*. 'Everyone should raise *his* hand when *he* is ready.'
>
> (Roberts 1967: 354–5)

Roberts's next suggestion has been offered by numerous grammarians from the nineteenth century right up to writers of textbooks now being used in the schools. They say, in effect, that if you cannot bring yourself to use 'he' for women then do not use a singular subject at all, but go back and start the sentence over again with a plural subject. 'Sometimes we avoid the issue by pluralizing the noun phrase to which the pronoun refers. "All the boys and girls should raise their hands when they are ready "' (1967: 355).

Actually, this advice to start the sentence over again with a clearly plural subject is a necessary escape, because some of the grammarians unable to see the frequent singular semantic content of the word 'they' are apparently equally unable to see the frequent plural semantic content of words like 'everyone' and 'everybody', for example, sentence 4. Sentence 8 was written by a 12-year-old boy in a school composition describing a dunking by a group of classmates; it is cited as an example of hypercorrection by Leonard (1929: 224 n. 57).

8   When I came up, everybody was laughing at me, but I was glad to see him just the same.

None of the modern textbook writers reviewed went quite so far as to recommend sentences like 8, but they did go so far as to condemn the use of 'them' even in a sentence like 8. Sentence 9 was given as an example of bad grammar in one textbook.

9   Everyone in the class worried about the midyear history examination, but they all passed (Tressler, Christ, and Starkey 1960; book 4: 343).

Tressler *et al.* could not quite bring themselves to recommend 'Everyone in the class worried about the midyear history examination, but *he* all passed', so they told the pupils to rewrite the sentence, 'The class members worried about the midyear history examination, but they all passed.'

The effect on actual written and spoken usage of the movement to eradicate 'he or she' and singular 'they' is complex. The continuing attack of textbook writers and teachers indicates that both forms are still very much a part of American English. On the other hand, the counter-attack on sex-indefinite 'he' by feminists indicates that sex-indefinite 'he' is also widely used.

The most clear-cut success of the movement to eradicate singular 'they' has been the near-universality of agreement in *discussions about* English, as opposed to its actual usage, that 'they' can not have singular meaning. A notable exception to the acceptance of the traditional analysis of English third person pronouns is Key (1972: 27–8). Key lists eight instances of lack of agreement of usage with the traditional analysis and implies that more may be found. Key's examples differ from those being discussed in this paper in that all are in some way special – non-native speakers, homosexuals, small children, humour – whereas this discussion concerns ordinary usage.

The persistence for almost two centuries of the original movement to eradicate 'he or she' and singular 'they' suggests that the counter-movement against sex-indefinite 'he' is unlikely to disappear.

Furthermore, since the countermovement has more explicit social and ideological buttresses as well as a larger number of supporters than the original movement had at its inception, it is reasonable to predict that the countermovement against sex-indefinite 'he' will affect English pronominal usage. Therefore, during the next few years students of language development may have the opportunity to follow the progress of a particularly visible type of language change.

Of course it is possible that the pronominal changes foreseen by this writer will not come to pass, and contrary predictions have indeed been made. For instance, Lakoff has suggested that the current feminist attack on sex-indefinite 'he' is misguided, since 'an attempt to change pronominal usage will be futile' (1973: 75). Conklin (1973) has also expressed doubt as to whether 'so stable a portion of language as the pronominal system will yield to change'. These writers do not recognize how widespread the use of singular 'they' is at present and they also tend to see the pronominal system as a categorical given. However, looking at the wider context of language change in general, it can be seen that pronominal systems are particularly susceptible to alteration in response to social change.

Comparison with changes in second person pronouns

The spread of the ideology of feudalism caused most European languages to develop two sets of second person singular pronouns, for the representation of hierarchy (Brown and Gilman 1960: 254–5; Jesperson 1938: 223–4). In both English and Russian this change came about by a process analogous to the inclusion of singularity in the pronoun 'they', i.e., the plural pronouns (English 'ye–you', Russian 'vy') were extended to include singularity. This resulted in two sets of second-person singular pronouns: English 'thou–thee' (nominative and accusative) and Russian 'ty' for an inferior or an intimate vs English 'ye–you' (nominative and accusative) and Russian 'vy' for a superior or a non-intimate (Brown and Gilman 1960; Friedrich 1966; Rendon 1973; Sampson 1973). Later, under the pressure of social structural changes and the beginnings of egalitarian ideology, English's second person singular pronouns contracted to a single word. More recently, second person pronouns have been undergoing change in a number of other European languages – French, German, Italian (Brown and Gilman 1960), Serbo-Croatian (Kocher 1967), and Swedish (Paulston 1971; Paulston and Featheringham 1974).[4]

These analyses of change in second-person pronoun usage rank among the most convincing demonstrations ever given of the social motivation of linguistic change. Their importance for linguistics is that they show the futility of attempting to explain language change as taking place on an autonomous linguistic level. Their importance for sociology is indicated by Grimshaw: 'I don't see how any sociologist could read the piece by Friedrich on Russian pronominal usage... without being persuaded of the imperative necessity of incorporating a sociolinguistic dimension into sociological research and theory' (1974: 5).

Implications

Careful observation of change in English pronominal usage could contribute to our understanding of a number of issues of general importance within linguistics including (*a*) continuing linguistic enculturation, (*b*) conscious vs unconscious change, and (*c*) compensatory adjustment within the linguistic system.

(*a*) The only aspect of post-childhood linguistic enculturation which has received much attention is vocabulary learning. Grimshaw is foremost among scholars calling for a broad investigation of all kinds of later language learning. He states,

> studies of language acquisition – like their companion studies of socialization done by sociologists – frequently tend...to ignore continuing linguistic and other socialization. I have recently had occasion to try and find out what is known about continuing language and other socialization of older adolescents and young adults. The answer thus far seems to be 'very little'.
>
> (1973: 584)

Because the particular language forms under discussion here have ties with age-related concerns and awareness they are a likely source of information on continuing language acquisition. No stable age differentiation is predicted, however, since as feminists grow older they are unlikely to return to the pronominal usage, sex-indefinite 'he', which they have rejected.

(*b*) Much of the writing on language change prior to 1960 pictures language change as slow, inexorable, unconscious, largely unmotivated drifting within free variation. Although sound change is still far from understood, the last dozen years of work by Labov and his followers have clearly demonstrated that free variation is not so free and sound change is not so unmotivated nor always so unconscious. The same has been documented for morphology and syntax by Rubin, who concludes,

> On the basis of the already reported cases, it seems reasonable to presume that any aspect of the language code or language usage is susceptible to conscious change provided that the necessary motivation and proper field for implementation exists.
>
> (1972: 8)

And, 'From the above examples, we can see that language structure has been molded deliberately to serve a number of different motivations, ranging from purely communicative to purely socio-political' (1972: 10).

Although the extent to which a speech community's members talk about talking varies from culture to culture, and between individuals within any single culture (Hymes 1961), most communities promote sufficient leisure, introspection, and argumentation to assure that differential acceptance and promotion of linguistic forms will play some role in lexical and grammatical change. As English pronominal usage is increasingly affected by the feminist countermovement discussed in this paper, it will provide an ideal opportunity to study differences in language change among those who make a conscious decision and deliberate effort to change, among those who are aware that the change is taking place but have no particular interest in the issue, among those who are oblivious to the change, and among those who are consciously resisting the change.

(*c*)   It is rare that linguists have the opportunity to analyse changes and adjustments in the relatively tightly structured pronominal system of a language at the very time when the systematic change is taking place. Such an opportunity is now being continuously exploited for Swedish second person pronouns by Paulston (1971: Paulston and Featheringham 1974) who is consequently able to provide an unusually complete record and analysis of the change. Baseline description of present day English third person pronominal usage coupled with continual monitoring of usage trends offers another such opportunity for the detailed investigation of systematic change in progress.

In most instances of multiple, related language changes it is impossible to extricate from the near-simultaneous changes what is cause and what is effect, especially when the changes are studied after the fact. However, if change (for example, the pronominal change discussed here) is anticipated, or detected at its inception, it should be possible to hypothesize about areas of language in which compensatory adjustments might take place (for example, a general weakening of number concord, for which there is no particular social pressure) and to subject those areas of potential instability to continuing observation.

Conclusion

Personal reference, including personal pronouns, is one of the most socially significant aspects of language. As such, it is particularly likely to become the target of deliberate efforts to bring symbolic representation of interpersonal relations into line with the way those relationships are structured in either the ideal or behavioural patterning of the members of a speech community. With the increase of opposition to sex-based hierarchy, the structure of English third person pronouns may be expected to change to reflect the new ideology and social practices, as second person pronouns did before them. Analysis of the processes and results of this change can further elucidate the contributions of social forces to language development.

Notes

1 Portions of this paper were presented at the Conference on Women and Language, Rutgers University, New Brunswick, New Jersey, April 1973 and at the 1973 Summer Meeting of the Linguistic Society of America. I am grateful to Adele Abrahamson, Dell Hymes, and Albert Marckwardt for valuable criticism. Helpful comments were also received from Nancy Bonvillain, Susan Davis, Anne Foner, Marilyn Johnson, Michael Moffatt, Gloria Nemerowicz, and Ann Parelius.

2 It is generally felt that there are constraints on the occurrence of singular 'they' such that singular 'they' can not be used for he/she indiscriminately, but only with distributive quantifiers: any, every, each, and the general 'a'. Although these are the contexts in which singular 'they' most commonly occurs, more recent research (Bodine 1974) indicates that singular 'they' can occur in all four contexts in which a singular, sex-indefinite third person pronoun is required in English, namely *a* mixed-sex, distributive; *b* mixed-sex, disjunctive; *c* sex-unknown; and *d* sex-concealed.

3 A panel of linguists, editors, writers, etc. was asked to vote on the acceptability of disputed English usages.

4 As thorough and insightful as these papers are with regard to manifestations of 'power and solidarity' in second person pronouns, the writers do not appear to notice analogous manifestations of sex-related 'power and solidarity', even in their own language use. For example, 'a *man's* consistent pronoun style gives away *his* class status and *his* political view' (Brown and Gilman 1960: 276),

emphasis added. 'The fact that the pronoun which is being extended to all *men* alike is T, the mark of solidarity, the pronoun of the nuclear family, expresses the radical's intention to extend *his* sense of *brotherhood*' (Brown and Gilman 1960: 276), emphasis added. To one who is, in 1974, investigating the linguistic manifestations of androcentrism, the above quotations seem ironically myopic. Of course, such a reaction is the result of a consciousness which had not been developed in 1960. A dozen years later consciousness of sex role hierarchy was well developed. Therefore, it is even more startling to find a writer such as Gouldner, who stands out among sociologists for the strength of his claims that language reflects and moulds social perception and social reality, to still be blind to *sex-related* 'ideological uses of ordinary languages and of the interests that these obscure and conceal', as shown in the following quotations (emphasis added), 'Rational theorizing means...dialectic and dialogue among committed *men* joined in a common-language-speaking community' (Gouldner 1972: 13). 'The manner in which...other forces mold *men's* behavior is not always known to them, partly because they simply may not have ways of perceiving them, given the ordinary languages with which they relate to the world' (1972: 14). 'It is essentially the task of social theory, and the social sciences more generally, to create new and "extraordinary" languages, to help *men* learn to speak them, and to mediate between the deficient understandings of ordinary language and the different and liberating perspectives of the extra-ordinary languages of social theory.... To say social theorists are concept-creators means that they are not merely in the knowledge-creating business, but also in the language-reform and language-creating business' (1972: 15–16). 'Social theory provides... an extraordinary language with which *men* can become aware of the ideological uses of ordinary languages and of the interests that these obscure and conceal' (1972: 54).

References

Aicken, J. (1693) *The English grammar*, Menston: Scolar Press Facsimile.

Bloomfield, M. and Newmark. L. (1967) *A Linguistic Introduction to the History of English*, New York: Alfred A. Knopf, Ch. VII.

Blumenthal, J. and Warriner, J. (1964) *English Workshop, Grades 9, 10, 11, 12*, New York: Harcourt, Brace and World.

Bodine, A. (1974) 'English third person pronouns', paper read at the 73rd Annual Meeting of the American Anthropological Association, Mexico City.

Brooks, C. and Warren, R. P. (1958) *Modern Rhetoric*, New York: Harcourt, Brace and World.

Brown, R. and Gilman, A. (1960) 'The pronouns of power and solidarity', in T. Sebeok (ed.) *Style in Language*, Cambridge, Mass.: M I T Press, 253–76.

Buchanan, J. (1762) *The British Grammar*, Menston: Scolar Press Facsimile.

Christ, H. (1961) *Heath Handbook of English, Grades 7, 8, 9, 10*, Boston: Heath.

Collyer, J. (1735) *The General Principles of Grammar*, Menston: Scolar Press Facsimile.

Conklin, N. F. (1973) 'Perspectives on the dialects of women', presented at the 1973 meeting of the American Dialect Society, Ann Arbor.

Conlin, D. and Herman, G. (1965) *Modern Grammar and Composition*, books 1, 2, 3, New York: American Book Co.

Curme, G. O. (1931) *A Grammar of the English Language*, vol. III (Syntax), Boston: D. C. Heath.

Evans, B. and Evans, C. (1957) *A Dictionary of Contemporary American Usage*, New York: Random House.

Fowler, H. W. (1926) *A Dictionary of Modern English Usage*, 2nd revised edn, 1965, New York: Oxford University Press.

Friedrich, P. (1966) 'Structural implications of Russian pronominal usage', in W. Bright (ed.), *Sociolinguistics: Proceedings of the UCLA Sociolinguistic Conference, 1964*, The Hague: Mouton.

Gildon, C. and Brighton, J. (1711) *A Grammar of the English Tongue*. Menston: Scolar Press Facsimile.

Gouldner, A. (1972) 'The politics of the mind', *Social Policy* 2 no. 6: 5–58.

Greaves, P. (1594) *Grammatica Anglicana*, Menston: Scolar Press Facsimile.

Greene, H. A., Loomis, K. A., Davis, P. C., and Biedenharn, N. W. (1965) *Building Better English, Grades 8, 9, 10*, New York: Harper and Row.

Grimshaw, A. D. (1973–4) 'On language and society: parts I and II', *Contemporary Society* 2 no. 6: 575–83; 3 no. 1: 3–11.

Haag, L. (1965–8) *Guidebook to Better English*, books 1, 2, 3, 4, Oklahoma City: Educational Guidelines Co.

Hymes, D. (1961) 'Linguistic aspects of cross-cultural personality study', in B. Kaplan (ed.), *Studying Personality Cross-Culturally*, New York: Harper and Row: 313–60.

Jesperson, O. (1938) *Growth and Structure of the English Language* (1968 edn), New York: Free Press.

Key, M. R. (1972) 'Linguistic behavior of male and female', *Linguistics* 88: 15–31.

Kirby, J. (1746) *A New English Grammar*, Menston: Scolar Press Facsimile.

Kocher, M. (1967) 'Second person pronouns in Serbo-Croatian', *Language* 43: 725–41.

Labov, W. (1972) *Sociolinguistic Patterns*, Philadelphia: University of Pennsylvania Press.

Lakoff, R. (1973) 'Language and woman's place', *Language in Society* 2: 45–79.

Lane, A. (1700) *A Key to the Art of Letters*, Menston: Scolar Press Facsimile.

Leonard, S. A. (1929) *The Doctrine of Correctness in English Usage, 1700–1800*, Madison: University of Wisconsin Studies in Language and Literature.

——(1932) *Current English Usage*, Chicago: Inland Press.

Lowth, R. (1762) *A Short Introduction to English Grammar*, Menston: Scolar Press Facsimile.

McCawley, J. (1974) Letter to the editor, *New York Times* Magazine, 10 November.

McKnight, G. H. (1925) 'Conservatism in American speech', *American Speech* 1: 1–17.

——(1928), *Modern English in the Making*, New York: Appleton and Company.

Murray, L. (1795) *English Grammar*, Menston: Scolar Press Facsimile.

Paulston, C. B. (1971) 'Language universals and socio-cultural implications in usage: personal questions in Swedish', paper read at the 46th Annual Meeting of the Linguistic Society of America, St Louis.

Paulston, C. B. and Featheringham, T. R. (1974) 'Language and social class: pronouns of address in Swedish', paper read at the 49th Annual Meeting of the Linguistic Society of America, New York.

Poole, J. (1646) *The English Accidence*, Menston: Scolar Press Facsimile.

Poutsma, H. (1916) *A Grammar of Late Modern English*, Groningen: P. Noordhoof.

Priestly, J. (1761) *The Rudiments of English Grammar*, Menston: Scolar Press Facsimile.

Rendon, B. (1973) '"Tu" and "vous": pronominal usage in French literature', paper presented at the 35th Summer Meeting of the Linguistic Society of America, Ann Arbor.

Roberts, P. (1967) *The Roberts English Series*, New York: Harcourt, Brace and World.

Rogers, R. and Stewart, P. (1967) *Keys to English Mastery, Grades 9, 10, 11, 12*, Oklahoma City: The Economy Co.

Rubin, J. (1972) 'Language planning offers new insights into the nature of language change', paper presented at the 71st Annual Meeting of the American Anthropological Association, Toronto.

Sampson, G. P. (1973) 'Sociolinguistic aspects of pronoun usage in Middle English', paper presented at the IXth International Congress of Anthropological and Ethnological Sciences, Chicago.

Saxon, S. (1737) *The English Scholar's Assistant*, Menston: Scolar Press Facsimile.

Tressler, J. C., Christ, H. I., and Starkey, M. (1960) *English in Action* books 1, 2, 3, 4, Lexington, Mass.: Heath.

Visser, F. Th, (1963) *An Historical Syntax of the English Language*, Leiden: E. J. Brill.

Wallis, J. (1653) *Grammatica Lingvae Anglicanae*, translated by J. A. Kemp (1972), London: Longman.

Ward, W. (1765) *An Essay on Grammar*, Menston: Scolar Press Facsimile.

Wharton, J. (1654) *The English Grammar*, Menston: Scolar Press Facsimile.

White, R. G. (1880) *Everyday English*, Boston: Houghton, Mifflin and Company.

——(1886) *Words and Their Uses*, Boston: Houghton, Mifflin and Company.

Wilson, T. (1553) *Arte of Rhetorique*, Gainsville: Scholars Facsimiles and Reprints, 1962. Also, Mair edition (1909), Oxford: Clarendon Press.

14

A person paper on purity in language

William Satire (alias Douglas Hofstadter)

Reprinted from D. Hofstadter, Metamagical Themas *(New York: Basic Books 1985; Harmondsworth: Penguin 1986)*

September 1983

It's high time someone blew the whistle on all the silly prattle about revamping our language to suit the purposes of certain political fanatics. You know what I'm talking about – those who accuse speakers of English of what they call 'racism'. This awkward neologism, constructed by analogy with the well-established term 'sexism', does not sit well in the ears, if I may mix my metaphors. But let us grant that in our society there may be injustices here and there in the treatment of either race from time to time, and let us even grant these people their terms 'racism' and 'racist'. How valid, however, are the claims of the self-proclaimed 'Black libbers', or 'Negrists' – those who would radically change our language in order to 'liberate' us poor dupes from its supposed racist bias?

Most of the clamour, as you certainly know by now, revolves around the age-old usage of the noun 'white' and words built from it, such as *chairwhite, mailwhite, repairwhite, clergywhite, middlewhite, Frenchwhite, forewhite, whitepower, whiteslaughter, oneupswhiteship, straw white, whitehandle,* and so on. The Negrists claim that using the word 'white', either on its own or as a component, to talk about *all* the members of the human species is somehow degrading to blacks and reinforces racism. Therefore the libbers propose that we substitute 'person' everywhere where 'white' now occurs. Sensitive speakers of our secretary tongue of course find this preposterous. There is great beauty to a phrase such as 'All whites are created equal.' Our forebosses who framed the Declaration of Independence well understood the poetry of our language. Think how ugly it would be to say 'All persons are created equal', or 'All whites and blacks are created equal.' Besides, as any schoolwhitey can tell you, such phrases are redundant. In most contexts, it is self-evident when 'white' is being used in an inclusive sense, in which case it subsumes members of the darker race just as much as fairskins.

There is nothing denigrating to black people in being subsumed under the rubric 'white' – no more than under the rubric 'person'. After all, white is a mixture of all the colours of the rainbow, including black. Used inclusively, the word 'white' has no connotations whatsoever of race. Yet many people are hung up on this point. A prime example is Abraham Moses, one of the more vocal spokeswhites for making such a shift. For years, Niss Moses, authoroon of the well-known Negrist tracts *A Handbook of Nonracist Writing* and *Words and Blacks*, has had nothing better to do than go around the country making speeches advocating the downfall of 'racist language' that ble objects to. But when you analyse bler objections, you find they all fall apart at the seams. Niss Moses says that words like 'chairwhite' suggest to people – most especially impressionable young whiteys and blackeys – that all chairwhites belong to the white race. How absurd! It is quite obvious, for instance, that the chairwhite of the League of Black Voters is going to be a black, not a white. Nobody need think twice about it. As a matter of fact, the suffix 'white' is usually not pronounced with a long 'i' as in the noun 'white', but like 'wit', as in the terms *saleswhite, freshwhite, penwhiteship, first basewhite*, and so on. It's just a simple and useful component in building race-neutral words.

But Niss Moses would have you sit up and start hollering 'Racism!' In fact, Niss Moses sees evidence of racism under every stone. Ble has written a famous article, in which ble vehemently objects to the immortal and poetic words of the first white on the moon, Captain Nellie Strongarm. If you will recall, whis words were: 'One small step for a white, a giant step for whitekind.' This noble sentiment is anything but racist; it is simply a celebration of a glorious moment in the history of White.

Another of Niss Moses's shrill objections is to the age-old differentiation of whites from blacks by the third-person pronouns 'whe' and 'ble'. Ble promotes an absurd notion: that what we really need in English is a single pronoun covering *both* races. Numerous suggestions have been made, such as 'pe', 'tey', and others. These are all repugnant to the nature of the English language, as the average white in the street will testify, even if whe has no linguistic training whatsoever. Then there are advocates of usages such as 'whe or ble', 'whis or bler', and so forth. This makes for monstrosities such as the sentence 'When the next President takes office, whe or ble will have to choose whis or bler cabinet with great care, for whe or ble would not want to offend any minorities.' Contrast this with the spare elegance of the normal way of putting it, and there is no question which way we ought to speak. There are, of course, some yapping black libbers who advocate writing 'bl/whe' everywhere, which, aside from looking terrible, has no reasonable pronunciation. Shall we say 'blooey' all the time when we simply mean 'whe'? Who wants to sound like a white with a chronic sneeze?

* * *

One of the more hilarious suggestions made by the squawkers for this point of view is to abandon the natural distinction along racial lines, and to replace it with a highly unnatural one along sexual lines. One such suggestion – emanating, no doubt, from the mind of a madwhite – would have us say 'he' for male whites (and blacks) and 'she' for female whites (and blacks). Can you imagine the outrage with which sensible folk of either sex would greet this 'modest proposal'?

Another suggestion is that the plural pronoun 'they' be used in place of the inclusive 'whe'. This would turn the charming proverb 'Whe who laughs last, laughs best' into the bizarre concoction 'They who laughs last, laughs best'. As if anyone in whis right mind could have thought that the original proverb applied only to the white race! No, we don't need a new pronoun to 'liberate' our minds. That's the lazy white's way of solving the pseudo-problem of racism. In any case, it's ungrammatical. The pronoun 'they' is a plural pronoun, and it grates on the civilized ear to hear it used to denote only one person. Such a usage, if adopted, would merely promote illiteracy and accelerate the already scandalously rapid nosedive of the average intelligence level of our society.

Niss Moses would have us totally revamp the English language to suit bler purposes. If, for instance, we are to substitute 'person' for 'white', where are we to stop? If we were to follow Niss Moses's ideas to their logical conclusion, we would have to conclude that ble would like to see small blackeys and whiteys playing the game of 'Hangperson' and reading the story of 'Snow Person and the Seven Dwarfs'. And would ble have us rewrite history to say. 'Don't shoot until you see the *persons* of their eyes!'? Will pundits and politicians henceforth issue *person* papers? Will we now have egg yolks and egg *persons*? And pledge allegiance to the good old Red, *Person*, and Blue? Will we sing, 'I'm dreaming of a *person* Christmas'? Say of a frightened white, 'Whe's *person* as a sheet!'? Lament the increase of *person*-collar crime? Thrill to the chirping of bob*persons* in our gardens? Ask a friend to *person* the table while we go visit the *persons'* room? Come off it, Niss Moses – don't personwash our language!

What conceivable harm is there in such beloved phrases as 'No white is an island', 'Dog is white's best friend', or 'White's inhumanity to white'? Who would revise such classic book titles as Bronob Jacowski's *The Ascent of White* or Eric Steeple Bell's *Whites of Mathematics*? Did the poet who wrote 'The best-laid plans of mice and whites gang aft agley' believe that blacks' plans gang *ne'er* agley? Surely not! Such phrases are simply metaphors; everyone can see beyond that. Whe who interprets them as reinforcing racism must have a perverse desire to feel oppressed.

'Personhandling' the language is a habit that not only Niss Moses but quite a few others have taken up recently. For instance, Nrs Delilah Buford has urged that we drop the useful distinction between 'Niss' and 'Nrs' (which, as everybody knows, is pronounced 'Nissiz', the reason for which nobody knows!). Bler argument is that there is no need for the public to know whether a black is employed or not. *Need* is, of course, not the point. Ble conveniently sidesteps the fact that there is a *tradition* in our society of calling unemployed blacks 'Niss' and employed blacks 'Nrs'. Most blacks – in fact, the vast majority – prefer it that way. They *want* the world to know what their employment status is, and for good reason. Unemployed blacks want prospective employers to know they are available, without having to ask embarrassing questions. Likewise, employed blacks are proud of having found a job, and wish to let the world know they are employed. This distinction provides a sense of security to all involved, in that everyone knows where ble fits into the scheme of things.

But Nrs Buford refuses to recognize this simple truth. Instead, ble shiftily turns the argument into one about whites, asking why it is that whites are universally addressed as 'Master', without any differentiation between employed and unemployed ones. The answer, of course, is that in Anerica and other northern societies, we set little store by the employment status of whites. Nrs Buford can do little to change that reality, for it seems to be tied to innate biological differences between whites and blacks. Many white-years of research, in fact, have gone into trying to understand why it is that employment status matters so much to blacks, yet relatively little to whites. It is true that both races have a longer life expectancy if employed, but of course people often do not act so as to maximize their life expectancy. So far, it remains a mystery. In any case, whites and blacks clearly have different constitutional inclinations, and different goals in life. And to I say, *Vive na différence!*

* * *

As for Nrs Buford's suggestion that both 'Niss' and 'Nrs' be unified into the single form of address 'Ns' (supposed to rhyme with 'fizz'), all I have to say is, it is arbitrary and clearly a thousand years ahead of its time. Mind you, this 'Ns' is an abbreviation concocted out of thin air: it stands for absolutely nothing. Who ever heard of such toying with language? And while we're on this subject, have you yet run across the recently founded *Ns* magazine, dedicated to the concerns of the 'liberated black'? It's sure to attract the attention of a trendy band of black airheads for a little while, but serious blacks surely will see through its thin veneer of slick, glossy Madison Avenue approaches to life.

Nrs Buford also finds it insultingly asymmetric that when a black is employed by a white, ble changes bler firmly name to whis firmly name. But what's so bad about that? Every firm's core consists of a boss (whis job is to make sure long-term policies are well charted out) and a secretary (bler job is to keep corporate affairs running smoothly on a day-to-day basis). They are both equally important and vital to the firm's success. No one disputes this. Beyond them there may of course be other firmly members. Now it's quite obvious that all members of a given firm should bear the same firmly name – otherwise, what are you going to call the firm's products? And since it would be nonsense for the boss to change whis name, it falls to the secretary to change bler name. Logic, not racism, dictates this simple convention.

What puzzles me the most is when people cut off their noses to spite their faces. Such is the case with the time-honoured coloured suffixes 'oon' and 'roon', found in familiar words such as *ambassadroon, stewardoon*, and *sculptroon*. Most blacks find it natural and sensible to add those suffixes on to nouns such as 'aviator' or 'waiter.' A black who flies an airplane may proudly proclaim, 'I'm an aviatroon!' But it would sound silly, if not ridiculous, for a black to say of blerself, 'I work as a waiter.' On the other hand, who could object to my saying that the lively Ticely Cyson is a great actroon, or that the hilarious Quill Bosby is a great comedioon? You guessed it – authoroons such as Niss Mildred

Hempsley and Nrs Charles White, both of whom angrily reject the appellation 'authoroon', deep though its roots are in our language. Nrs White, perhaps one of the finest poetoons of our day, for some reason insists on being known as a 'poet'. It leads one to wonder, is Nrs White *ashamed* of being black, perhaps? I should hope not. White needs Black, and Black needs White, and neither race should feel ashamed.

Some extreme Negrists object to being treated with politeness and courtesy by whites. For example, they reject the traditional notion of 'Negroes first', preferring to open doors for themselves, claiming that having doors opened for them suggests implicitly that society considers them inferior. Well, would they have it the other way? Would these incorrigible grousers prefer to open doors for whites? What do blacks want?

* * *

Another unlikely word has recently become a subject of controversy: 'blackey'. This is, of course, the ordinary term for black children (including teenagers), and by affectionate extension it is often applied to older blacks. Yet, incredible though it seems, many blacks – even teenage blackeys – now claim to have had their 'consciousness raised', and are voguishly skittish about being called 'blackeys'. Yet it's as old as the hills for Blacks employed in the same office to refer to themselves as 'the office blackeys'. And for their superior to call them 'my blackeys' helps make the ambiance more relaxed and comfy for all. It's hardly the mortal insult that libbers claim it to be. Fortunately, most blacks are sensible people and realize that mere words do not demean; they know it's how they are *used* that counts. Most of the time, calling a black – especially an older black – a 'blackey' is a thoughtful way of complimenting bler, making bler feel young, fresh, and hirable again. Lord knows, I certainly wouldn't object if someone told me that I looked whiteyish these days!

Many young blackeys go through a stage of wishing they had been born white. Perhaps this is due to popular television shows like *Superwhite* and *Batwhite*, but it doesn't really matter. It is perfectly normal and healthy. Many of our most successful blacks were once tomwhiteys and feel no shame about it. Why should they? Frankly, I think tomwhiteys are often the cutest little blackeys – but that's just my opinion. In any case, Niss Moses (once again) raises a ruckus on this score, asking why we don't have a corresponding word for young whiteys who play blackeys' games and generally manifest a desire to be black. Well, Niss Moses, if this were a common phenomenon, we most assuredly *would* have such a word, but it just happens not to be. Who can say why? But given that tomwhiteys are a dime a dozen, it's nice to have a word for them. The lesson is that White must learn to fit language to reality; White cannot manipulate the world by manipulating mere words. An elementary lesson, to be sure, but for some reason Niss Moses and others of bler ilk resist learning it.

Shifting from the ridiculous to the sublime, let us consider the Holy Bible. The good book is, of course, the source of some of the most beautiful language and profound imagery to be found anywhere. And who is the central character of the Bible? I am sure I need hardly remind you; it is God. As everyone knows, Whe is male and white, and that is an indisputable fact. But have you heard the latest joke promulgated by tasteless Negrists? It is said that one of them died and went to Heaven and then returned. What did ble report? 'I have seen God, and guess what? Ble's female!' Can anyone say that this is not blasphemy of the highest order? It just goes to show that some people will stoop to any depths in order to shock. I have shared this 'joke' with a number of friends of mine (including several blacks, by the way), and, to a white, they have agreed that it sickens them to the core to see Our Lord so shabbily mocked. Some things are just in bad taste, and there are no two ways about it. It is scum like this who are responsible for some of the great problems in our society today, I am sorry to say.

* * *

Well, all of this is just another skirmish in the age-old Battle of the Races, I guess, and we shouldn't take it too seriously. I am reminded of words spoken by the great British philosopher Alfred West Malehead in whis commencement address to my *alma secretaria*, the University of North Virginia: 'To enrich the language of whites is, certainly, to enlarge the range of their ideas.' I agree with this admirable sentiment wholeheartedly. I would merely point out to the over-zealous that there are some extravagant notions about language that should be recognized for what they are: cheap attempts to let dogmatic, narrow minds enforce their views on the speakers lucky enough to have inherited the richest, most beautiful, and flexible language on earth, a language whose traditions run back through the centuries to such deathless poets as Milton, Shakespeare, Wordsworth, Keats, Walt Whitwhite, and so many others.... Our language owes an incalculable debt to these whites for their clarity of vision and expression, and if the shallow minds of bandwagon-jumping Negrists succeed in destroying this precious heritage for all whites of good will, that will be, without any doubt, a truly female day in the history of Northern White.

Post scriptum

Perhaps this piece shocks you. It is meant to. The entire point of it is to use something that we find shocking as leverage to illustrate the fact that something that we usually close our eyes to is also very shocking. The most effective way I know to do so is to develop an extended analogy with something known as shocking and reprehensible. Racism is that thing, in this case. I am happy with this piece, despite – but also because of – its shock value. I think it makes its point better than any factual article could. As a friend of mine said, 'It makes you so uncomfortable that you can't ignore it.' I admit that rereading it makes even me, the author, uncomfortable!

Numerous friends have warned me that in publishing this piece I am taking a serious risk of earning myself a reputation as a terrible racist. I guess I cannot truly believe that anyone would see this piece that way. To misperceive it this way would be like calling someone a vicious racist for telling other people 'The word 'nigger' is extremely offensive'. If *allusions* to racism, especially for the purpose of satirizing racism and its cousins, are confused with racism itself, then I think it is time to stop writing.

Some people have asked me if to write this piece, I simply took a genuine William Safire column (appearing weekly in the *New York Times Magazine* under the title 'On language') and 'fiddled' with it. That is far from the truth. For years I have collected examples of sexist language, and in order to produce this piece, I dipped into this collection, selected some of the choicest, and ordered them very carefully. 'Translating' them into this alternate world was sometimes extremely difficult, and some words took weeks. The hardest terms of all, surprisingly enough, were 'Niss', 'Nrs' and 'Ns', even though 'Master' came immediately. The piece itself is not based on any particular article by William Safire, but Safire has without doubt been one of the most vocal opponents of non-sexist language reforms, and therefore merits being safired upon.

Interestingly, Master Safire has recently spoken out on sexism in whis column (5 August 1984). Lamenting the inaccuracy of writing either 'Mrs Ferraro' or 'Miss Ferraro' to designate the Democratic vice-presidential candidate whose husband's name is 'Zaccaro', whe writes:

> It breaks my heart to suggest this, but the time has come for *Ms*. We are no longer faced with a theory, but a condition. It is unacceptable for journalists to dictate to a candidate that she call herself *Miss* or else use her married name; it is equally unacceptable for a candidate to demand that newspapers print a blatant inaccuracy by applying a married honorific to a maiden name.

How disappointing it is when someone finally winds up doing the right thing but for the wrong reasons! In Safire's case, this shift was entirely for journalistic rather than humanistic reasons! It's as if Safire wished that women had never entered the political ring, so that the Grand Old Conventions of English – good enough for our grandfathers – would never have had to be challenged. How heartless of women! How heartbreaking the toll on our beautiful language!

* * *

A couple of weeks after I finished this piece, I ran into the book *The Nonsexist Communicator*, by Bobbye Sorrels. In it, there is a satire called 'A Tale of Two Sexes', which is very interesting to compare with my 'Person paper'. Whereas in mine, I slice the world orthogonally to the way it is actually sliced and then perform a mapping of worlds to establish a disorienting yet powerful new vision of our world, in hers, Ms Sorrels simply reverses the two halves of our world as it is actually sliced. Her satire is therefore in some ways very much like mine, and in other ways extremely different. It should be read.

I do not know too many publications that discuss sexist language in depth. The finest I have come across are the aforementioned *Handbook of Nonsexist Writing* by Casey Miller and Kate Swift; *Words and Women* by the same authors; *Sexist Language: A Modern Philosophical Analysis* edited by Mary Vetterling-Braggin; *The Nonsexist Communicator* by Bobbye Sorrels; and a very good journal titled *Women and Language News*.

My feeling about non-sexist English is that it is like a foreign language that I am learning. I find that even after years of practice, I still have to translate sometimes from my native language, which is sexist English. I know of no human being who speaks non-sexist as their native tongue. It will be very interesting to see if such people come to exist. If so, it will have taken a lot of work by a lot of people to reach that point.

Figure 3 From a 'Peggy Mills' comic strip, c. 1930.

One final footnote: my book *Gödel, Escher, Bach*, whose dialogues were the source of my very first trepidations about my own sexism, is now being translated into various languages, and to my delight, the Tortoise, a green-blooded male if ever there was one in English, is becoming *Madame Tortue* in French, *Signorina Tartaruga* in Italian, and so on. Full circle ahead!

References

Miller, C. and Swift, K. (1976) *Words and Women: New Language in New Times*, Harmondsworth: Penguin.

——(1980) *The Handbook of Nonsexist Writing*, London: Women's Press.

Sorrels, B. (1983) *The Nonsexist Communicator*, Englewood Cliffs, NJ: Prentice Hall.

Vetterling-Braggin, M. (ed.) *Sexist Language: A Modern Philosophical Analysis*, Totowa, NJ: Rowman & Littlefield.

Part Three

DOMINANCE AND DIFFERENCE IN WOMEN'S LINGUISTIC BEHAVIOUR

Introduction

The third and last part of this book concentrates on investigations of sex differences in verbal behaviour (some readers may wonder why *sex* differences rather than gender differences, as it is surely the social construct, gender, which is at issue: the reason is that the word *gender* in writings on language is used to refer to systems of grammatical concord, so that a book on 'language and gender' would suggest different concerns to linguists and other readers).

We begin with the work of Jespersen which has inspired so much feminist critique, and move on to an extract from Robin Lakoff's ground-breaking *Language and Woman's Place* (it may be appropriate to point out here that the author is a woman; British readers are often misled by her first name, though it is very interesting to note the apparent existence of a rule which says 'when in doubt, assume someone is male'!).

The last two papers exemplify two important approaches to differences between men and women's speech style. Pamela Fishman's work on interaction between couples (that is, *heterosexual* couples) represents the 'dominance' approach while Deborah Jones's paper on 'Gossip' represents the 'difference' approach, stressing the existence and the value of specifically female traditional modes of speech. The distinction between the two approaches is discussed in the general introduction (pp. 23–4).

One obvious omission from this section is any consideration of whether women and men *write* differently. Part One, of course, contains examples of theoretical speculation on the topic of 'feminine language', but little actual evidence that women writers have in practice differed systematically from men. There is in fact relatively little work on this question, and what has been done (for example, computer analyses of popular fiction and non-fiction written by women and men) has yielded negative results: there are few significant differences.[1] It could of course be argued that computation of sentence lengths, numbers of adjectives, and other measures of the same sort are intolerably crude instruments with which to probe subtle stylistic differences. But there again it could also be plausibly argued that writing is unlikely to display dramatic sex differences unless and until women choose (and are permitted) to forge a distinctive style in the manner advocated by the writers of Part One. Recently it has been claimed that just such a style, characterized (not unlike *écriture féminine*) by fragmentation and shifting perspective, has come into being among women writers identified with the Women's Liberation Movement.[2] For the most part, however, both now and in the past, women writers have worked in male traditions with male critics, as it were, looking over their shoulders. The form this internalized male surveillance has taken, its extent and its effects in different cultures and periods, is an interesting topic for further research.

Notes

1 For example, Mary Hiatt, *The Way Women Write* (New York: Teachers Press 1977).
2 See Julia Penelope and Susan Wolfe, 'Consciousness as style, style as aesthetic', in B. Thorne *et al.* (eds), *Language, Gender and Society* (Rowley, Mass.: Newbury House 1983).

15

The woman

Otto Jespersen

Reprinted from O. Jespersen, Language: Its Nature, Development and Origin *(London: Allen & Unwin 1922)*.

Women's languages

There are tribes in which men and women are said to speak totally different languages, or at any rate distinct dialects. It will be worth our while to look at the classical example of this, which is mentioned in a great many ethnographical and linguistic works, *viz.* the Caribs or Caribbeans of the Small Antilles. The first to mention their distinct sex dialects was the Dominican Breton, who, in his *Dictionnaire Caraïbe-français* (1664), says that the Caribbean chief had exterminated all the natives except the women, who had retained part of their ancient language. This is repeated in many subsequent accounts, the fullest and, as it seems, most reliable of which is that by Rochefort, who spent a long time among the Caribbeans in the middle of the seventeenth century (Rochefort 1665: 449ff.). Here he says that

> the men have a great many expressions peculiar to them, which the women understand but never pronounce themselves. On the other hand, the women have words and phrases which the men never use, or they would be laughed to scorn. Thus it happens that in their conversations it often seems as if the women had another language than the men.... The savage natives of Dominica say that the reason for this is that when the Caribs came to occupy the islands these were inhabited by an Arawak tribe which they exterminated completely, with the exception of the women, whom they married in order to populate the country. Now, these women kept their own language and taught it to their daughters.... But though the boys understand the speech of their mothers and sisters, they nevertheless follow their fathers and brothers and conform to their speech from the age of five or six.... It is asserted that there is some similarity between the speech

of the continental Arawaks and that of the Carib women. But the Carib men and women on the continent speak the same language, as they have never corrupted their natural speech by marriage with strange women.

This evidently is the account which forms the basis of everything that has since been written on the subject. But it will be noticed that Rochefort does not really speak of the speech of the two sexes as totally distinct languages or dialects, as has often been maintained, but only of certain differences within the same language. If we go through the comparatively full and evidently careful glossary attached to his book, in which he denotes the words peculiar to the men by the letter H and those of the women by F, we shall see that it is only for about one-tenth of the vocabulary that such special words have been indicated to him, though the matter evidently interested him very much, so that he would make all possible efforts to elicit them from the natives. In his lists, words special to one or the other sex are found most frequently in the names of the various degrees of kinship; thus, 'my father' in the speech of the men is *youmáan*, in that of the women *noukóuchili*, though both in addressing him say *bába*, 'my grandfather' is *itámoulou* and *nárgouti* respectively, and thus also for maternal uncle, son (elder son, younger son), brother-in-law, wife, mother, grandmother, daughter, cousin – all of these are different according as a man or a women is speaking. It is the same with the names of some, though far from all, of the different parts of the body, and with some more or less isolated words, as friend, enemy, joy, work, war, house, garden, bed, poison, tree, sun, moon, sea, earth. This list comprises nearly every notion for which Rochefort indicates separate words, and it will be seen that there are innumerable ideas for which men and women use the same word. Further, we see that where there are differences these do not consist in small deviations, such as different prefixes or suffixes added to the same root, but in totally distinct roots. Another point is very important to my mind: judging by the instances in which plural forms are given in the lists, the words of the two sexes are inflected in exactly the same way; thus the grammar is common to both, from which we may infer that we have not really to do with two distinct languages in the proper sense of the word.

Now, some light may probably be thrown on the problem of this women's language from a custom mentioned in some of the old books written by travellers who have visited these islands. Rochefort himself

(1665: 497) very briefly says that 'the women do not eat till their husbands have finished their meal', and Lafitau (1724) says that women never eat in the company of their husbands and never mention them by name, but must wait upon them as their slaves; with this Labat agrees.

Taboo

The fact that a wife is not allowed to mention the name of her husband makes one think that we have here simply an instance of a custom found in various forms and in varying degrees throughout the world – what is called verbal taboo: under certain circumstances, at certain times, in certain places, the use of one or more definite words is interdicted, because it is superstitiously believed to entail certain evil consequences, such as exasperate demons and the like. In place of the forbidden words it is therefore necessary to use some kind of figurative paraphrase, to dig up an otherwise obsolete term, or to disguise the real word so as to render it more innocent.

Now as a matter of fact we find that verbal taboo was a common practice with the old Caribs: when they were on the war-path they had a great number of mysterious words which women were never allowed to learn and which even the young men might not pronounce before passing certain tests of bravery and patriotism: these war-words are described as extraordinarily difficult ('un baragoin fort difficile', Rochefort 1665: 450). It is easy to see that when once a tribe has acquired the habit of using a whole set of terms under certain frequently recurring circumstances, while others are at the same time strictly interdicted, this may naturally lead to so many words being reserved exclusively for one of the sexes that an observer may be tempted to speak of separate 'languages' for the two sexes. There is thus no occasion to believe in the story of a wholesale extermination of all male inhabitants by another tribe, though on the other hand, it is easy to understand how such a myth may arise as an explanation of the linguistic difference between men and women, when it has become strong enough to attract attention and therefore has to be accounted for.

In some parts of the world the connection between a separate women's language and taboo is indubitable. Thus among the Bantu people of Africa. With the Zulus a wife is not allowed to mention the name of her father-in-law and of his brothers, and if a similar word or even a similar syllable occurs in the ordinary language, she must substitute something else of a similar meaning. In the royal family the difficulty of understanding the women's language is further increased by the woman's being forbidden to mention the names of her husband, his father, and grandfather as well as brothers. If one of these names means something like 'the son of the bull', each of these words has to be avoided, and all kinds of paraphrases have to be used. According to Kranz the interdiction holds good not only for meaning elements of the name, but even for certain sounds entering into them; thus, if the name contains the sound *z*, *amanzi* 'water' has to be altered into *amandabi*. If a woman were to contravene this rule she would be indicted for sorcery and put to death. The substitutes thus introduced tend to be adopted by others and to constitute a real women's language.

With the Chiquitos in Bolivia the difference between the grammars of the two sexes is rather curious (see Henry 1879). Some of Henry's examples may be thus summarized: men indicate by the addition of *-tii* that a male person is spoken about, while the women do not use this suffix and thus make no distinction between 'he' and 'she', 'his' and 'her'. Thus in the men's speech the following distinctions would be made:

He went to his house: *yebotii ti n-ipoostii*.
He went to her house: *yebotii ti n-ipoos*.
She went to his house: *yebo ti n-ipoostii*.

But to express all these different meanings the women would have only one form, *viz*.:

yebo ti n-ipoos,

which in the men's speech would mean only 'She went to her house.'

To many substantives the men prefix a vowel which the women do not employ, thus *o-petas* 'turtle', *u-tamokos* 'dog', *i-pis* 'wood'. For some very important notions the sexes use distinct words; thus, for the names of kinship, 'my father' is *iyai* and *išupu*, 'my mother' *ipaki* and *ipapa*, 'my brother' *tsaruki* and *ičibausi* respectively.

Among the languages of California, Yana, according to Dixon and Kroeber (*The American Anthropologist*, n.s. 5.15) is the only language that shows a difference in the words used by men and women – apart from terms of relationship, where a distinction according to the sex of the speaker is made among many Californian tribes as well as in other parts of the world, evidently 'because the relationship itself is to them different, as the sex is different'. But in Yana the distinction is a linguistic one, and curiously enough, the few specimens given all present a trait found already in the Chiquito forms, namely, that the forms spoken by women are shorter than those of the men, which appear as extensions, generally by suffixed -(*n*)*a*, of the former.

It is surely needless to multiply instances of these customs, which are found among many wild tribes; the curious reader may be referred to S. Lasch: pp. 7–13, and Ploss and Bartels 1908. The latter says that the Suaheli system is not carried through so as to replace the ordinary language, but the Suaheli have for every object which they do not care to mention by its real name a symbolic word understood by everybody concerned. In especial such symbols are used by women in their mysteries to denote obscene things. The words chosen are either ordinary names for innocent things or else taken from the old language or other Bantu languages, mostly Kiziguha, for among the Waziguha secret rites play an enormous role. Bartels finally says that with us, too, women have separate names for everything connected with sexual life, and he thinks that it is the same feeling of shame that underlies this custom and the interdiction of pronouncing the names of male relatives. This, however, does not explain everything, and, as already indicated, superstition certainly has a large share in this as in other forms of verbal taboo. See on this the very full account in the third volume of Frazer's *The Golden Bough*.

Competing languages

A difference between the language spoken by men and that spoken by women is seen in many countries where two languages are struggling for supremacy in a peaceful way – thus without any question of one nation exterminating the other or the male part of it. Among German and Scandinavian immigrants in America the men mix much more with the English-speaking population, and therefore have better opportunities, and also more occasion, to learn English than their wives, who remain more within doors. It is exactly the same among the Basques, where the school, the military service, and daily business relations contribute to the extinction of Basque in favour of French, and where these factors operate much more strongly on the male than on the female population: there are families in which the wife talks Basque, while the husband does not even understand Basque and does not allow his children to learn it (Bornecque and Mühlen, *Les Provinces françaises*: 53). Vilhelm Thomsen informs me that the old Livonian language, which is now nearly extinct, is kept up with the greatest fidelity by the women, while the men are abandoning it for Lettish. Albanian women, too, generally know only Albanian, while the men are more often bilingual.

Sanskrit drama

There are very few traces of real sex dialects in our Aryan languages, though we have the very curious rule in the old Indian drama that women talk Prakrit (*pràkrta*, the natural or vulgar language) while men have the privilege of talking Sanskrit (*samskrta*, the adorned language). The distinction, however, is not one of sex really, but of rank, for Sanskrit is the language of gods, kings, princes, brahmans, ministers, chamberlains, dancing-masters, and other men in superior positions, and of a very few women of special religious importance, while Prakrit is spoken by men of an inferior class, like shopkeepers, law officers, aldermen, bathmen, fishermen and policemen, and by nearly all women. The difference between the two 'languages' is one of degree only: they are two strata of the same language, one higher, more solemn, stiff, and archaic, and another lower, more natural, and familiar, and this easy, or perhaps we should say slipshod, style is the only one recognized for ordinary women. The difference may not be greater than that between the language of a judge and that of a costermonger in a modern novel, or between Juliet's and her nurse's expressions in Shakespeare, and if all women, even those we should call the 'heroines' of the plays, use only the lower stratum of speech, the reason certainly is that the social position of women was so inferior that they ranked only with men of the lower orders and had no share in the higher culture which, with the refined language, was the privilege of a small class of selected men.

Conservatism

As Prakrit is a 'younger' and 'worn-out' form of Sanskrit, the question here naturally arises: what is the general attitude of the two sexes to those changes that are constantly going on in languages? Can they be ascribed exclusively or predominantly to one of the sexes? Or do both equally participate in them? An answer that is very often given is that as a rule women are more conservative than men, and that they do nothing more than keep to the traditional language which they have learnt from their parents and hand on to their children, while innovations are due to the initiative of men. Thus Cicero in an often-quoted passage says that

when he hears his mother-in-law Lælia, it is to him as if he heard Plautus
or Nævius, for it is more natural for women to keep the old language
uncorrupted, as they do not hear many people's way of speaking and
thus retain what they have first learnt (*De oratore*, III. 45). This,
however, does not hold good in every respect and in every people. The
French engineer, Victor Renault, who lived for a long time among the
Botocudos (in South America) and compiled vocabularies for two of
their tribes, speaks of the ease with which he could make the savages
who accompanied him invent new words for anything.

One of them called out the word in a loud voice, as if seized by a
sudden idea, and the others would repeat it amid laughter and excited
shouts, and then it was universally adopted. But the curious thing is
that it was nearly always the women who busied themselves in
inventing new words as well as in composing songs, dirges and
rhetorical essays. The word-formations here alluded to are probably
names of objects that the Botocudos had not known previously . . . as
for horse, *krainejoune*, 'head-teeth'; for ox, *po-kekri*, 'foot-cloven';
for donkey, *mgo-jonne-orône*, 'beast with long ears.' But well-
known objects which have already got a name have often similar new
denominations invented for them, which are then soon accepted by
the family and community and spread more and more.

(Martius, Beitr. zur Ethnogr. u. Sprachenkunde
Amerikas 1867: i. 330)

I may also quote what E. R. Edwards says in his *Etude phonétique de
la langue japonaise* (1903: 79):

In France and in England it might be said that women avoid
neologisms and are careful not to go too far away from the written
forms: in Southern England the sound written *wh* [ʍ] is scarcely ever
pronounced except in girls' schools. In Japan, on the contrary,
women are less conservative than men, whether in pronunciation or
in the selection of words and expressions. One of the chief reasons is
that women have not to the same degree as men undergone the
influence of the written language. As an example of the liberties
which the women take may be mentioned that there is in the actual
pronunciation of Tokyo a strong tendency to get rid of the sound (*w*),
but the women go further in the word *atashi*, which men pronounce
watashi or *watakshi*, 'I'. Another tendency noticed in the language of

Japanese women is pretty widely spread among French and English women, namely, the excessive use of intensive words and the exaggeration of stress and tone-accent to mark emphasis. Japanese women also make a much more frequent use than men of the prefixes of politeness *o-*, *go-* and *mi-* .

Phonetics and grammar

In connection with some of the phonetic changes which have profoundly modified the English sound system we have express statements by old grammarians that women had a more advanced pronunciation than men and characteristically enough these statements refer to the raising of the vowels in the direction of [i]; thus in Sir Thomas Smith (1567), who uses expressions like 'mulierculæ quædam delicatiores, et nonnulli qui volunt isto modo videri loqui urbanius', and in another place 'fœminæ quædam delicatiores', further in Mulcaster (1582)[1] and in Milton's teacher, Alexander Gill (1621), who speaks about 'nostræ Mopsæ, quæ quidem ita omnia attenuant'.

In France, about 1700, women were inclined to pronounce *e* instead of *a*; thus Alemand (1688) mentions *Barnabé* as 'façon de prononcer mâle' and *Bernabé* as the pronunciation of 'les gens polis et délicats ... les dames surtout'; and Grimarest (1712) speaks of 'ces marchandes du Palais, qui au lieu de *madame, boulevart*, etc., prononcent *medeme, boulevert*' (Thurot i. 12 and 9).

There is one change characteristic of many languages in which it seems as if women have played an important part even if they are not solely responsible for it: I refer to the weakening of the old fully trilled tongue-point *r*. I have elsewhere (*Fonetik*, p. 417 ff.) tried to show that this weakening, which results in various sounds and sometimes in a complete omission of the sound in some positions, is in the main a consequence of, or at any rate favoured by, a change in social life: the old loud trilled point sound is natural and justified when life is chiefly carried on out-of-doors, but indoor life prefers, on the whole, less noisy speech habits, and the more refined this domestic life is, the more all kinds of noises and even speech sounds will be toned down. One of the results is that this original *r* sound, the rubadub in the orchestra of language, is no longer allowed to bombard the ears, but is softened down in various ways, as we see chiefly in the great cities and among the educated classes, while the rustic population in many countries keeps up the old sound with much greater conservatism. Now we find that women are not unfrequently mentioned in connection with this reduction of the trilled *r*; thus in the sixteenth century in France there was a tendency to leave off the trilling and even to go further than to the present English untrilled point *r* by pronouncing [z] instead, but some of the old grammarians mention this pronunciation as characteristic of women and a few men who imitate women (Erasmus: mulierculæ Parisinæ; Sylvius: mulierculæ...Parrhisinæ et earum modo quidam parum viri; Pillot: Parisinæ mulierculæ . . . adeo delicatulæ sunt, ut pro *pere* dicant *pese*). In the ordinary language there are a few remnants of this tendency; thus, when by the side of the original *chaire* we now have also the form *chaise*, and it is worthy of note that the latter form is reserved for the everyday signification (English chair, seat) as belonging more naturally to the speech of women, while *chaire* has the more special signification of 'pulpit, professorial chair'. Now the same tendency to substitute [z] – or after a voiceless sound [s] – for *r* is found in our own days among the ladies of Christiania, who will say *gzuelig* for *gruelig* and *fsygtelig* for *frygtelig* (Brekke, *Bidrag til dansknorskens lydlære* 1881: 17; I have often heard the sound myself). And even in far-off Siberia we find that the Chuckchi women will say *nízak* or *nízak* for the male *nírak* 'two', *zërka* for *rërka* 'walrus', etc. (Nordqvist; see fuller quotations in my *Fonetik* 431).

In present-day English there are said to be a few differences in pronunciation between the two sexes; thus according to Daniel Jones, *soft* is pronounced with a long vowel [sɔ·ft] by men and with a short vowel [sɔft] by women; similarly [gɛəl] is said to be a special ladies' pronunciation of *girl*, which men usually pronounce [g3·l]; cf. also on *wh* above, p. 207. So far as I have been able to ascertain, the pronunciation [tʃuldrən] for [tʃildrən] *children* is much more frequent in women than in men. It may also be that women are more inclined to give to the word *waistcoat* the full long sound in both syllables, while men, who have occasion to use the word more frequently, tend to give it the historical form [weskət] (for the shortening compare *breakfast*). But even if such observations were multiplied – as probably they might easily be by an attentive observer – they would be only more or less isolated instances, without any deeper significance, and on the whole we must say that from the phonetic point of view there is scarcely any difference between the speech of men and that of women: the two sexes speak for all intents and purposes the same language.

Choice of words

But when from the field of phonetics we come to that of vocabulary and style, we shall find a much greater number of differences, though they have received very little attention in linguistic works. A few have been mentioned by Greenough and Kittredge: 'The use of *common* in the sense of "vulgar" is distinctly a feminine peculiarity. It would sound effeminate in the speech of a man. So, in a less degree, with *person* for "woman", in contrast to "lady." *Nice* for "fine" must have originated in the same way' (1901: 54).

Others have told me that men will generally say 'It's very *good* of you', where women will say 'It's very *kind* of you.' But such small details can hardly be said to be really characteristic of the two sexes. There is no doubt, however, that women in all countries are shy of mentioning certain parts of the human body and certain natural functions by the direct and often rude denominations which men, and especially young men, prefer when among themselves. Women will therefore invent innocent and euphemistic words and paraphrases, which sometimes may in the long run come to be looked upon as the plain or blunt names, and therefore in their turn have to be avoided and replaced by more decent words.

In Pinero's *The Gay Lord Quex* (p. 116) a lady discovers some French novels on the table of another lady, and says: 'This is a little – h'm – isn't it?' – she does not even dare to say the word 'indecent,' and has to express the idea in inarticulate language. The word 'naked' is paraphrased in the following description by a woman of the work of girls in ammunition works: 'They have to take off every stitch from their bodies in one room, and run *in their innocence and nothing else* to another room where the special clothing is' (Bennett *The Pretty Lady*: 176).

On the other hand, the old-fashioned prudery which prevented ladies from using such words as *legs* and *trousers* ('those manly garments which are rarely mentioned by name', says Dickens, *Dombey and Son*: 335) is now rightly looked upon as exaggerated and more or less comical (cf. my GS §247).

There can be no doubt that women exercise a great and universal influence on linguistic development through their instinctive shrinking from coarse and gross expressions and their preference for refined, and (in certain spheres) veiled and indirect expressions. In most cases that influence will be exercised privately and in the bosom of the family; but there is one historical instance in which a group of women worked in that direction publicly and collectively. I refer to those French ladies who in the seventeenth century gathered in the Hôtel de Rambouillet and are generally known under the name of *Précieuses*. They discussed questions of spelling and of purity of pronunciation and diction, and favoured all kinds of elegant paraphrases by which coarse and vulgar words might be avoided. In many ways this movement was the counterpart of the literary wave which about that time was inundating Europe under various names – Gongorism in Spain, Marinism in Italy, Euphuism in England; but the Précieuses went further than their male confrères in desiring to influence everyday language. When, however, they used such expressions as, for 'nose', 'the door of the brain', for 'broom', 'the instrument of cleanness', and for 'shirt' 'the constant companion of the dead and the living' (la compagne perpétuelle des morts et des vivants), and many others, their affectation called down on their heads a ripple of laughter, and their endeavours would now have been forgotten but for the immortal satire of Molière in *Les Précieuses ridicules* and *Les Femmes savantes*. But apart from such exaggerations the feminine point of view is unassailable, and there is reason to congratulate those nations, the English among them, in which the social position of women has been high enough to secure greater purity and freedom from coarseness in language than would have been the case if men had been the sole arbiters of speech.

Among the things women object to in language must be specially mentioned anything that smacks of swearing;[2] where a man will say 'He told an infernal lie', a women will rather say, 'He told a most dreadful fib.' Such euphemistic substitutes for the simple word 'hell' as 'the other place', 'a very hot,' or 'a very uncomfortable place' probably originated with women. They will also use *ever* to add emphasis to an interrogative pronoun, as in 'Whoever told you that?' or 'Whatever do you mean?', and avoid the stronger 'who the devil' or 'what the dickens'. For surprise we have the feminine exclamations 'Good gracious', 'Gracious me', 'Goodness gracious', 'Dear me' by the side of the more masculine 'Good heavens', 'Great Scott'. 'To be sure' is said to be more frequent with women than with men. Such instances might be multiplied, but these may suffice here. It will easily be seen that we have here civilized counterparts of what was above mentioned as sexual taboo; but it is worth noting that the interdiction in these cases is ordained by the women themselves, or perhaps rather by the older among them, while the young do not always willingly comply.

Men will certainly with great justice object that there is a danger of the language becoming languid and insipid if we are always to content ourselves with women's expressions, and that vigour and vividness count for something. Most boys and many men have a dislike to some words merely because they feel that they are used by everybody and on every occasion: they want to avoid what is commonplace and banal and to replace it by new and fresh expressions, whose very newness imparts to them a flavour of their own. Men thus become the chief renovators of language, and to them are due those changes by which we sometimes see one term replace an older one, to give way in turn to a still newer one, and so on. Thus we see in English that the old verb *weorpan*, corresponding to German *werfen*, was felt as too weak and therefore supplanted by *cast*, which was taken from Scandinavian; after some centuries *cast* was replaced by the stronger *throw*, and this now, in the parlance of boys especially, is giving way to stronger expressions like *chuck* and *fling*. The old verbs, or at any rate *cast*, may be retained in certain applications, more particularly in some fixed combinations and in figurative significations, but it is now hardly possible to say, as Shakespeare does, 'They cast their caps up.' Many such innovations on their first appearance are counted as slang, and some never make their way into received speech: but I am not in this connection concerned with the distinction between slang and recognized language, except in so far as the inclination or disinclination to invent and to use slang is undoubtedly one of the 'human secondary sexual characters'. This is not invalidated by the fact that quite recently, with the rise of the feminist movement, many young ladies have begun to imitate their brothers in that as well as in other respects.

Vocabulary

This trait is indissolubly connected with another: the vocabulary of a woman as a rule is much less extensive than that of a man. Women move preferably in the central field of language, avoiding everything that is out of the way or bizarre, while men will often either coin new words or expressions or take up old-fashioned ones, if by that means they are enabled, or think they are enabled, to find a more adequate or precise expression for their thoughts. Woman as a rule follows the main road of language, where man is often inclined to turn aside into a narrow footpath or even to strike out a new path for himself. Most of those who are in the habit or reading books in foreign languages will have experienced a much greater average difficulty in books written by male than by female authors, because they contain many more rare words, dialect words, technical terms, etc. Those who want to learn a foreign language will therefore always do well at the first stage to read many ladies' novels, because they will there continually meet with just those everyday words and combinations which the foreigner is above all in need of, what may be termed the indispensable small-change of a language.

This may be partly explicable from the education of women, which has up to quite recent times been less comprehensive and technical than that of men. But this does not account for everything, and certain experiments made by the American professor Jastrow would tend to show that we have here a trait that is independent of education. He asked twenty-five university students of each sex, belonging to the same class and thus in possession of the same preliminary training, to write down as rapidly as possible a hundred words, and to record the time. Words in sentences were not allowed. There were thus obtained 5,000 words, and of these many were of course the same. But the community of thought was greater in the women; while the men used 1,375 different words, their female classmates used only 1,123. Of 1,266 unique words used, 29.8 per cent were male, only 20.8 per cent female. The group into which the largest number of the men's words fell was the animal kingdom; the group into which the largest number of women's words fell was wearing apparel and fabrics; while the men used only fifty-three words belonging to the class of foods, the women used 179.

> In general the feminine traits revealed by this study are an attention to the immediate surroundings, to the finished product, to the ornamental, the individual, and the concrete; while the masculine preference is for the more remote, the constructive, the useful, the general and the abstract.
>
> (Havelock Ellis 1904: 189)

Another point mentioned by Jastrow is the tendency to select words that rhyme and alliterative words; both these tendencies were decidedly more marked in men than in women. This shows what we may also notice in other ways, that men take greater interest in words as such and in their acoustic properties, while women pay less attention to that side of words and merely take them as they are, as something given once for all. Thus it comes that some men are confirmed punsters, while women are generally slow to see any point in a pun and scarcely ever perpetrate one themselves. Or, to get to something of greater value; the science of language has very few votaries among women, in spite of the fact that foreign languages, long before the reform of female education, belonged to those things which women learnt best in and out of schools, because, like music and embroidery, they were reckoned among the specially feminine 'accomplishments'.

Woman is linguistically quicker than man: quicker to learn, quicker to hear, and quicker to answer. A man is slower: he hesitates, he chews the cud to make sure of the taste of words, and thereby comes to discover similarities with and differences from other words, both in sound and in sense, thus preparing himself for the appropriate use of the fittest noun or adjective.

Adverbs

While there are a few adjectives, such as *pretty* and *nice*, that might be mentioned as used more extensively by women than by men, there are greater differences with regard to adverbs. Lord Chesterfield wrote (*The World*; 5 December 1754):

> Not contented with enriching our language by words absolutely new, my fair countrywomen have gone still farther, and improved it by the application and extension of old ones to various and very different significations. They take a word and change it, like a guinea into shillings for pocket-money, to be employed in the several occasional purposes of the day. For instance, the adjective *vast* and its adverb *vastly* mean anything and are the fashionable words of the most fashionable people. A fine woman . . . is *vastly* obliged, or *vastly* offended, *vastly* glad, or *vastly* sorry. Large objects are *vastly* great, small ones are *vastly* little; and I had lately the pleasure to hear a fine woman pronounce, by a happy metonymy, a very small gold snuff-box, that was produced in company, to be *vastly* pretty, because it was so *vastly* little.

Even if that particular adverb to which Lord Chesterfield objected has now to a great extent gone out of fashion, there is no doubt that he has here touched on a distinctive trait: the fondness of women for hyperbole will very often lead the fashion with regard to adverbs of intensity, and these are very often used with disregard of their proper meaning, as in German *riesig klein*, English *awfully pretty, terribly nice*, French *rudement joli, affreusement délicieux*, Danish *roedsom morsom* (horribly amusing), Russian *strast' kakoy lovkiy* (terribly able), etc. *Quite*, also, in the sense of 'very', as in 'she was quite charming; it makes me quite angry', is, according to Fitzedward Hall, due to the ladies. And I suspect that *just sweet* (as in Barrie: 'Grizel thought it was just sweet of him') is equally characteristic of the usage of the fair sex.

There is another intensive which has also something of the eternally feminine about it, namely *so*. I am indebted to Stoffel (Int. 101) for the following quotation from *Punch* (4 January 1896): 'This little adverb is a great favourite with ladies, in conjunction with an adjective. For instance, they are very fond of using such expressions as "He is *so* charming!" "It is *so* lovely!" etc.' Stoffel adds the following instances of strongly intensive *so* as highly characteristic of ladies' usage: 'Thank you *so* much!' 'It was *so* kind of you to think of it!' 'That's *so* like you!' 'I'm *so* glad you've come!' 'The bonnet is *so* lovely!'

The explanation of this characteristic feminine usage is, I think, that women much more often than men break off without finishing their sentences, because they start talking without having thought out what they are going to say; the sentence 'I'm so glad you've come' really requires some complement in the shape of a clause with *that*, 'so glad that I really must kiss you', or, 'so glad that I must treat you to something extra', or whatever the consequence may be. But very often it is difficult in a hurry to hit upon something adequate to say, and 'so glad that I cannot express it' frequently results in the inexpressible remaining unexpressed, and when that experiment has been repeated time after time, the linguistic consequence is that a strongly stressed *so* acquires the force of 'very much indeed'. It is the same with *such*, as in the following two extracts from a modern novel (in both it is a lady who is speaking): 'Poor Kitty! she has been in *such* a state of mind', and 'Do you know that you look *such* a duck this afternoon. . . This hat suits you *so* – you are *such* a *grande dame* in it.' Exactly the same thing has happened with Danish *så* and *sådan*, German *so* and *solch*; also with French *tellement*, though there perhaps not to the same extent as in English.

We have the same phenomenon with *to a degree*, which properly requires to be supplemented with something that tells us what the degree is, but is frequently left by itself, as in 'His second marriage was irregular to a degree.'

Periods

The frequency with which women thus leave their exclamatory sentences half finished might be exemplified from many passages in our novelists and dramatists. I select a few quotations. The first is from the beginning of *Vanity Fair*: 'This almost caused Jemima to faint with terror. "Well, I never," said she. "What an audacious" – emotion prevented her from completing either sentence.' Next from one of Hankin's plays. 'Mrs. Eversleigh: I must say! (but words fail her).' And finally from Compton Mackenzie's *Poor Relations*: '"The trouble you must have taken," Hilda exclaimed.' These quotations illustrate types of sentences which are becoming so frequent that they would seem soon to deserve a separate chapter in modern grammars, 'Did you ever!' 'Well, I never!' being perhaps the most important of these 'stop-short' or 'pull-up' sentences, as I think they might be termed.

These sentences are the linguistic symptoms of a peculiarity of feminine psychology which has not escaped observation. Meredith says of one of his heroines: 'She thought in blanks, as girls do, and some women', and Hardy singularizes one of his by calling her 'that novelty among women – one who finished a thought before beginning the sentence which was to convey it'.

The same point is seen in the typical way in which the two sexes build up their sentences and periods; but here, as so often in this paper, we cannot establish absolute differences, but only preferences that may be broken in a great many instances and yet are characteristic of the sexes as such. If we compare long periods as constructed by men and by women, we shall in the former find many more instances of intricate or involute structures with clause within clause, a relative clause in the middle of a conditional clause or vice versa, with subordination and sub-subordination, while the typical form of long feminine periods is that of co-ordination, one sentence or clause being added to another on the same plane and the gradation between the respective ideas being marked not grammatically, but emotionally, by stress and intonation, and in writing by underlining. In learned terminology we may say that men are fond of hypotaxis and women of parataxis. Or we may use the simile that a male period is often like a set of Chinese boxes, one within another, while a feminine period is like a set of pearls joined together on a string of *ands* and similar words. In a Danish comedy a young girl is relating what has happened to her at a ball, when she is suddenly interrupted by her brother, who has slyly taken out his watch and now exclaims: 'I declare! you have said *and then* fifteen times in less than two and a half minutes.'

General characteristics

The greater rapidity of female thought is shown linguistically, among other things, by the frequency with which a woman will use a pronoun like *he* or *she*, not of the person last mentioned, but of somebody else to whom her thoughts have already wandered, while a man with his slower intellect will think that she is still moving on the same path. The difference in rapidity of perception has been tested experimentally by Romanes: the same paragraph was presented to various well-educated persons, who were asked to read it as rapidly as they could, ten seconds being allowed for twenty lines. As soon as the time was up the paragraph was removed, and the reader immediately wrote down all that he or she could remember of it. It was found that women were usually more successful than men in this test. Not only were they able to read more quickly than the men, but they were able to give a better account of the paragraph as a whole. One lady, for instance, could read exactly four times as fast as her husband, and even then give a better account than he of that small portion of the paragraph he had alone been able to read. But it was found that this rapidity was no proof of intellectual power, and some of the slowest readers were highly distinguished men. Ellis (1904: 195) explains this in this way: with the quick reader it is as though every statement were admitted immediately and without inspection to fill the vacant chambers of the mind, while with the slow reader every statement undergoes an instinctive process of cross-examination; every new fact seems to stir up the accumulated stores of facts among which it intrudes, and so impedes rapidity of mental action.

This reminds me of one of Swift's 'Thoughts on Various Subjects':

The common fluency of speech in many men, and most women, is owing to the scarcity of matter, and scarcity of words; for whoever is a master of language, and hath a mind full of ideas, will be apt in speaking to hesitate upon the choice of both: whereas common speakers have only one set of ideas, and one set of words to clothe them in; and these are always ready at the mouth. So people come faster out of a church when it is almost empty, than when a crowd is at the door.

(1735: i. 305)

The volubility of women has been the subject of innumerable jests: it has given rise to popular proverbs in many countries;[3] as well as to Aurora Leigh's resigned 'A woman's function plainly is – to talk' and Oscar Wilde's sneer, 'Women are a decorative sex. They never have anything to say, but they say it charmingly.' A woman's thought is no sooner formed than uttered. Says Rosalind, 'Do you not know I am a woman! When I think, I must speak' *As You Like It*, III. 2. 264). And in a modern novel a young girl says: 'I talk so as to find out what I think. Don't you? Some things one can't judge of till one hears them spoken' (Housman *John of Jingalo*: 346).

The superior readiness of speech of women is a concomitant of the fact that their vocabulary is smaller and more central than that of men. But this again is connected with another indubitable fact, that women do not reach the same extreme points as men, but are nearer the average in most respects. Havelock Ellis, who establishes this in various fields, rightly remarks that the statement that genius is undeniably of more frequent occurrence among men than among women has sometimes been regarded by women as a slur upon their sex, but that it does not appear that women have been equally anxious to find fallacies in the statement that idiocy is more common among men. Yet the two statements must be taken together. Genius is more common among men by virtue of the same general tendency by which idiocy as more common among men. The two facts are but two aspects of a larger zoological fact – the greater variability of the male (Ellis 1904: 420).

In language we see this very clearly: the highest linguistic genius and the lowest degree of linguistic imbecility are very rarely found among women. The greatest orators, the most famous literary artists, have been men; but it may serve as a sort of consolation to the other sex that there are a much greater number of men than of women who cannot put two words together intelligibly, who stutter and stammer and hesitate, and are unable to find suitable expressions for the simplest thought. Between these two extremes the woman moves with a sure and supple tongue which is ever ready to find words and to pronounce them in a clear and intelligible manner.

Nor are the reasons far to seek why such differences should have developed. They are mainly dependent on the division of labour enjoined in primitive tribes and to a great extent also among more civilized peoples. For thousands of years the work that especially fell to men was such as demanded an intense display of energy for a comparatively short period, mainly in war and in hunting. Here, however, there was not much occasion to talk, nay, in many circumstances talk might even be fraught with danger. And when that rough work was over, the man would either sleep or idle his time away, inert and torpid, more or less in silence. Woman, on the other hand, had a number of domestic occupations which did not claim such an enormous output of spasmodic energy. To her was at first left not only agriculture, and a great deal of other work which in more peaceful times was taken over by men; but also much that has been till quite recently her almost exclusive concern – the care of the children, cooking, brewing, baking, sewing, washing, etc. – things which for the most part demanded no deep thought, which were performed in company and could well be accompanied with a lively chatter. Lingering effects of this state of things are seen still, though great social changes are going on in our times which may eventually modify even the linguistic relations of the two sexes.

Notes

1 '*Ai* is the man's diphthong, and soundeth full: *ei*, the woman's, and soundeth finish [i.e. fineish] in the same both sense, and vse: a *woman is deintie, and feinteth soon, the man fainteth not bycause he is nothing daintie.*' Thus what is now distinctive of refined as opposed to vulgar pronunciation was then characteristic of the fair sex.

2 There are great differences with regard to swearing between different nations; but I think that in those countries and in those circles in which swearing is common it is found much more extensively among men than among women: this at any rate is true of Denmark. There is, however, a general social movement against swearing, and now there are many men who never swear. A friend writes to me: 'The best English men hardly swear at all....I imagine some of our fashionable women now swear as much as the men they consort with.'

3 'Où femme y a, silence n'y a.' 'Deux femmes font un plaid, trois un grant caquet, quatre un plein marché.' 'Due donne e un' oca fanno una fiera' (Venice). 'The tongue is the sword of a woman, and she never lets it become rusty' (China). 'The North Sea will sooner be found wanting in water than a woman at a loss for a word' (Jutland).

References

Edwards, E. R. (1903) *Etude phonétique de la langue japonaise*, Leipzig.
Ellis, Havelock (1904) *Man and Woman*, London, 4th edn.
Greenough and Kittredge (1901) *Words and Their Ways in English Speech*, New York.

Henry, V. (1879) 'Sur le parler des hommes et le parler des femmes dans la langue chiquita', *Revue de linguistique* xii: 305.

Ploss, H. and Bartels, M. (1908) *Das Weib in der Natur und Völkerkunde*, Leipzig, 9th edn.

Rochefort (1665) *Histoire naturelle et morale des Iles Antilles*, Rotterdam, 2nd edn.

Swift, Jonathan (1735) 'Thoughts on Various Subjects' in *Works*, Dublin.

16

Extract from *Language and Woman's Place*

Robin Lakoff

Reprinted from Language and Woman's Place (*New York: Harper & Row 1975*).

If a little girl 'talks rough' like a boy, she will normally be ostracized, scolded, or made fun of. In this way society, in the form of a child's parents and friends, keeps her in line, in her place. This socializing process is, in most of its aspects, harmless and often necessary, but in this particular instance – the teaching of special linguistic uses to little girls – it raises serious problems, though the teachers may well be unaware of this. If the little girl learns her lesson well, she is not rewarded with unquestioned acceptance on the part of society; rather, the acquisition of this special style of speech will later be an excuse others use to keep her in a demeaning position, to refuse to take her seriously as a human being. Because of the way she speaks, the little girl – now grown to womanhood – will be accused of being unable to speak precisely or to express herself forcefully.

I am sure that the preceding paragraph contains an oversimplified description of the language-learning process in American society. Rather than saying that little boys and little girls, from the very start, learn two different ways of speaking, I think, from observation and reports by others, that the process is more complicated. Since the mother and other women are the dominant influences in the lives of most children under the age of 5, probably both boys and girls first learn 'women's language' as their first language. (I am told that in Japanese, children of both sexes use the particles proper for women until the age of 5 or so; then the little boy starts to be ridiculed if he uses them, and so soon learns to desist.) As they grow older, boys especially go through a stage of rough talk, as described by Spock and others; this is probably discouraged in little girls more strongly than in little boys, in whom parents may often find it more amusing than shocking. By the time children are 10 or so, and split up into same-sex peer groups, the two languages are already present, according to my recollections and observations. But it seems that what has happened is that the boys have unlearned their original form of expression and adopted new forms of expression, while the girls retain their old ways of speech. (One wonders whether this is related in any way to the often-noticed fact that little boys innovate, in their play, much more than little girls.) The ultimate result is the same, of course, whatever the interpretation.

So a girl is damned if she does, damned if she doesn't. If she refuses to talk like a lady, she is ridiculed and subjected to criticism as unfeminine; if she does learn, she is ridiculed as unable to think clearly, unable to take part in a serious discussion: in some sense, as less than fully human. These two choices which a woman has – to be less than a woman or less than a person – are highly painful.

An objection may be raised here that I am overstating the case against women's language, since most women who get as far as college learn to switch from women's to neutral language under appropriate situations (in class, talking to professors, at job interviews, and such). But I think this objection overlooks a number of problems. First, if a girl must learn two dialects, she becomes in effect a bilingual. Like many bilinguals, she may never really be master of either language, though her command of both is adequate enough for most purposes, she may never feel really comfortable using either, and never be certain that she is using the right one in the right place to the right person. Shifting from one language to another requires special awareness to the nuances of social situations, special alertness to possible disapproval. It may be that the extra energy that must be (subconsciously or otherwise) expended in this game is energy sapped from more creative work, and hinders women from expressing themselves as well, as fully, or as freely as they might otherwise. Thus, if a girl knows that a professor will be receptive to comments that sound scholarly, objective, unemotional, she will of course be tempted to use neutral language in class or in conference. But if she knows that, as a man, he will respond more approvingly to her at other levels if she uses women's language, and sounds frilly and feminine, won't she be confused as well as sorely tempted in two directions at once? It is often noticed that women participate less in class discussion than men – perhaps this linguistic indecisiveness is one reason why. (Incidentally, I don't find this true in my classes.)

It will be found that the overall effect of 'women's language' – meaning both language restricted in use to women and language descriptive of women alone – is this: it submerges a woman's personal identity, by denying her the means of expressing herself strongly, on the one hand, and encouraging expressions that suggest triviality in subject matter and uncertainty about it; and, when a woman is being discussed, by treating her as an object – sexual or otherwise – but never a serious person with individual views. Of course, other forms of behaviour in this society have the same purpose; but the phenomena seem especially clear linguistically.

The ultimate effect of these discrepancies is that women are systematically denied access to power, on the grounds that they are not capable of holding it as demonstrated by their linguistic behaviour along with other aspects of their behaviour; and the irony here is that women are made to feel that they deserve such treatment, because of inadequacies in their own intelligence and/or education. But in fact it is precisely because women have learned their lessons so well that they later suffer such discrimination. (This situation is of course true to some extent for all disadvantaged groups: white males of Anglo-Saxon descent set the standards and seem to expect other groups to be respectful of them but not to adopt them – they are to 'keep in their place'.)

Talking like a lady

'Women's language' shows up in all levels of the grammar of English. We find differences in the choice and frequency of lexical items; in the situations in which certain syntactic rules are performed; in intonational and other supersegmental patterns. As an example of lexical differences, imagine a man and a woman both looking at the same wall, painted a pinkish shade of purple. The woman may say (1):

(1) The wall is mauve,

with no one consequently forming any special impression of her as a result of the words alone; but if the man should say (1), one might well conclude he was imitating a woman sarcastically, or was a homosexual, or an interior decorator. Women, then, make far more precise discriminations in naming colours than do men; words like *beige, ecru, aquamarine, lavender*, and so on are unremarkable in a woman's active vocabulary, but absent from that of most men. I have seen a man helpless with suppressed laughter at a discussion between two other people as to whether a book jacket was to be described as 'lavender' or 'mauve'. Men find such discussion amusing because they consider such a question trivial, irrelevant to the real world.

We might ask why fine discrimination of colour is relevant for women, but not for men. A clue is contained in the way many men in our society view other 'unworldly' topics, such as high culture and the church, as outside the world of men's work, relegated to women and men whose masculinity is not unquestionable. Men tend to relegate to women things that are not of concern to them, or do not involve their egos. Among these are problems of fine colour discrimination. We might rephrase this point by saying that since women are not expected to make decisions on important matters, such as what kind of job to hold, they are relegated the non-crucial decisions as a sop. Deciding whether to name a colour 'lavender' or 'mauve' is one such sop.

If it is agreed that this lexical disparity reflects a social inequity in the position of women, one may ask how to remedy it. Obviously, no one could seriously recommend legislating against the use of the terms 'mauve' and 'lavender' by women, or forcing men to learn to use them. All we can do is give women the opportunity to participate in the real decisions of life.

Aside from specific lexical items like colour names, we find differences between the speech of women and that of men in the use of particles that grammarians often describe as 'meaningless'. There may be no referent for them, but they are far from meaningless: they define the social context of an utterance, indicate the relationship the speaker feels between himself and his addressee, between himself and what he is talking about.

As an experiment, one might present native speakers of standard American English with pairs of sentences, identical syntactically and in terms of referential lexical items, and differing merely in the choice of 'meaningless' particle, and ask them which was spoken by a man, which a woman. Consider:

(2) *a* Oh dear, you've put the peanut butter in the refrigerator again.
     b Shit, you've put the peanut butter in the refrigerator again.

It is safe to predict that people would classify the first sentence as part of 'women's language', the second as 'men's language'. It is true that many self-respecting women are becoming able to use sentences like (2)*b* publicly without flinching, but this is a relatively recent development, and while perhaps the majority of Middle America might condone the use of *b* for men, they would still disapprove of its use by women. (It is of interest, by the way, to note that men's language is increasingly being used by women, but women's language is not being adopted by men, apart from those who reject the American masculine image (for example, homosexuals). This is analogous to the fact that men's jobs are being sought by women, but few men are rushing to become housewives or secretaries. The language of the favoured group, the group that holds the power, along with its non-linguistic behaviour, is generally adopted by the other group, not vice versa. In any event, it is a truism to state that the 'stronger' expletives are reserved for men, and the 'weaker' ones for women.)

Now we may ask what we mean by 'stronger' and 'weaker' expletives. (If these particles were indeed meaningless, none would be stronger than any other.) The difference between using 'shit' (or 'damn', or one of many others) as opposed to 'oh dear', or 'goodness', or 'oh fudge' lies in how forcefully one says how one feels – perhaps, one might say, choice of particle is a function of how strongly one allows oneself to feel about something, so that the strength of an emotion conveyed in a sentence corresponds to the strength of the particle. Hence in a really serious situation, the use of 'trivializing' (that is, 'women's') particles constitutes a joke, or at any rate is highly inappropriate. (In conformity with current linguistic practice, throughout this work an (*) will be used to mark a sentence that is inappropriate in some sense, either because it is syntactically deviant or used in the wrong social context.)

(3) *a* *Oh fudge, my hair is on fire.
     b *Dear me, did he kidnap the baby?

As children, women are encouraged to be 'little ladies'. Little ladies don't scream as vociferously as little boys, and they are chastised more severely for throwing tantrums or showing temper: 'high spirits' are expected and therefore tolerated in little boys; docility and resignation are the corresponding traits expected of little girls. Now, we tend to excuse a show of temper by a man where we would not excuse an identical tirade from a woman: women are allowed to fuss and complain, but only a man can bellow in rage. It is sometimes claimed that there is a biological basis for this behaviour difference, though I don't believe conclusive evidence exists that the early differences in behaviour that have been observed are not the result of very different treatment of babies of the two sexes from the beginning; but surely the use of different particles by men and women is a learned trait, merely mirroring non-linguistic differences again, and again pointing out an inequity that exists between the treatment of men, and society's expectations of them, and the treatment of women. Allowing men stronger means of expression than are open to women further reinforces men's position of strength in the real world: for surely we listen with more attention the more strongly and forcefully someone expresses opinions, and a speaker unable – for whatever reason – to be forceful in stating his views is much less likely to be taken seriously. Ability to use strong particles like 'shit' and 'hell' is, of course, only incidental to the inequity that exists rather than its cause. But once again, apparently accidental linguistic usage suggests that women are denied equality partially for linguistic reasons, and that an examination of language points up precisely an area in which inequity exists. Further, if someone is allowed to show emotions, and consequently does, others may well be able to view him as a real individual in his own right, as they could not if he never showed emotion. Here again, then, the behaviour a woman learns as 'correct' prevents her from being taken seriously as an individual, and further is considered 'correct' and necessary for a woman precisely because society does *not* consider her seriously as an individual.

Similar sorts of disparities exist elsewhere in the vocabulary. There is, for instance, a group of adjectives which have, besides their specific and literal meanings, another use, that of indicating the speaker's approbation or admiration for something. Some of these adjectives are neutral as to sex of speaker: either men or women may use them. But another set seems, in its figurative use, to be largely confined to women's speech. Representative lists of both types are below:

neutral	*women only*
great	adorable
terrific	charming
cool	sweet
neat	lovely
	divine

As with the colour words and swear words already discussed, for a man to stray into the 'women's' column is apt to be damaging to his reputation, though here a woman may freely use the neutral words. But it should not be inferred from this that a woman's use of the 'women's' words is without its risks. Where a woman has a choice between the neutral words and the women's words, as a man has not, she may be suggesting very different things about her own personality and her view of the subject-matter by her choice of words of the first set or words of the second.

(4) *a* What a terrific idea!
    b What a divine idea!

It seems to me that *a* might be used under any appropriate conditions by a female speaker. But *b* is more restricted. Probably it is used appropriately (even by the sort of speaker for whom it was normal) only in case the speaker feels the idea referred to to be essentially frivolous, trivial, or unimportant to the world at large – only an amusement for the speaker herself. Consider, then, a woman advertising executive at an advertising conference. However feminine an advertising executive she is, she is much more likely to express her approval with (4)*a* than with *b*, which might cause raised eyebrows, and the reaction: 'That's what we get for putting a woman in charge of this company.'

On the other hand, suppose a friend suggests to the same woman that she should dye her French poodles to match her cigarette lighter. In this case, the suggestion really concerns only her, and the impression she will make on people. In this case, she may use *b*, from the 'women's language'. So the choice is not really free: words restricted to 'women's language' suggest that concepts to which they are applied are not relevant to the real world of (male) influence and power.

One may ask whether there really are no analogous terms that are available to men – terms that denote approval of the trivial, the personal; that express approbation in terms of one's own personal emotional reaction, rather than by gauging the likely general reaction. There does in fact seem to be one such word: it is the hippie invention 'groovy', which seems to have most of the connotations that separate 'lovely' and 'divine' from 'great' and 'terrific' excepting only that it does not mark the speaker as feminine or effeminate.

(5) *a* What a terrific steel mill!
    b *What a lovely steel mill! (male speaking)
    c What a groovy steel mill!

I think it is significant that this word was introduced by the hippies, and, when used seriously rather than sarcastically, used principally by people who have accepted the hippies' values. Principal among these is the denial of the Protestant work ethic: to a hippie, something can be worth thinking about even if it isn't influential in the power structure, or money-making. Hippies are separated from the activities of the real world just as women are – though in the former case it is due to a decision on their parts, while this is not uncontroversially true in the case of women. For both these groups, it is possible to express approval of things in a personal way – though one does so at the risk of losing one's credibility with members of the power structure. It is also true, according to some speakers, that upper-class British men may use the words listed in the 'women's' column, as well as the specific colour words and others we have categorized as specifically feminine, without raising doubts as to their masculinity among other speakers of the same dialect. (This is not true for lower-class Britons, however.) The reason may be that commitment to the work ethic need not necessarily be displayed: one may be or appear to be a gentleman of leisure, interested in various pursuits, but not involved in mundane (business or political) affairs, in such a culture, without incurring disgrace. This is rather analogous to the position of a woman in American middle-class society, so we should not be surprised if these special lexical items are usable by both groups. This fact points indeed to a more general conclusion. These words aren't, basically, 'feminine'; rather, they signal 'uninvolved', or 'out of power'. Any group in a society to which these labels are applicable may presumably use these words; they are often considered 'feminine', 'unmasculine', because women are the 'uninvolved', 'out of power' group *par excellence*.

Another group that has, ostensibly at least, taken itself out of the search for power and money is that of academic men. They are frequently viewed by other groups as analogous in some ways to women – they don't really work, they are supported in their frivolous pursuits by others, what they do doesn't really count in the real world, and so on. The suburban home finds its counterpart in the ivory tower: one is supposedly shielded from harsh realities in both. Therefore it is not too surprising that many academic men (especially those who emulate British norms) may violate many of these sacrosanct rules I have just laid down: they often use 'women's language'. Among themselves, this does not occasion ridicule. But to a truck driver, a professor saying 'What a lovely hat!' is undoubtedly laughable, all the more so as it reinforces his stereotype of professors as effete snobs.

When we leave the lexicon and venture into syntax, we find that syntactically too women's speech is peculiar. To my knowledge, there is no syntactic rule in English that only women may use. But there is at least one rule that a woman will use in more conversational situations than a man. (This fact indicates, of course, that the applicability of syntactic rules is governed partly by social context – the positions in society of the speaker and addressee, with respect to each other, and the impression one seeks to make on the other.) This is the rule of tag-question formation.[1]

A tag, in its usage as well as its syntactic shape (in English) is midway between an outright statement and a yes–no question: it is less assertive than the former, but more confident than the latter. Therefore it is usable under certain contextual situations: not those in which a statement would be appropriate, nor those in which a yes–no question is generally used, but in situations intermediate between these.

One makes a statement when one has confidence in his knowledge and is pretty certain that his statement will be believed; one asks a question when one lacks knowledge on some point and has reason to believe that this gap can and will be remedied by an answer by the addressee. A tag question, being intermediate between these, is used when the speaker is stating a claim, but lacks full confidence in the truth of that claim. So if I say

(6) Is John here?

I will probably not be surprised if my respondent answers 'no'; but if I say

(7) John is here, isn't he?

instead, chances are I am already biased in favour of a positive answer, wanting only confirmation by the addressee. I still want a response from him, as I do with a yes–no question; but I have enough knowledge (or think I have) to predict that response, much as with a declarative statement. A tag question, then, might be thought of as a declarative statement without the assumption that the statement is to be believed by the addressee: one has an out, as with a question. A tag gives the addressee leeway, not forcing him to go along with the views of the speaker.

There are situations in which a tag is legitimate, in fact the only legitimate sentence form. So, for example, if I have seen something only indistinctly, and have reason to believe my addressee had a better view, I can say:

(8) I had my glasses off. He was out at third, wasn't he?

Sometimes we find a tag question used in cases in which the speaker knows as well as the addressee what the answer must be, and doesn't need confirmation. One such situation is when the speaker is making 'small talk', trying to elicit conversation from the addressee:

(9) Sure is hot here, isn't it?

In discussing personal feelings or opinions, only the speaker normally has any way of knowing the correct answer. Strictly speaking, questioning one's own opinions is futile. Sentences like (10) are usually ridiculous.

(10) * I have a headache, don't I?

But similar cases do, apparently, exist, in which it is the speaker's opinions, rather than perceptions, for which corroboration is sought, as in (11):

(11) The way prices are rising is horrendous, isn't it?

While there are of course other possible interpretations of a sentence like this, one possibility is that the speaker has a particular answer in mind – 'yes' or 'no' – but is reluctant to state it baldly. It is my impression, though I do not have precise statistical evidence, that this sort of tag question is much more apt to be used by women than by men. If this is indeed true, why is it true?

These sentence types provide a means whereby a speaker can avoid committing himself, and thereby avoid coming into conflict with the addressee. The problem is that, by so doing, a speaker may also give the impression of not being really sure of himself, of looking to the addressee for confirmation, even of having no views of his own. This last criticism is, of course, one often levelled at women. One wonders how much of it reflects a use of language that has been imposed on women from their earliest years.

Related to this special use of a syntactic rule is a widespread difference perceptible in women's intonational patterns.[2] There is a peculiar sentence intonation pattern, found in English as far as I know only among women, which has the form of a declarative answer to a question, and is used as such, but has the rising inflection typical of a yes–no question, as well as being especially hesitant. The effect is as though one were seeking confirmation, though at the same time the speaker may be the only one who has the requisite information.

(12) *a* When will dinner be ready?
     b Oh. . . around six o'clock . . .?

It is as though *b* were saying, 'Six o'clock, if that's OK with you, if you agree.' *a* is put in the position of having to provide confirmation, and *b* sounds unsure. Here we find unwillingness to assert an opinion carried to an extreme. One likely consequence is that these sorts of speech patterns are taken to reflect something real about character and play a part in not taking a woman seriously or trusting her with any real responsibilities, since 'she can't make up her mind' and 'isn't sure of herself'. And here again we see that people form judgements about other people on the basis of superficial linguistic behaviour that may have nothing to do with inner character, but has been imposed upon the speaker, on pain of worse punishment than not being taken seriously.

Such features are probably part of the general fact that women's speech sounds much more 'polite' than men's. One aspect of politeness is as we have just described: leaving a decision open, not imposing your mind, or views, or claims on anyone else. Thus a tag question is a kind of polite statement, in that it does not force agreement or belief on the addressee. A request may be in the same sense a polite command, in that it does not overtly require obedience, but rather suggests something be done as a favour to the speaker. An overt order (as in an imperative) expresses the (often impolite) assumption of the speaker's superior position to the addressee, carrying with it the right to enforce compliance, whereas with a request the decision on the face of it is left up to the addressee. (The same is true of suggestions: here, the implication is not that the addressee is in danger if he does not comply – merely that he will be glad if he does. Once again, the decision is up to the addressee, and a suggestion therefore is politer than an order.) The more particles in a sentence that reinforce the notion that it is a request, rather than an order, the politer the result. The sentences of 13 illustrate these points: (13)*a* is a direct order, *b* and *c* simple requests, and *d* and *e* compound requests.[3]

(13) *a* Close the door.
     b Please close the door.
     c Will you close the door?
     d Will you please close the door?
     e Won't you close the door?

Let me first explain why *e* has been classified as a compound request. (A sentence like *Won't you please close the door* would then count as a doubly compound request.) A sentence like (13)*c* is close in sense to 'Are you willing to close the door?' According to the normal rules of polite conversation, to agree that you are willing is to agree to do the thing asked of you. Hence this apparent enquiry functions as a request, leaving the decision up to the willingness of the addressee. Phrasing it as a positive question makes the (implicit) assumption that a 'yes' answer will be forthcoming. Sentence (13)*d* is more polite than *b* or *c* because it combines them: *please* indicating that to accede will be to do something for the speaker, and *will you*, as noted, suggesting that the addressee has the final decision. If, now, the question is phrased with a negative, as in (13)*e*, the speaker seems to suggest the stronger likelihood of a negative response from the addressee. Since the assumption is then that the addressee is that much freer to refuse, (13)*e* acts as a more polite request than (13)*c* or *d*: *c* and *d* put the burden of refusal on the addressee, as *e* does not.

Given these facts, one can see the connection between tag questions and tag orders and other requests. In all these cases, the speaker is not committed as with a simple declarative or affirmative. And the more one compounds a request, the more characteristic it is of women's speech, the less of men's. A sentence that begins *Won't you please* (without special emphasis on *please*) seems to me at least to have a distinctly unmasculine sound. Little girls are indeed taught to talk like little ladies, in that their speech is in many ways more polite than that of boys or men, and the reason for this is that politeness involves an absence of a strong statement, and women's speech is devised to prevent the expression of strong statements.

Notes

1 Within the lexicon itself, there seems to be a parallel phenomenon to tag-question usage, which I refrain from discussing in the body of the text because the facts are controversial and I do not understand them fully. The intensive *so*, used where purists would insist upon an absolute superlative, heavily stressed, seems more characteristic of women's language than of men's, though it is found in the latter, particularly in the speech of male academics. Consider, for instance, the following sentences:

a I feel *so* unhappy!
b That movie made me *so* sick!

Men seem to have the least difficulty using this construction when the sentence is unemotional, or non-subjective – without reference to the speaker himself:

   c That sunset is *so* beautiful!
   d Fred is *so* dumb!

Substituting an equative like *so* for absolute superlatives (like *very, really, utterly*) seems to be a way of backing out of committing oneself strongly to an opinion, rather like tag questions (cf. discussion on p. 229). One might hedge in this way with perfect right in making aesthetic judgements, as in *c*, or intellectual judgements, as in *d*. But it is somewhat odd to hedge in describing one's own mental or emotional state: who, after all, is qualified to contradict one on this? To hedge in this situation is to seek to avoid making any strong statement: a characteristic, as we have noted already and shall note further, of women's speech.

2 For analogues outside of English to these uses of tag questions and special intonation patterns, see my discussion of Japanese particles in 'Language in context', *Language*, 48 (1972), pp. 907–27. It is to be expected that similar cases will be found in many other languages as well. See, for example, M. R. Haas's very interesting discussion of differences between men's and women's speech (mostly involving lexical dissimilarities) in many languages, in D. Hymes (ed.) *Language in Culture and Society* (New York: Harper & Row 1964).

3 For more detailed discussion of these problems, see Lakoff, 'Language in context'.

17

Conversational insecurity[1]

Pamela Fishman

Reprinted from H. Giles, W. Robinson, and P. Smith (eds), Language: Social Psychological Perspectives *(Oxford: Pergamon Press 1980).*

Abstract

Concrete ways that women talk are frequently explained as a result of female 'personality' and socialization. This paper offers an alternative social explanation for the depiction of women as 'insecure', using data from tape recordings of three male–female couples in their homes. Looking at the seemingly insecure behaviour of women in actual conversational settings, their activity can be demonstrated to be embedded in the necessary work involved in producing successful interactions.

Introduction

Discussions of the way women act, including the way they talk, often rely on some notion of a female 'personality'. Usually, socialization is used to explain this personality. Women are seen as more insecure, dependent and emotional than men because of the way that they are raised. Socialization is seen as the means by which male–female power differences are internalized and translated into behaviour producing properly dominant men and submissive women (Bardwick and Douvan 1977; Lakoff 1975). Lakoff (1979) has probably been the most explicit in offering this personality–socialization explanation for women's speech patterns:

> Linguistic behavior, like other facets of the personality is heavily influenced by training and education. Women speak as they do – and men speak as *they* do – because they have from childhood been rewarded for doing so, overtly or subtly. Also they speak as they do because their choice of speech style reflects their self-image.
>
> (p. 141)

I want to propose an altogether different analysis. Instead of viewing the behaviour of adult women as indicative of a gender identity acquired through childhood socialization, I will examine the behaviour in terms of the interactional situation in which it is produced. As a methodological strategy, I advocate that *first* we examine the situational context for the forces that explain why people do what they do. If no such forces can be found in the immediate context, only then should we rely on prior socialization to explain present behaviour.

In this paper I will consider two examples of women's conversational style: *question-asking* and the use of *'you know'*. Both are seen as indicative of women's tendency to be more 'insecure' and 'hesitant', and are said to arise from a socialized female personality. Rather than using these as evidence of personality traits, I shall explore the character of conversational interaction in which they occur. By doing so, we will see that these speech patterns are attempted solutions to the problematics of conversation.

The illustrative data in this paper come from fifty-two hours of taped natural conversation, twelve and a half hours of which have been transcribed. Three male–female couples agreed to have tape recorders placed in their apartments for periods ranging from four to fourteen days. Because the couples operated the recorders manually, uninterrupted recording lengths ran from one to four hours. The apartments were all small one-bedroom units, and the recorders picked up all kitchen and living room conversation as well as louder talk from the bedroom and bath. The six participants were between the ages of 25 and 35, white, and professionally oriented. The three men were graduate students, as were two of the women. The third woman was a social worker. Two of the women were feminists. The other woman and all of the men were sympathetic to the women's movement. The participants could erase anything they wished before giving me the tapes, though this was done in only three instances.

Asking questions

Lakoff argues that the asking of questions is a prime example of women's insecurity and hesitancy. She deals with women's extensive use of two interrogatory devices: tag questions ('Isn't it?' 'Couldn't we?') (1975) and questions with declarative functions ('Did you see this in the paper?' 'Should we do a grocery shopping?') (1979):

[W]omen are more apt than men to use a question when there is a choice for this reason: a woman has traditionally gained reassurance in this culture from presenting herself as concerned about her accept-ance as well as unsure of the correctness of what she's saying ... a woman, believing that a hesitant style will win her acceptance, will adopt it, and phrase her opinions ... deferentially. ... The single great-est problem women are going to have in achieving parity is surely this pervasive tendency toward hesitancy, linguistic and otherwise.

(1979: 143)

My transcripts support Lakoff's claim that women use tags and declarative questions much more often than men. In fact, women ask more questions of any kind. Out of a total of 370 questions asked in twelve and a half hours of conversation, the women asked 263, two and a half times as many as the men. About a third of the women's questions (87) were tags, or were ones that could have been phrased as declaratives. The women asked three times as many tags or declarative questions as the men (87 to 29) and twice as many requests for information or clarification (152 to 74). (There were 28 questions which I could not categorize, half because of the lack of transcribable words. Twenty-four were asked by the females, four by the males.) A substantial number of women's questions theoretically need not have been questions at all. Why do women speak this way? And why do women ask so many more questions generally?

Instead of interpreting question-asking as the expression of an insecure personality, let us consider the question's interactive attributes. What work does a question do? Question-asking attempts to establish one of the prerequisites of conversation. In order for two or more people to talk to one another, they must agree to do so. They must display that agreement by entering into mutual orientation to one another, and they must speak and respond to one another as one aspect of their mutual orientation. They must take turns speaking, and they must display connectedness between what they say to one another.

Sacks, working within this interactional perspective, has noted that questions are part of a category of conversational sequencing devices; questions form the first part of a pair of utterances, answers being the second part (Sacks 1972). Questions and answers are linked together, conversationally and normatively. Questions are both explicit invitations to the listener to respond and demands that they do so. The questioner has rights to complain if there is no response forthcoming.

Questions are stronger forms interactively than declaratives. A declarative can be more easily ignored. The listener can claim they did not know the speaker was finished, or that they thought the speaker was musing aloud.

Evidence for the strength of the question–answer sequence can be seen from an analysis of who succeeds in getting their topics adopted in conversation. In earlier work (Fishman 1978) I found that women, using a variety of utterance types to introduce topics, succeeded only 36 per cent of the time in getting their topics to become actual conversations. In contrast, all but one of the men's topic attempts succeeded. However, when we look at the number of topic attempts that women introduced with a question, their success rate jumps considerably. Of eighteen introductory attempts which were questions, thirteen succeeded. This 72 per cent success rate is exactly double the women's overall success rate of 36 per cent. Men used questions to introduce topics 6 times out of 29, all of which succeeded.

Women ask questions so often because of the conversational power of questions, not because of personality weakness. Women have more trouble starting conversation and keeping it going when they are talking with men. Their greater use of questions is an attempt to solve the *conversational* problem of gaining a response to their utterances.

'You know'

Lakoff discusses hedging as another aspect of women's insecurity. By hedges, she is referring to the frequent use of such phrases as 'sorta', 'like', and 'you know'. I shall deal here with 'you know', since it is a device which I have addressed in my own analyses of conversations (1979). In my transcripts, just as Lakoff would predict, the women used 'you know' five times more often than the men (87 to 17). Why is this?

Let us consider where 'you know'; appears in conversation. According to Lakoff, one would expect 'you know' to be randomly scattered throughout women's speech, since its usage is supposed to reflect the general insecurity of the speaker. If, however, 'you know' does some kind of work in conversation, we would expect its occurrence to cluster at points in conversation where the interactional context seems to call for its usage. And this is just what I found. Thirty of the women's 87 'you know's' occur during six short segments of talk. These were all places where the women were unsuccessfully attempting to pursue topics. The six segments of talk total 10 minutes. This means that nearly

35 per cent of the uses occur in less than 2 per cent of the transcribed hours of conversation. (The 'you know's' were not counted for one and a half hours of transcript where four people, rather than the couple, were conversing. Thus, the total transcript time here is eleven hours ($^{10}/_{660}$ = 1.5 per cent). Also during two hours of one couple there were no clustered 'you know's'. Subtracting those two hours, we are left with $^{10}/_{540}$ = 1.9 per cent; a ratio well under the 35 per cent of the total 'you know's' which fall in that time.)

'You know' displays conversational trouble, but it is often an attempt to solve the trouble as well. 'You know' is an attention-getting device, a way to check with one's interactional partner to see if they are listening, following and attending to one's remarks. When we consider 'you know' interactively, it is not surprising to find that its use is concentrated in long turns at talk where the speaker is unsuccessfully attempting to carry on a conversation. If we look briefly at the two longest segments in which 'you know' clusters, we can clarify how it works in actual conversation.

In the two transcripts which follow, the numbers in brackets are the time in seconds of the pauses. The vertical lines in the second transcript indicate overlapping talk. The first segment is five minutes long and only parts of it are reprinted (the full text can be found in Fishman 1979). Here, the woman is attempting to engage the man in conversation about an article she has just read. During the five minutes the man responds only six times, and the woman uses 'you know' sixteen times. Ten of her sixteen uses fall in the two minutes when there is no response from the man at all:

F   he's talking about the differences, that the women [1.3] uhm [0.8] that the black women represent to the black men, [0.5] white society [0.8] and that uhm [1.5] they stand for all the white values like they're dressed much neater than the men. They're obviously trying much harder, y'know, and they're more courteous and polite etcetera, etcetera, you know. [1.5] It seems to me that the women because of our [0.7] chauvinism in this society are constantly being put down for things that the same set of the same traits in a man would be put up. [1.5] Like this – he uses different words, you know? [1.5] uhmm [1]. For instance you know they try more they're more conscientious. This sort of thing the goddamn blighter used to say about a man, 'n'-, and so on. [1] It's just obvious that – [3] uhh [1], he doesn't know what to do with the fact that the women, the black women [1] uh you know, for a multitude of reasons probably, have come out to be much stronger in many ways than black men. [1] Y'know they hold families together, they're also the bread earners, [1] they just have to go through a lot more shit than the men it seems, and they're stronger for it. [1] and uhm [1.5] he doesn't know what to make of the fact that [0.9] they do all these things, [2] y'know, and so he just puts them down. In a blind and chauvinistic way. [2.5] In other words black women are white. [2] Y'know it's really a simplistic article [0.5] you know he starts off saying – this – [1] y'know, [0.8] sort of this gross, indiscriminate, black versus white [1] vision and ....

Eight out of ten of the 'you know's' occur immediately prior to or after pauses in the woman's speech. Pauses are places where speaker change might occur, i.e., where the man might have responded. Because the man does not respond and the woman continues talking to keep the conversation going, the pauses become internal to the woman's speech. 'You know' seems to be an explicit invitation to respond. At the same time, it displays the man's position as a co-participant when he has not displayed it himself.

'You know' appears to be used somewhat differently in the second segment. In this two-minute piece, the woman uses 'you know' five times. (The 'Richard' referred to in this segment is a mutual friend. He was born in a foreign country which the couple were discussing immediately prior to this piece of conversation.)

F   Many of the men I've met have been incredibly uhh provincial [2] in a sense [1] Umm and it also you know you've got a-, mind you, I know that Richard has had a very good education [2] but he's a very taciturn man and very bitter [0.6] very bitter about the way he's been treated. He's ve-, you know old family in regards

M   umphhh

F   Well you know some people got caught up in it I mean

M   oh of course [1.1]

F   You know I mean [0.6] yes I'm sure I mean he's very conservative, right? I mean I'm [1] he hates everything [0.7] and I am I am sure he didn't before but [1] whenever you talk to his father about it [0.6] he [1.5] he is very confused. I mean apparently he, he was [0.7] very active [0.6] hated Germany [2] and yet turned around afterwards [1] you know which is sort of

M   Oh the trouble is that he turned against everything, even the war.

(F then makes another attempt to pursue the topic of Richard's politics, which M responds to with a discussion of cities in the country of Richard's birth.)

Two of the five 'you know's' here follow internal pauses, as in the first transcript we examined. The other three cluster around the man's two minimal responses. Minimal responses display minimal orientation but not full participation. They fill the necessity of turn-taking but add nothing to the substantive progress of the talk, to the content of the conversation.

The use of 'you know' around minimal responses displays and attempts to solve the same problem as its use around pauses. In both cases there is a speaker change problem. The women are either trying to get a response or have gotten an unsatisfactory one. The evidence for women's insecurity is in fact evidence of the work they are doing to try to turn insecure conversations into successful ones.

Concluding remarks

I do not mean to imply that women may not find themselves feeling insecure and hesitant in such conversations. The point is that the feelings are not necessarily something women carry around with them as a result of early socialization. Rather, the feelings arise in situations where the women's attempts at conversation are faltering or failing and they are forced to do considerable work for dubious results.

And why do women have more conversational trouble than men do? Because men often do not do the necessary work to keep conversation going. Either they do not respond, or they respond minimally to conversational attempts by the women. In the few instances where men have trouble in conversations with women they use the same devices to try to solve their problems. I suspect that in conversations with their superiors men use what has been regarded as women's conversational style. The underlying issue here is likely to be hierarchy, not simply gender. Socially-structured power relations are reproduced and actively maintained in our everyday interactions. Women's conversational troubles reflect not their inferior social training but their inferior social position.

Note

1 I thank Mark Fishman and Linda Marks for their comments.

References

Bardwick, J. M. and Douvan, E. (1977) 'Ambivalence: the socialization of women', in P. J. Stein, J. Richman, and N. Hannon (eds) *The Family: Functions, Conflicts and Symbols*, Reading, Mass.: Addison-Wesley.

Fishman, P. M. (1978) 'Interaction: the work women do', *Social Problems* 25: 397–406.

——(1979) 'What do couples talk about when they're alone?' in D. Butturff and E. L. Epstein (eds) *Women's Language and Style*, Akron: University of Akron.

Lakoff, R. (1975) *Language and Woman's Place*, New York: Harper & Row.

——(1979) 'Women's language', in D. Butturff and E. L. Epstein (eds) *Women's Language and Style*, Akron: University of Akron.

Sacks (1972) 'On the analyzability of stories by children', in J. Gumperz and D. Hymes (eds) *Directions in Sociolinguistics: The Ethnography of Communication*, New York: Holt, Rinehart & Winston.

18

Gossip: notes on women's oral culture

Deborah Jones

Reprinted from Women's Studies International Quarterly, *3 (1980), pp. 193–8.*

Synopsis

Little is known about language use in all-female groups. In this paper an approach to the study of women's oral culture is proposed, based on the researcher's own participation in a female speech community and her knowledge of its norms. Women's gossip is an aspect of female language use, distinguished from more general concepts of women's speech style and of gossip. Gossip is described here in terms of its socio-linguistic features, with an emphasis on its functions which form the basis for the division of gossip into four categories: house-talk, scandal, bitching, and chatting.

Introduction

The problems of studying women's language are those of women's studies in general: the lack of concrete data, the sexist bias of the data available, the necessity of generating new perspectives from 'nowhere' – from our own experience, our own intuition.

The new wave of studies about women's language is characterized in its beginnings by Lakoff's *Language and Woman's Place* (1975). Wide-ranging, intuitive, arbitrary, it has been ground-breaking in spite of criticisms that it fails to conform to academic norms (Dubois and Crouch 1975). Inevitably, the more recent studies have tended to be more specific, controlled in contrast and measurement, focusing on particular communities, particular speech forms and functions.[1] Where these studies have focused on language use, their field has generally been the interface of male and female language, the linguistic transactions between men and women. Such studies facilitate specific comparisons, as well as describing in a variety of concrete ways the linguistic mechanisms of the oppression of women by men (for example, Zimmerman and West 1975).

What I will be concerned with in this paper, however, is the study of female oral culture, language use in women's natural groups, which as Thorne and Henley have pointed out is a 'virtually untouched' area (1975: 30).[2] These notes on gossip are one kind of approach to this investigation, an approach based on *our* own experience as members of the female speech community. In this case the experience is mine, supplemented by the writings of other women: novelists, critics, sociologists, and anthropologists, as well as sociolinguists. I am not concerned so much to present a specific thesis or body of data but to point ahead in new directions. I hope to map out a field for future and more specific study.

Women and gossip

I will initially define gossip as a way of talking between women in their roles as women, intimate in style, personal and domestic in topic and setting, a female cultural event which springs from and perpetuates the restrictions of the female role, but also gives the comfort of validation.

It seems to me that women form a speech community,[3] with language skills and attitudes of our own, as well as those shared by the wider speech community.[4] There continues to be a debate about how best to describe 'women's language' as Lakoff calls it (1975: 45); as a style (Thorne and Henley 1975: p. 11), or as a 'genderlect' (Kramer 1974: 54 n 1). Gossip is a narrower term than these, a specific type of women's 'language' or 'style'.

My use of the term gossip as a type of women's language is also, of course, more specific than the term 'gossip' as it is generally used. However the anthropological literature on gossip in this broader sense is relevant to a discussion of women's gossip, emphasizing as it does the social functions of gossip.

Anthropologist Gluckman's main thesis is that gossip, defined as a 'general interest in the doings, the virtues and vices of others', has a social function in maintaining 'the unity, morals and values of social groups' (Gluckman 1963: 308, 312). Paine emphasizes, on the other hand, the importance of gossip as 'a genre of informal communication' (1967: 278). Women's gossip illuminates the 'unity, morals, and values' of women as a social group, and provides the informal communications network that transmits these female values and concerns.

The elements of gossip

The description of gossip which follows is organized in terms of a sociolinguistic framework presented by Ervin-Tripp, a framework in which 'verbal behaviour' is studied 'in terms of the relations between the setting, the participants, the topic, the functions of an interaction, the form, and the values held by the participants about each of these' (Ervin-Tripp 1964: 192).

Setting

Ervin-Tripp uses the term *setting* in both the specific sense of 'time and place' and the more general sense of the cultural situation and its norms (1964: 193). The cultural and physical settings of gossip are, like those of women's lives, characterized by restriction. The private, the personal domain – this is the cultural setting. In concrete terms, the setting is the house, the hairdressers', the supermarket: locales associated with the female role both at home and outside it. There are also domestic enclaves within male institutions: the women's toilets or cloakrooms, the cluster of women in the corridor or the tearoom.

Time to gossip is usually snatched from work time, and work – in the shape of a child, a telephone, or a boiling pot – frequently intervenes. Gossip is necessarily serial and, like the knitting which often accompanies it, can be taken up and put down as opportunities permit.

Participants

Gossip is essentially talk between women in our common role *as* women. Gossip is a 'language of intimacy ' as Rubin describes it, an intimacy arising from the solidarity and identity of women as members of a social group with a pool of common experience (Rubin 1972: 513).

It is the nature of this common experience which not only gives gossip its topics and style, but makes gossip a basic element of the female subculture. As Millett puts it 'like the members of any repressed group, [women] are verbal persons, talking because they are permitted no other form of expression', and 'those out of power must settle for talk' (Millett 1971: 61). Gossip may be derogated by men as trivial (what could be more trivial than women's concerns?), but it is also seen as a threat. Women have been prevented from talking together by ridicule, interruption, physical constraint, and even by statute (Oakley 1972: 10), and the fear of gossip and its subversive power has been associated with witchcraft (Gluckman 1963: 314; Oakley 1974: 16).

Gossip, a language of female secrets, is one of women's strengths and, like all our strengths, it is both discounted and attacked. The secretive, even furtive air of much gossip is one index of the extent to which these male attitudes have been internalized. The linguistic precocity of female children has been well established,[5] but the likelihood that this facility develops into a rich and subtle oral art in the talk of adult women is not seen as an obvious corollary.

Topic

Women are an occupational group of a special kind, and our occupation and training as wives, girlfriends, and mothers are reflected in the topics of gossip. We are expected to be knowledgeable in our field: housework (cooking, cleaning, sewing, interior decoration, etc.); child-rearing; the wifely role (sexuality, appearance, psychological expertise).

Whatever the specific topic, the wider theme of gossip is always personal experience; it is in terms of the details of the speakers' lives and the lives of those around them that a perspective on the world is created.

Formal features

Little is known about any distinctive formal features of women's language in all-female groups, and what is known is not necessarily relevant to a description of gossip.[6] The suggestions that follow below are largely the result of my own observations.

In the excerpt below, the two heroines of Lessing's *The Golden Notebook* are discussing friends:

'Didn't he write to you?' asked Anna, cautious.
'Both he and Marion wrote – ever such *bonhomous* letters. Odd, isn't it?'
This *odd, isn't it* was the characteristic note of the intimate conversations they designated gossip.

(Lessing 1973: 25)

245

Gossip is allusive; its 'characteristic note' is the rising inflection, sometimes accompanying a tag question, the implicit reference to common knowledge, common values – the group values to which Gluckman refers. Women are not only sharing information, but are asking each other: what does this add to what we know about these people? What is its significance? What do we feel about it?

The replies to these questions, like the questions themselves, are frequently paralinguistic in form: the raised eyebrows, the pursed lips, the sigh, or the silence. Paralinguistic responses are also important to acknowledgement and validation of each speaker's contribution; Hirschman found that women are more likely than men to give minimal responses (for example, mm-hmm) as feedback to another speaker's statements, especially another woman's. Hirschman further suggests that 'males tend to dispute the other person's utterance or ignore it, while females acknowledge it, or often build on it' (1973: 249).

The implications of each piece of information presented are contemplated, rather than argued, as the participants in turn contribute their own experience to the picture. Reciprocity forms the pattern of discourse in female gossip.

Functions

I have divided gossip into four functional categories: house-talk, scandal, bitching, and chatting. As function varies, there are some accompanying variations in topic and formal features.

a   *House-talk.* If shop-talk is a term for the male occupational register, house-talk can describe the female version.[7] Its distinguishing function is the exchange of information and resources connected with the female role as an occupation. This usually centres around concrete tasks, as in the exchange of recipes, household hints, and dress patterns. It also includes the discussion of relationships from a strictly practical point of view: how to catch a husband, how to manage a child. House-talk provides an informal but thorough training in the female role.

House-talk may also take on a secondary function in meeting emotional needs for support and recognition. House-talk may then become a more intimate sharing of feelings and attitudes about women's work, and thus merge into other categories of gossip: complaint, (bitching) or more intimate self-disclosure (chatting).

b   *Scandal.*   Women's gossip is often dismissed as malicious scandal-mongering. However, this is only one aspect of gossip, and rather than being distinguished by malice, it is marked by a considered judging of the behaviour of others, and women in particular. This judgement is usually made in terms of the domestic morality of which women have been appointed guardians. The 'misbehaviour' of other women, especially sexual misbehaviour, is frequently seen as an attack on the job security of all women, and therefore behaviour which must be policed.[8] In as much as this judgement is harmful to other women, the fault lies not in female maliciousness, but in sexist moral codes which women enforce but do not create.

The second function of scandal is to cater for women's interest in each other's lives, providing a cultural medium which reflects female reality, and a connection between the lives of women who are otherwise isolated from each other. There also seems to be a kind of entertainment value for women in hearing how others live, perhaps a kind of vicarious enjoyment of a range of experience beyond the small sphere to which the individual woman is restricted. When judging the behaviour of others is minimal, while an interest in the lives of others as meaningful for one's own is predominant, scandal merges into the category of more intimate gossip, chatting.

c   *Bitching.*   While scandal keeps women's dissatisfaction focused on each other, and so does not threaten men, bitching is the kind of gossip that men feel most uneasy about. Bitching is the overt expression of women's anger at their restricted role and inferior status.[9] Overt, that is, in that it *is* expressed, but in private and to other women only.[10] The anger expressed in bitching is privatized; women's oppression is not discussed as a general concept, but in the relating of specific, personal complaints. Consciousness-raising in the women's movement is bitching in its political form.

As a form of gossip, bitching is essentially cathartic. The women speaking do not expect to change, but want only to make their complaints in an environment where their anger will be understood and expected.

d   *Chatting.*   Chatting is the most intimate form of gossip, a mutual self-disclosure, a transaction where the skills that women have learned as part of their job of nurturing others are turned to their own advantage. Chesler's description cannot be bettered:

[M]any dialogues between women seem 'senseless' or 'mindless' to men. Two women talking often seem to be reciting monologues at each other, neither really listening to (or 'judging') what the other is saying. Two personal confessions, two sets of feelings, seem to be paralleling one another, rather 'mindlessly', and without 'going anywhere'. In fact, what the women are doing – or where they are going – is toward some kind of emotional resolution or comfort. Each woman comments on the other's feelings by reflecting them in a very sensitive matching process. The two women share their feelings by alternating the retelling of the entire experience in which their feelings are embedded and from which they cannot be 'abstracted' or 'summarized'. Their theme, method and goal are non-verbal and/or non-verbalized. Facial expressions, pauses, sighs and seemingly unrelated (or 'non-abstract') responses to statements are crucial to such dialogue. A very special prescience is at work here. On its most ordinary level, it affords women a measure of emotional reality and a kind of comfort that they cannot find with men. On its highest level, it constitutes the basic tools of art and psychic awareness.

(Chesler 1972: 268).

Chatting sessions such as this provide a continuous chorus and commentary on the incidents of women's daily lives, in an evaluative process that also provides emotional sustenance.

Gossip is a staple of women's lives, and the study of gossip is the study of women's concerns and values, a key to the female subculture.

Notes

1 See, for example, Dubois and Crouch (1978).
2 Bethany Dumas, for instance, recommends research on language use in women's natural groups that is similar to Labov's research into the language use of Black male adolescents (Dumas 1975: 15). Oakley (1972: 15), looking at gossip from a sociological perspective, suggests a 'systematic study of gossip as a form of unarticulated female power'.
3 According to Labov (1972: 250–1), 'the speech community is not defined by any marked agreement in the use of language elements so much as by participation in a set of shared norms'.
4 I refer to my own white, English-speaking community. The relevance of these ideas to the language of other communities can only be guessed at.
5 See Oakley (1972: 79–80) for a brief summary.
6 For instance, the subjects in Crosby and Nyquist's (1977: 316) female dyads were constrained by unusual laboratory conditions, for example, assigned topics, blocked view of each other.

7 Women in paid occupations are usually competent in the shop-talk of their occupational group, as well as being competent in house-talk even if they do not do housework for a living.

8 Summers (1975) has borrowed the phrase 'God's police' from nineteenth-century Australian philanthropist Caroline Chisholm in her description of women's role as enforcers of a traditional moral code (see especially pp. 291–316).

9 See Meade's book *Bitching* (1973).

10 When women complain to men it is called 'nagging'.

References

Chesler, P. (1972) *Women and Madness*, New York: Avon.

Crosby, F. and Nyquist, L. (1977) 'The female register: an empirical study of Lakoff's hypothesis', *Language in Society* 6, pp. 313–22.

Dubois, B. L. and Crouch, I. (1975) 'The question of tag questions in women's speech: They don't really use more of them, do they?', *Language in Society*, 4, pp. 289–94.

——(eds) (1978) 'American minority women in sociolinguistic perspective', *International Journal of the Sociology of Language* 17, The Hague: Mouton.

Dumas, B. (1975) 'Women's language model: a proposal', Washington, DC: Educational Resources Information Center (ED, 134–031).

Ervin-Tripp, S. (1964) 'An analysis of the interaction of language, topic, and listener', *American Anthropologist* 66 (6: part 2), 86–102. Rpt. in Joshua A. Fishman (ed.) *Readings in the Sociology of Language*, The Hague: Mouton.

Gluckman, M. (1963) 'Gossip and scandal', *Current Anthropology*, 4 (3), pp. 307–15.

Hirschman, L. (1973) 'Female–male difference in conversational interaction', abstract in Barrie Thorne and Nancy Henley (eds) *Language and Sex: Difference and Dominance*, Rowley, Mass.: Newbury House.

Kramer, C. 'Women's speech: separate but unequal?' *Quarterly Journal of Speech* 60: 14–24. Rpt. in Barrie Thorne and Nancy Henley (eds) *Language and Sex: Difference and Dominance*, Rowley, Mass.: Newbury House.

Labov, W. (1972) 'The reflections of social processes in linguistic structure', in Joshua A. Fishman (ed.) *Readings in the Sociology of Language*, The Hague: Mouton.

Lakoff, R. (1975) *Language and Women's Place*, New York: Harper & Row.

Lessing, D. (1973) *The Golden Notebook*, Herts: Panther.

Meade, M. (1973) *Bitching*, London: Garnstone Press.

Millett, K. (1971) 'Prostitution: a quartet for female voices', in V. Gornick and B. K. Moran (eds) *Woman in Sexist Society*, New York: Basic Books.

Oakley, A. (1972) *Sex, Gender and Society*, Melbourne: Sun Books.

——(1974) *The Sociology of Housework*, New York: Pantheon/Random House.

Paine, R. (1967) 'What is gossip about? An alternative hypothesis', *Man* 2, pp. 278–85.

Rubin, J. (1972) 'Bilingual usage in Paraguay', in Joshua A. Fishman (ed.) *Readings in the Sociology of Language*, The Hague: Mouton.

Summers, A. (1975) *Damned Whores and God's Police: The Colonisation of Women in Australia*, Harmondsworth: Penguin.

Thorne, B. and Henley, N. (1975) 'Difference and dominance: an overview of language, gender and society', in B. Thorne and N. Henley (eds) *Language and Sex: Difference and Dominance*, Rowley, Mass.: Newbury House.

Zimmerman, D. and West, C. (1975) 'Sex roles, interruptions, and silences in conversation', in B. Thorne and N. Henley (eds) *Language and Sex: Difference and Dominance*, Rowley, Mass.: Newbury House.

Further reading

With this list of references I aim to lead readers either to texts which will take them deeper into the issues raised by this collection or to material which, dipped into, might widen their acquaintance with the field as a whole. This certainly is not an exhaustive bibliography, and in particular I have avoided citing either difficult, specialized, and technical work in linguistics (the interested reader may refer to the bibliographies in those volumes listed under 'General texts' below, p. 252) or work in literary criticism which makes use of ideas about language and gender as opposed to expounding them directly (teachers and students of literature will doubtless know where to look for critical works on specific texts much better than I do).

Collections of articles on women and language

(Mainly on 'linguistic' rather than 'literary' topics.)

1 Thorne, B. and Henley, N., (eds) (1975) *Language and Sex: Difference and Dominance*, Rowley, Mass.: Newbury House.
Contains several 'classic' papers on a number of subjects and an annotated bibliography of published and unpublished material.

2 Thorne, B., Kramarae, C., and Henley, N., (eds) (1983) *Language, Gender and Society*, Rowley, Mass: Newbury House.
Also has an updated bibliography and some useful introductory material.

3 McConnell-Ginet, S., Borker, N., and Furman, R. (eds) (1980) *Women and Language in Literature and Society*, New York: Praeger.
Covers literary as well as sociolinguistic subjects.

4 Philips, S. U., Steele, S., and Tanz, C. (eds) (1987) *Language, Gender and Sex in Comparative Perspective*, Cambridge: CUP.
The papers in here are more technical than in 1–3, but the focus of the collection is interesting: it is good on cross-cultural variation and addresses the question of how culture and biology interact.

5 Coates, J. and Cameron, D. (eds) (1989) *Women in Their Speech Communities: New Perspectives on Language and Sex*, London: Longman.

A collection of specifically British material, including papers dealing with minority ethnic groups in Britain.

General texts

1 Lakoff, R. (1975) *Language and Woman's Place*, New York: Harper & Row.
A ground-breaking book, much criticized for its lack of empirical back-up; but the arguments about women's use of language and her examples of sexism are still worth discussing.

2 Spender, D. (1980) *Man Made Language*, London: Routledge.
Wide-ranging and provocative introduction; though you should start rather than finish with it.

3 Cameron, D. (1985) *Feminism and Linguistic Theory*, London: Macmillan.
Covers both sex differences in usage and sexism in language, and has an introduction to linguistic theory *per se*.

4 Coates, J. (1986) *Women, Men and Language*, London: Longman.
Very thorough survey of the literature on men's and women's speech.

5 Smith, P. (1985) *Language, the Sexes and Society*, Oxford: Blackwell.
Dense text by a social psychologist, but interesting in parts.

Language, sexual difference, psychoanalysis

These references deal with the thought of mainly French theorists and place their perspective in context.

1 Moi, T. (1985) *Sexual/Textual Politics*, London: Methuen.
Good clear exposition of the ideas of Cixous, Irigaray and Kristeva; also a critical section on Anglo-American feminist linguists. See also Moi's *Kristeva Reader* (Oxford: Blackwell 1986), for more detailed exposition of and extracts from Kristeva's work – though it is not an easy read.

2 Marks, E. and de Courtivron, I. (eds) (1981) *New French Feminisms*, Brighton: Harvester.

3 Duchen, C. (ed.) (1986) *French Connections*, London: Hutchinson.
Two collections selected and edited from rather different standpoints, containing writings by French feminists on language among other things. They are both rather 'bitty' but provide a useful sampling of the range of French thought. Helpful introductory material putting the work in context.

Feminist dictionaries and glossaries

1 Kramarae, C. and Treichler, P. (eds) (1985) *A Feminist Dictionary*, London: Pandora Press.

2 Daly, M. and Caputi, J. (1988) *Webster's New Intergalactic Wickedary of the English Language*, London: Women's Press.

Two volumes which both criticize and wittily subvert the practices of traditional lexicography. The *Wickedary* has the hallmarks of Mary Daly's iconoclastic approach to language, displayed also in her other work (for example, *Gyn/Ecology* (London: Women's Press 1978)). See also M. Wittig and S. Zeig (1979) *Lesbian Peoples, Materials Towards a Dictionary*, New York: Avon.

Women writers on women and writing

1 Woolf, V. (1979) *Women and Writing*, ed. M. Barrett, London: Women's Press.
2 Olsen, T. (1980) *Silences*, London: Virago.
3 Rich, A. (1980) *On Lies, Secrets and Silence*, London: Virago.
4 Walker, A. (1984) *In Search of our Mothers' Gardens*, London: Women's Press.
5 Ncobo, L. (ed.) (1988) *Let it be Told: Black Women Writers in Britain*, London: Virago.

All these collections deal with other things besides language and gender, but all have stimulating observations to make about it. Ncobo in addition contains pieces which pose the question of Black women's relation to non-standard and non-western linguistic and literary traditions.

Index

A note on using this index

This index is designed so that some entries – those most central to the concerns of the book – are very detailed (e.g. the entry for *sexist language*, which contains a number of subdivisions and cross-references narrowing the topic down still further), while others are much less detailed (for instance, the entry for *psychoanalysis*. If you want to look up a specific concept like *Oedipus complex*, and there is no entry for it, you should go to the more general entry for *psychoanalysis* and work through the references.) The index does not contain references for every single name mentioned in the text: only for the more important names and those mentioned several times.